ADVENTURES ON The HIGH TEAS

D1494192

For The English Roses

STUART MACONIE

IN SEARCH OF MIDDLE ENGLAND

ADVENTURES On The HIGH TEAS

EBURY
PRESS

5 7 9 10 8 6 4

Published in 2010 by Ebury Press, an imprint of Ebury Publishing
A Random House Group Company
First published in the UK by Ebury Publishing in 2009
This edition published 2010

The Random House Group Limited Reg. No. 954009

Addresses for companies within the Random House Group can be found at
www.randomhouse.co.uk

A CIP catalogue record for this book is available from the British Library

The Random House Group Limited supports The Forest Stewardship Council (FSC),
the leading international forest certification organisation. All our titles that are printed
on Greenpeace approved FSC certified paper carry the FSC logo. Our paper
procurement policy can be found at www.rbooks.co.uk/environment

Mixed Sources
Product group from well-managed
forests and other controlled sources
www.fsc.org Cert no. TT-COC-2139
© 1996 Forest Stewardship Council

Designed and set by seagulls.net

Printed in the UK by CPI Cox & Wyman, Reading, RG1 8EX

ISBN 9780091926519

To buy books by your favourite authors and register for offers visit www.rbooks.co.uk

Contents

The land of embarrassment and breakfast.

Julian Barnes

CHAPTER 1
The Heart of the Matter

Imagine that you are a very particular kind of Englishman or woman. One burdened by strange and terrible fears. You are terrified of the sea, suspicious of the Scots and consumed by a loathing of France and all things French. Your notion of hell involves not fire and brimstone but bladderwrack, bagpipes and brie. And so profound and dreadful runs this fear that it drives you as far into your beloved realm as you can go: deep into the bosom of your native land, putting as much space as you can between you and your Gallic, Celtic and aquatic demons.

Well, this is where you would come. Meriden, Warwick-shire. Population 2,734. Grid Ref SP240824, 93 miles equally from the Irish Sea, the Wash and the North Sea. Now I like the Scots and I like the sea. I really, really like Debussy and Roquefort. But I have come here too, on A Journey to the Centre of the Earth. Well, A Journey to the Centre of England, at least. I was not trying to get to the bottom of things, but to the middle.

It's an ash-grey Sunday at the fag end of an unremarkable year early in the twenty-first century and I am standing in the dead centre of England. Appropriately enough, it's a village green. A village green of sorts, anyway, in that Meriden isn't really a village and this isn't really a green; more a functional lozenge of clipped municipal grass. (Nicely kept, mind you, and plenty of benches.) But no other phrase will quite do here. If Meriden is the centre of England – and its residents will tell you proudly and without much provocation that it is – then it is fitting that the very middle of the very middle of Middle England should be a sort of village green, albeit one with a charity shop, a Lloyds pharmacy and a branch of Spar where the stocks and the maypole and the blacksmiths should be.

Middle England. Depending on how you say it, it can mean entirely different things. Said with a snort and a roll of the eyes – maybe in a private members' club frequented by media types in Soho – it means stifling conservatism, the *Daily Mail* and bringing back the birch. Said with a swell of pride and a raised glass of warm flat beer in a saloon bar in the Shires, though, it means tradition, dependability, decency, the pleasing swish not of birch on buttock but of willow on leather. All this and, of course, a notorious gang of British bikers, those famous spinsters cycling to evensong.

The cycling spinsters attained the status of modern retro-myth in 1993 when John Major mentioned them in his speech to the Conservative Party conference, the infamous 'Back To Basics' address. They were one of a litany of icons of Englishness he cited, some lifted from George Orwell's introduction to *The Lion and the Unicorn*. Orwell's essay was a socialist call to arms, its original context suggesting either that

a) John Major was a skilled and witty ironist or b) he hadn't read it. Major talked of 'old maids cycling to Holy Communion, long shadows on cricket grounds, warm beer, invincible green suburbs, dog lovers and pools fillers'. Orwell actually had his maids 'hiking', which sounds oddly transatlantic; Major's misquotation is the one that has passed into legend. Orwell, though, and this is telling, also wrote in his piece of 'the clatter of clogs in the Lancashire mill towns, the to-and-fro of the lorries on the Great North Road, the queues outside the Labour Exchanges, the rattle of pin-tables in the Soho pubs'. None of which, perhaps understandably, Major thought would get the blue-rinses and retired colonels moist-eyed and palpitating. In some ways Major – Pooterish, decent, normal, went to a cricket match on the afternoon he stood down as PM – embodied Middle England; well, as much as the Brixtonian son of a trapeze artist who had a passionate illicit romance with Edwina Currie can be said to be in any way normal. That's the thing with Middle England, you see. Hidden depths.

Orwell himself loved and loathed Middle England in a way that I can easily understand. He disliked the Establishment even though he was a lapsed former member of it, having been to Eton and served as a colonial policeman in Burma. He called England 'a land of snobbery and privilege, ruled largely by the old and silly'. But he was fiercely patriotic for all that, not for queen and country and fox-hunting but for pubs and architecture and people. In that same wonderful essay (I would vote for any political party that had *The Lion and the*

Unicorn as its manifesto) he says of England: 'It is a culture as individual as that of Spain. It is somehow bound up with solid breakfasts and gloomy Sundays, smoky towns and winding roads, green fields and red pillar-boxes.'

The French have a word for their mythic geographical soul: La France Profonde. Deepest France. In the USA, they call it Middle America; culturally and geographically the nation's heartland. Middle America is actually and physically central – the flyover states, as NY and LA cosmopolites call them – but it's also a synonym for the real America, more truly American than Hollywood or Manhattan, Miami Beach or Cape Cod.

Back in Blighty, others apart from Orwell and Major have come up with their own pen portraits and icon litanies. With a mischievous smirk, George MacDonald Fraser, author of the Flashman novels, characterised 'Merrie England', a bawdy, busty, tankard-clinking predecessor of Middle England, as 'the old and golden days of England ... when all the hedgerows were green and the roads dusty, when hawthorn and wild roses bloomed, when big-bellied landlords brewed rich October ale at a penny a pint ... when squires ate roast beef ... while their faithful hounds slumbered on the rushes by the hearth, when summers were long and warm and drowsy, with honeysuckle and hollyhocks by cottage walls'. When the Department of Media, Culture and Sport, in its relentlessly upbeat, trendy sandal-wearing teacher way, asked Britain to name its 'icons of Britishness', the first twelve 'we' came up with were Stonehenge, Punch and Judy, SS *Empire Windrush*, Holbein's portrait of Henry VIII, a cup of tea, the FA Cup, *Alice in*

Wonderland, the Routemaster bus, the King James Bible, the Angel of the North, the Spitfire and Jerusalem (the song not the place).

Journeying through the Shires for this book, though, from service station to farmers' market, along branch lines and country lanes, through countless gift shops, gastropubs and hotel receptions, I came to see that there is a new iconography of Middle England beyond spinsters and cycle clips. If I were compiling the new *I-Spy Book of Middle England*, you would score points not just for spinsters but for Ginsters, not just for evensong but for loft conversions, CCTV cameras, adverts for firms doing patio improvements on people's drives, white-towelling-clad hen parties in health spas, trampolines in suburban gardens, those yellow 'Cleaning In Progress' signs in the shape of jaunty commissionaires, yummy mummies in black Suzuki jeeps, *Top Gear* DVDs, phone-in speak ('long-time listener, first-time caller', 'As I told your researcher ...'), Polish chambermaids, Diana Princess of Wales, cheery little knots of smokers round patio heaters in beer gardens and sad little bouquets of flowers taped to pelican crossings.

Middle England. It's not really a place. It's more a certain kind of Englishness, one distilled to its very essence like sloe gin, dark and potent. Granted it's not the only kind of Englishness. There's the raw, bold, virile, doomed northern variety, composed of jutting crags, sleet, Joy Division, Ted Hughes, roaring winds and silent foundries. There's the rich, strange otherness of the deep south with its shanties, tin mines, smugglers, witches, Poldark and pasties. But Middle England is different. Comfortable, maybe ... if you call flooded cathedral towns and post-Apocalypse Slough comfortable. Straight-laced, yes; if your definition includes Cromwell Street, Gloucester. Cosy, perhaps, in the way that the gruesome, feral ritual of mayhem and bloodletting that goes on every Sunday night in the county of Midsomer is cosy.

It is not just the literal middle of England, not just its ample, well-fed midriff rising and falling in a post-Sunday-lunch snooze across the Chilterns, the Cotswolds, the Mendips and the Peak District. It is a state of mind. I would use the word Psycho-Geography but they don't talk like that here. They call a spade a spade. Unless of course they mean the edging iron or the Dutch hoe.

That said, and this is real geography, I am still standing in the very middle of England. Meriden, Warwickshire. Not much is happening, I have to say, on this slate-coloured Sunday. A fifty-something lady in fleecy pink jogging bottoms with a perky spaniel surreptitiously watches me whilst pretending to have seen something utterly compelling in the window of the charity shop. A passing teenager, with studied insouciance, flips his skateboard up with a foot and into his grasp and dodges triumphantly into the Spar. Somewhere, faintly, a radio is playing 'Hey Jude'. It is Sunday. Middle England is napping or hoeing or, more likely, getting two litres of Autumn Cornflower mixed at B&Q. Meriden is no exception. In fact, it's the rule.

Back in the 1960s and early 1970s, had those cycling spinsters fancied upgrading to something a little sportier, they would have soon known the name of Meriden. Then the village was synonymous with British motorcycling and had been since 1942 when Triumph motorcycles had moved to a new plant here after the bombing of Coventry. The company became world famous when Marlon Brando rode one of their bikes in *The Wild One*. Triumph, BSA, Norton, Villiers … names to make a Hells Angel cry into his cider. And he would have shed tears aplenty in 1983 when the last Triumph Bonneville rolled off the production line. With help from that kindly uncle of international socialism Anthony Wedgwood Benn, as he then was, a workers' cooperative had run the Meriden plant since 1973 when Norton Villiers Triumph pulled out.

Now the village, and in particular the green, is a place of pilgrimage for devotees of a, well, 'greener' form of biking. Dominating one end of the green is a big, quite forbidding stone cone. It's the kind of architecture they favoured for police stations in 1970s Romania. In fact, it was erected by cyclists in 1921 as a memorial to their fellows killed in the Great War. It is, in fact, I realise as I stand before it, chewing thoughtfully on a Werther's butter candy, a massive, quite imposing sort of mini-cenotaph.

But why Meriden? The lady in the pink jogging bottoms didn't know. She was really nice, though, once she'd seen my notebook and packet of Werther's and established that, though I was clearly some kind of nut to be wandering around Meriden jotting furtive notes on a dull, chilly Sunday after-noon, I wasn't a dangerous one. It turns out that the cyclists put the memorial here for no other reason than Meriden is in the centre of England and therefore equally accessible to all.

Some 200,000 turned up for its official unveiling. The logic of its location is unassailable, but why then isn't Meriden festooned, crammed, overrun with such monuments erected by the British Association of Plumbers, or Cheesemongers, Netball Players and Vintage Traction Engine Enthusiasts? Obviously cyclists think a little differently. Well done, cyclists. But please stay off the pavement, or you'll be needing another monument to fallen comrades soon.

Every year, there's a memorial service and celebration here on the green which attracts cyclists from all over Britain. As I write, it's just happened. In the afternoon there was a pace-judging competition starting at the village hall. Competitors cycle a 9km route twice, once in each direction. The winner is the one whose times match most closely. Presumably you could do this incredibly slowly if you liked, whilst wobbling in the saddle, as long as you did the same speed twice. In its gentle, formal absurdity, this sounds such a wonderfully Middle English kind of race.

There's another bit of bicycle-related commemorative statu-ary at the other end of the green, a handsome seat 'To the memory of Wayfarer (WM Robinson) who died on 17 Sept 1956. His devotion to the pastime of cycling inspired many to enjoy'. Wayfarer was the pen name of Walter MacGregor Robinson, pioneer of modern cycling. Someone's been enjoying themselves on Wayfarer's seat pretty recently judging by the bottle of Lucozade and the half-eaten tray of chips and congealed gravy underneath it. Nearby stands a flagpole sans flag.

At this end of the green, though, much smaller than the

cyclists' obelisk, is a more significantly 'Meriden' artefact. This is a grade-II ancient monument, a 500-year-old sandstone pillar bearing testimony to the fact that this is the traditional, mythic middle of England. The people of Meriden like their monuments. Apart from this, there's the village's war memorial, a crucifix, just across from the duck pond. In the courtyard of the Bull's Head pub, a sign indicates that it was open for travellers needing rest and stabling for their horses as far back as 1603, and a fingerpost tells you the distance to various major cities, letting you know that, yes indeed, this is the 'Centre of England'.

The Centre of Englandness is affirmed even more proudly by the half-a-millennium-old landmark on the green. It has seen better days. The head seems to be missing for one thing. When the writer Caroline Hillier came here in 1976, the Spar was a village shop and the girl in it said that the cross had been 'like that for as long as I remember and I've been here sixteen years'. Maybe it got knocked about a bit when it was lent to the Festival of Britain in 1951, given pride of place in the model village.

There is something very Middle English about how Meriden markets its geographical claim to fame. I once spent a week in a town called Fairmont, Indiana, whose USP, to coin a phrase, is that it's the birthplace of James Dean. From the colossal 1950s rock and roll and vintage motorbike festival to the rock-lassoing competition (Dean performed this odd trick in *Giant*) to the diners stuffed with cheesy, evocative memorabilia, Fairmont had no qualms about trading on their dead son. Their only real reservation was about his rumoured homosexuality – lots of burly men told me that 'there was no way old Jimmy Dean was that way inclined, son' – and the fact that he took attention away from other luminaries of the town they were equally proud of, other such famous sons as Jim Davis, the creator of Garfield, and a chap who had once been head of the National Hurricane Centre. I found this fierce small-town pride utterly charming, and still do.

So I also like how Meriden shows a quiet, unshowy but very English self-confidence. 'Welcome to Meriden, please drive carefully' asks the first sign on the outskirts, meekly. But the next proclaims with a little more swagger, 'Welcome to Meriden, centre of England'. All else is largely undemonstrative, save for the balloons and bunting tied to the gates of a very nice property where someone is having a party.

Meriden Fish and Chips resists the temptation to offer anything as crass as 'the most centrally positioned cod and chips in England' but the Centre of England Florists has no such qualms. A passer-by in his thirties offers to take my picture outside it. Neither of us has a camera but it seems churlish to point this out. 'Thought you wanted a souvenir. Most of them do.' Checking in the local paper later, I find that this is true. The shop owner, one Tracy Gardiner, told their reporter: 'Tourists and media always use my shop as a backdrop for photos and things like that … I have actually had an order placed from the United States by a man who saw a picture of the shop.' Today, though, I have this photo opportunity to myself. My friend without a camera, by the way, and here you will have to believe me, was a tall, slim Rastafarian in full dreads dressed in a red replica England shirt with 'Gerrard' emblazoned on the back.

I wander along the small row of businesses overlooking the green to the charity shop. 'Please do not leave any items outside this shop while it is closed,' it warns. Other notices are more tantalising, offering a glimpse of a different, racier Meriden. 'Inspired by "Strictly"? Want to dance? Ballroom at Heart of England Leisure centre.' 'Strictly', I should point out in case this reference means nothing by the time these words are printed, is/was the official popular designation of *Strictly Come Dancing*, the BBC's astonishingly successful TV show hosted by octogenarian Light Entertainment titan Bruce Forsyth and itself a contemporary bulwark of Middle English taste.

They clearly like to cut a rug hereabouts, as another photocopied flyer offers 'Dancing to the Fabulous Ambassadors at the RSPCA Xmas Party'. If you want to sit this one out, there's 'Wind of Change, a Pentecostal musical by Phillip Shapiro'. In the gathering Warwickshire dusk I peer beyond the signs into the interior of the closed shop and the sundry items for sale. There is a quite horrible ceramic owl 'sold to John', some curious balls, a child's car seat, several Dick Francis paperbacks and a large wooden contraption whose sign reads 'Good when new, all in working order, lovly [*sic*] sound, 75 pounds with stool'. I have no idea what it is but assume from this that it's some kind of musical instrument. Appearances suggest a harpsichord that you could milk a cow with and possibly travel the countryside selling pegs from. A postcard in the Post Office window reads, simply and intriguingly, 'Stay At Home Mums Wanted'.

At the end of the row is the village shop, now a branch of Spar as noted. National Lottery ads jostle with lined postcards offering 'Hay and Straw' and the services of odd-job men: new and old Middle England in a single window. In another small but significant change, the shop is open, brightly lit and crackling with the sounds of a radio on a late Sunday afternoon. Stepping inside, the most significant change in the face – literally – of Middle England becomes apparent.

The shop is run by a Sikh family. Dad, seventy-ish, is gently rearranging some cauliflowers in the green plastic vegetable rack. Son sports a snazzy bandana-style headdress rather than the more traditional turban and is sifting through the tidal detritus of the day's papers, the *Observers, Telegraphs* and *Sunday Mercuries,* sold or returned. Suddenly hungry, I turn left along the food racks: vegetable pakora, corned beef and Branston pickle baguettes, Eccles cakes. Tottenham are at home to Blackburn on Radio 5 Live and Father and Son are chatting animatedly about the game, switching between English, Punjabi and a dazzling, colourful hybrid of the two. I decide on pakora, subconsciously hoping perhaps that this will be taken as credentials of my faultless cosmopolitan liberalism, before noticing that both Father and Son are dipping regularly and enthusiastically into bags of Monster Munch. This, along with the Eccles cakes, the quickfire Punjabi, the Rastas, chips and gravy, cycling memorials, *Strictly Come Dancing,* pakoras and Steven Gerrard, makes this late Sunday in Meriden a nicely bamboozling hors d'oeuvre for the hearty repast that is Middle England.

Meriden is Middle England but doesn't quite sound it. Chipping Norton does, though: it sounds of high-torque wheels crunching on gravel, fishing lure falling on stream water, clotted cream spreading on scone. Whenever I heard it mentioned as a child, along with its cosy companions Sodbury, Camden and Ongar, I assumed it was made up. I thought it was a suburb of Camberwick Green or possibly a dormitory town for Chigley. A place where, after Mr Cresswell the biscuit-factory manager had headed off in the Audi for a hard day with the Hobnobs, Mrs Cresswell might carry on a steamy illicit affair with Harry Farthing from the Pottery. Yes, these were all residents of Chigley. Just because in our celebrity-obsessed culture Windy Miller and Mrs Honeyman are never out of *Heat* magazine, you forget the little people, don't you? But they also serve who only stand and pot.

Incidentally, when he was interviewed on Radio 4 in 1995, the creator of Trumptonshire Gordon Murray was asked where exactly he thought Trumptonshire was. Kent? Sussex? Apparently not. 'There are mountains in the background so I would think it's probably in the middle of the country somewhere. Because the mountains look rather nice in the background.'

The Cotswolds, then, I'd say, and this thought occurs en route to CN (as I'm sure no one calls it), driving through Banbury in the warm ripe light of a late Friday afternoon in September. It's more built up and urban than its nursery rhyme name suggests. There's a hulking 24-hour Tesco on the fringes of town and some grimly utilitarian commercial developments. But they are having a canal day, which is reassuring, and Ralph McTell is playing at the extremely pretty St Mary's church in Banbury and, best of all, I pass a fancy obelisk decorated with cock horses; obviously the site of the famous Banbury Cross. Up the road is Bloxham, a posh independent school for boys and girls. The villages have thatched roofs but there are still signs for the National Lottery in the Post Office window. A phalanx of kids of all shapes and ages in black blazers is strolling down the hill from evensong. The boys look like Prince William and the girls like Kate Middleton, each bright with the carefree self-possession of their golden youth and boundless promise. Even the most hardened class warrior would find it rather sweet.

Through a very windy village called Fenbury and things start to get nicely rolling and hilly, the way I like it. We climb upwards gently into 'Chippy', as the locals call it, or 'Gateway to the Cotswolds' as the brochures proclaim. For all its self-evident gentility and charm – the Georgian townhouses, the shy, pretty mews, the tree-lined streets – 'Chippy' is still a real town, not a tourist trap like Bourton-on-the-Water or Broadway. The locals will tell you that it has the last fish and chip shop for thirty miles in the Cheltenham direction. Chipping Norton stands alone from the surrounding Shires geographically (high on the North Oxfordshire ridge), and culturally, being handsome rather than twee, having some of the few Labour councillors around here and a thriving co-op presence with sizeable investments and property holdings in the town. They've always made real things here: wool and tweed at the nearby Bliss Mill rather than cream teas and souvenir doilies.

The Crown and Cushion Hotel was once owned by Keith Moon, the 'hilarious' wild man drummer of The Who, much given to dressing as a Nazi and driving cars into swimming pools. Moon's influence, it is fair to say, does not pervade the old coaching inn today. The boy who greets us is painfully shy and diffident, blond and softly spoken, like the slow, childlike boy in a Frankenstein movie's alpine village who saves everyone from the terrible fire at the end. The restaurant is almost deserted, apart from three generations of the women of a rather posh family, dressed in silk and organic cottons all, languidly mulling over dessert. The waitresses are Polish, naturally.

In the two years after EU regulations were relaxed, half a million young Polish people came to Britain in search of work and many of them came right to the heart of Middle England: to the Wolds and the Shires, to wait on our tables, build our conservatories and fold down the top sheet on our hotel beds. Polite, hard-working and frequently possessed of fabulous cheekbones, they were no problem for me. For others they were. Even that paragon of liberalism *Guardian* columnist Polly Toynbee claimed that supporting economic migration was an act of treachery to the indigenous British working class. Having seen *The Jeremy Kyle Show*, I was less convinced that Jacek and Ludmila were putting Jason and Kylie out of work.

Then the Bulgarians and Latvians and Romanians started to come too, and the papers frothed, the government got twitchy and as of 2008 the numbers are well down. But if you stay in any hotel in Britain, you will still meet young Eastern Europeans gamely and sweetly struggling with the oddities of British idioms. My waitress came over during my meal (rib-eye steak with oven-baked aubergine followed by Grand Marnier parfait, since you ask) and asked, charmingly, 'How is your very good meal?'

'Very good,' I replied.

In truth, the food is OK but not helped by the atmosphere of the deserted dining room. Weird martial music is piped across the unoccupied tables, lit by sad dim candelabras. It feels like a scene from a Thomas Mann novel, with me cast as the doomed consumptive academic working on his magnum opus in a failing sanatorium. To dispel this mood, it seems a tour of Friday-night Chipping Norton is in order.

In many an English market town of a weekend, you will be 'treated', if that is the word, to a display of cornering, gear-crunching and acceleration by a succession of acned youth in souped-up Vauxhall Novas. Penrith is a great place for students of this faintly tragic sub-culture. Chipping Norton has its own version in the shape of one solitary youth on a trials bike buzzing around the town like a vexed but languid hornet for about four hours every weekend evening. I assume it's a youth anyway. Hard to tell with the leathers and full-face helmet. It speaks volumes for the tolerance and patience of Chipping Norton folk that they haven't murdered him yet in some grisly fashion, since he must be known to everyone in the town. Unless, of course, like a superhero in reverse, his identity is unknown and he changes from mild-mannered chorister into his Irritating Bikeboy garb in a phone box.

Aside from this, the streets are quiet though the pubs look busy and welcoming. On this mild evening, the recently introduced Smoking Ban on enclosed spaces seems indubitably A Good Thing. Not, I should add, for any puritanical reason but because it's the end of September and, against their will or not, groups of people are chatting and drinking on patios and under awnings and it all feels deliciously warm and lively and al fresco and continental. Maybe it will look less inviting come the first stinging sleet of January.

Though the town feels vaguely genteel, there are hints of a darker modernity. In one window, a scrolling red LED advert offers 'No Mercy' tattoos. Through another, in what looked like a DSS hostel, a scrawny kid is sprawled on a moth-eaten sofa looking blankly at a TV set. On arriving in the town and popping into the chemists, I had seen a sad, sweating man conducting a furtive transaction that looked to me like the weekly methadone pick-up.

Elsewhere, there are bookshops, health food shops and a cute Greco-Roman town hall. It's hosting a craft fair tomorrow and I make a note to be there. A poster in a shop window advertises the *Chipping Norton News* whose recent headlines include 'Chip Shop Goes Green' and 'Police Apologise'. There are several antique shops and outside one, standing in a pool of light on the pavement, two elderly gentlemen are gazing lustfully at some crockery in the window as if it were a particularly fleshy *FHM* supplement.

The combination of antiques and lusty, eye-rolling middle-aged men reminds me instantly of Chipping Norton's most famous ex-resident. When Ronnie Barker, the larger of Middle England's adored double act The Two Ronnies, retired in 1987 and whilst still hugely popular, his announcement that he intended to run an antique shop in Chipping Norton was taken as a joke. But he meant to do just that, and for most of the next couple of decades could be found with wife Joy among the walking sticks, knick-knacks and wind-up gramophones of the Emporium. The town was quietly proud of him though he never became a local celebrity. He wasn't often glimpsed in the pubs or restaurants. If you spotted him about town in one of his 'Stick of Rock' sports coats, he would politely turn down your request for a photo or autograph. Unlike his famous creation Arkwright in *Open All Hours*, he was no lurid, leering presence behind the counter. But he did contribute much to the town's successful bid to bring live professional theatre to Chippy at the converted Salvation Army citadel. And in his shop you could buy some of the duplicates from his 40,000-strong collection of that uniquely British celebration of innocent smut, the saucy seaside postcard. They're worth another look, along with some other things that make Middle England laugh, a little later in our journey.

By the time I get back to the hotel bar, there's been a transformation: from gloomy alpine sanatorium to hearty hub of the community. Many of you will remember the scene in Jon Landis's film *American Werewolf in London* where the travellers arrive at that daunting wayside inn, the Slaughtered

Lamb. The clientele of slack-jawed yokels all fall silent as the newcomers enter and much unpleasantness ensues. This sadly has become a lazy shorthand gag for metropolitan types horrified to find that country pubs don't do frappuccino or have a crèche with wi-fi.

There was nothing of the Slaughtered Lamb about the Crown and Cushion this autumn Friday evening. Everyone seemed to know each other, yes, but there was a definite lack of goitres, eye patches and slack jaws, and I was made implicitly welcome without recourse to slapped backs or clanking tankards. Three smart middle-aged women, clearly enjoying a regular rendezvous, were playing cards and gently gossiping. A woman with a ledger under her arm, high-ranking WI I reckoned, plonked herself at the bar and without a word a tall, misted G&T arrived. There were dogs and body-warmers and dimple glasses and soft accents and it was a warm, welcoming place to sit and sip whisky and write up my notes under the guise of completing the *Times* crossword.

Breakfast was a buffet, an increasingly ubiquitous but problematic start to the day for the English traveller. If you're pennywise or greedy or maybe both it has its advantages in that you can pile your plate high with sausage, egg, hash browns, mushrooms, bacon, beans and fried bread and then brazenly go back for several more artery-hardening platefuls. However, no anguished curling bacon, no flaccid sausage congealing under a high-wattage lamp, no tomato-half slowly cooling like a dying planet can ever match the sheer heartiness of a plate brought to your table with a kindly, 'Now these plates are very hot so be careful. Toast? White or brown?' by a bun-haired septuagenarian or white-pinnied young waitress. Standing in that peculiar limbo that is the space before the breakfast tureens, gingerly trying to scrape solidified beans off a ladle, the man in the neat pullover at my side says cheerily, 'This is a bit like being in prison, isn't it? … Not that I'd know, of course!'

Breakfast consumed, I had a date with a craft fair. Inside the rather nice town hall, designed in 1842 by G.S. Repton and, according to the town's website, 'Neo-classical with a pedimented Tuscan portico placed strangely to one side and not facing the Market Square as might be expected', under the gilded portraits of various well-upholstered aldermen like Albert Brassey and J.H. Langston, I was treated to the full, baffling panoply of bewildering produce that is a typical English craft fair. A delightful, giggly Filipino lady is selling the chunky, quirky jewellery that she and her sister produce. 'You like it! It's very pretty! Your lady will love it!' She giggles again as I hand over the cash. On other stalls, there were more traditional craft fair staples too. And I use 'traditional' here in the sense of 'crap': coasters with poorly mounted pictures of Golden Labradors, tiny turquoise soaps that smell of Toilet Duck, twenty quid for a wicker basket stuffed randomly with cloth and serving no discernible purpose. If these were on a trestle table at a church hall 'bring and buy' sale, they'd be charming. But touted as the small, aggressive flagships of prospective craft empires, encouraged perhaps by a million avaricious daytime bargain shows, they are taking the piss. I wouldn't have told Mrs Labrador Coasters this though, as she looked a bit like Patricia Routledge's cruel ex-Gestapo half-sister.

Chippy's high-street department store is called Westgate and though at first it strikes one as grimly, depressingly 1950s with its acidic strip-lighting and forlorn displays, it soon reveals its shy, old-world charms. One gets the sense, negotiating its little aisles and racks, that for generations this has been where Chipping Nortonians have come to get everything from a roasting tin to a corset to a dog lead to a family pack of mothballs. What they didn't seem to have, though, was men's socks, precisely the items I needed, having packed both in haste and with a hangover. 'Try Burtons,' they said. I did. They didn't have any either – no, really – although they did have a large selection of washable polyester bow-ties. What does this say about the menfolk of Chipping Norton, I wonder. That they are barefooted free spirits who nevertheless often have to attend messy formal functions? I went back to Westgate and the girl expressed shock and outrage that Burtons menswear didn't have any men's socks. 'You don't either,' I pointed out. She paused, smiled coyly and said, 'Oh, come on … these are really you,' producing a pair of pink ankle socks encrusted with little stars.

The little Museum of Chipping Norton is closed – it is Saturday, after all – so I sit on a bench in the mild sunshine with a copy of that supposed bible of Middle England, the *Daily Mail*. For weeks it has been full of high dudgeon over a supposed moral holocaust at the BBC wherein some admitted errors of judgement on a few radio shows and some cheeky editing of a documentary trailer featuring the Queen have been presented as evidence that the corporation is a vile, satanic monolith where cackling lizard men disguised in rubber humanoid masks eat live hamsters and plot world domination via Radio 2's *Friday Night is Music Night*.

I am biased here, of course. I am fond and proud of the BBC, not least for employing me, and the *Mail* knows that public-service bashing will always go down well with its red-faced, golfing rump. But while the *Mail* is undoubtedly popular in these cosy Shires, knows its audience well and must have its temperature on some matters, I don't like the implication that Middle England can be characterised by fear and rage or that its predominant tone is censorious, illiberal and vindictive. Already I have seen it to be as much kindly, easy-going and tolerant. Funny too.

Putting such matters behind me, I embark on an afternoon fact-finding mission around this patch of the Cotswolds, 'the Heart of England' as a hundred guidebooks and websites have it. Here are some facts I learned. Shipton-under-Wychwood has a railway station, surely only because Dr Beeching sloped off early that Friday to go to his caravan; more of him anon. They also like their heavy-horse ploughing championships round here. The local stone is lovely (a yellow oolitic limestone, geology fans) and the colour of runny honey, making even the most overcast day look like high summer. Also, there's a fine example outside the Red Lion hereabouts of the heated smokers' gazebo – emblem of Middle England, just as the hi-viz tabard and Greggs pasty are the new standards of the north.

On the road to Burford the scenery rolls by: ploughed

land and gently rolling Cotswold Hills and sweet green pasture. Burford nestles in trees and, to paraphrase *The Wizard of Oz*, you know you aren't in Wigan or Stockport or Goole any more when the local boozer has a Michelin award. That boozer, by the way, is the Carpenters Arms. It's on Walnut Road leading to Meadow Way. I bet Windy Miller and Chippy Minton drink there.

Like Chipping Norton, in fact like a dozen or so places hereabouts, Burford styles itself as the Gateway to the Cotswolds. On a North American scale of distance, I suppose Halifax could claim the title too. Basically, the Cotswolds has more Gates than a scandal-obsessed tabloid. Burford is essentially one big street. But what a street. Long and steep and fabulously higgledy-piggledy with scarcely a right angle to be seen. It was originally a street of shops, each a single storey with workshops and stores behind and the craftsman or artisan's living quarters above. It's still retail heaven: art shops, antique shops, cheese shops, clothes shops. There's even a preserve shop. Burford clearly likes its jam. There is another shop selling, bizarrely, Staffordshire pottery, which I fully expect to be burned out and ransacked fairly soon.

As you may recall, I am still sockless so I make for the gents' outfitters, viz. the Oxford Shirt Company. If I was expecting the local clothes emporium to offer me Vivienne Westwood, leather-studded ponchos or bling jewellery (and I wasn't) I'd have been disappointed. Here all is Barbour, Gore-Tex, Rohan and Aquascutum. It is a riot of tweed, if that isn't a contradiction in terms. The clothes on offer are both fantastically expensive and shockingly bad, with a heavy emphasis on those bright scarlet or salmon-pink corduroy trousers that Edward Stourton and David Cameron wear to Sunday afternoon drinks parties. What is it with the upper classes and these comedy clothes? Is it that having worn a grey suit and a Windsor knot all week they want to shed their adulthood and go about like overgrown children or playschool refugees at the weekend? There was a man browsing in the shop who looked like Rupert the Bear's gay farmer cousin.

My spies tell me – well, if you count Wikipedia as espionage – that Cameron, along with fellow locals Kate Moss, Liz Hurley, Gary Barlow, Kate Winslet and Radiohead, can often be spotted getting their bark chips and barbecue lighter fluid from the Burford Garden Company. It's a garden centre with two restaurants. That tells you a lot about Burford. Not far away is Daylesford Organic Farm Shop, 'the poshest shop in England', as it's been described, and where all of the above can be found as well as many another 'Cotswold highflier', to use the name coined by Alex James of Blur, now local country squire and cheesemaker.

On the way to Windrush I jetwash the car. I mention this only because of the wonderful sign that says 'Jetwash available till half an hour before closing or when darkness falls'. According to my sat nav, this is the only Windrush in Britain, so this tiny, secluded hamlet gave its name to the ship that brought the first wave of commonwealth immigrants to Britain. A curious and sweet juxtaposition. My wife's family are from Windrush. I would say my wife's 'people' but that would make me feel like Tom Parker Bowles and I would have to gouge my own heart out with the nearest scissors. Anyway, I find lots of them on the commemorative stone to the war dead in the church, as well as something quite remarkable. A plaque on the church wall commemorates 'Sgt Pilot Bruce Hancock RAFVR who sacrificed his life by ramming and destroying an enemy Heinkel bomber while flying an unarmed training aircraft from Windrush landing ground during Battle of Britain 18th August 1940'.

Even by the superior standards of courage and toughness of our grandfathers' generation, a generation when even conscripted service men did not baulk at danger, knew death was ever at hand and didn't blub for their iPods when they were taken prisoner, this stopped me in my tracks. It is a bravery that humbles and astonishes. Why on earth, I wondered, did he not receive the Victoria Cross? So I went away and found out. It's a sad and strange story.

On the glorious summer Sunday of 18 August 1940, the Battle of Britain was drawing to an end when 26-year-old Sergeant Bruce Hancock was completing his training with No. 6 SFTS at nearby RAF Little Rissington. The course was almost over and he was excited about his forthcoming leave. That evening he took off from RAF Windrush on a night-training flight alone in his unarmed training plane, an Anson L9164, when just before midnight he was spotted by the Heinkel bomber, No. 1408 of the Luftwaffe's 5/KG27. Originally, it's thought, the Heinkel had been en route to attack RAF Brize Norton but for some reason had chosen instead to bomb Windrush. The German nose gunner opened fire on Sgt Hancock's aircraft and it slowed, causing the Heinkel to overtake it from above.

Instantly Hancock's Anson climbed, rammed the Heinkel from below and both aircraft plunged to earth as fireballs, killing Sgt Hancock along with the four crew aboard the Heinkel. The wreck of the Heinkel was found at Blackpits Farm, near Aldbourne, and such was the carnage that it was thought at first there were five bodies. Sgt Hancock's body was found the following day, some hundred yards from the wreckage of his Anson. Local firewatchers who found his body believed that had more of an effort been made to find him on the night of the crash, he might have lived.

The question, of course, is did Hancock deliberately sacrifice himself? There were several witnesses on the ground that night, both military and civilian, and most stated unequivocally that Sgt Hancock must have sacrificed his life deliberately in an effort to bring down the German aircraft. However, this was never formally accepted by the RAF and Sgt Hancock was never posthumously decorated for what most accept must have been astonishing courage. Sgt Hancock had even told his brother-in-law that he would 'deliberately ram an enemy aircraft' if he had to.

The four Luftwaffe crew were afforded a full military funeral in Britain organised by the Home Office and are interred in Cannock, Staffordshire. Sgt Hancock, because he was not serving with a front-line squadron, is not commemorated on any 'Battle of Britain' roll of honour, was never decorated and is remembered by this small brass plaque on the wall of a country church. One is tempted to talk of 'lions led by donkeys' but perhaps that is presumptuous. But when someone is sneering at Middle England's foibles and foolishness, remember that August night above the sleepy Cotswolds and young Bruce Hancock, giving his life at twenty-six so that Jasmine Cottage and Vine Cottage and the Old Church House could sleep on.

There is nowhere to park at Bourton-on-the-Water. There never is. They call it a tourist trap but it doesn't so much trap tourists as stun them into submission with its sheer cream-tea-and-ducks-on-the-pond niceness. Eventually, by killing a man with my bare hands, setting fire to his Audi and having my brigands force his grieving family into the hills, I get a parking spot for an hour just by Radish Designer Outlet. Radish is unusual amongst Bourton retail outlets for not having the word 'Cotswolds' as a prefix. There is a Cotswolds Perfumery. There is a Cotswolds Bakery. There is a Cotswolds Knitting Shop. I wonder if anything would be deemed too outlandish or inapt. The Cotswolds Nerve Gas Outlet perhaps.

Zombified by the sheer pleasantness, I lope past the model village, the car museum and the discount china and cookwear shop to the Rose Tree café for that cream tea which in these surroundings is luring craving, lusting tourists with the addictive power of a crackhouse. Just as I am spooning on the cream with shaking hand, two foreign tourists are denied their fix of scone by the proprietor as 'it's gone five'. It is two minutes past. This, in its own way, is very Middle England. I hope they scored some in Stow-on-the-Wold later.

Or possibly Lower Slaughter, called by some the most beautiful village in England. That's fighting talk in Chaddesley Corbett, Cerne Abbas and Acton Burnell, but it seems entirely plausible as you cross the languid river Eye and gaze in wonder and a little envy at the place with its quaint footbridges, its delicious church, its lovingly restored water wheel with red-brick tower, its gorgeous, unaffordable houses. Don't be put off by the name. It has nothing to do with death and slaying but refers to the fact that before it became as des as res can be, Lower Slaughter was a 'slough' or quagmire. It has certainly scrubbed up nicely now although there's still plenty of places to get your feet wet. In fact, the first time I ever came across the place was as a tiny tot watching a public information film about testing your brakes after driving through a deep ford. 'Deep Ford Ahead' said the sign and 'Lower Slaughter' too, bringing a chortle from the plummy voiceover man. The ford and the sign are still here, and I get a nostalgic thrill from driving through with a splash. Whatever happened to PIFs? Maybe with the new Health and Safety mania, they'll be back soon and we can all be terrified again by Donald Pleasance and the cowled Spirit of Dark and Lonely Water.

By contrast to its neighbour, Upper Slaughter is a hell-hole, a 1960s planners' nightmare of brutalist concrete tower blocks riven by organised crime and gang violence where feral youths congregate in darkened underpasses to shoot smack and no one is safe after nightfall. Only joking. It's actually incredibly lovely too. Just not as well known. It sits aslant the river Windrush and has a small paved square with medieval almshouses restored by none other than Sir Edward Lutyens. Ramblers ramble, dazed by the place. Ivy creeps up the walls of a row of detached cottages and the medieval/Tudor manor house is now a swanky hotel. There are only so many cream teas a man can have, though, so it's back via crowded B roads to Saturday night in Chippy.

The pubs are filling up, the lights are coming on and I have a table booked in town at a restaurant called, rather winningly, the Thai Shire. It was a good idea to make a reservation. The place was packed, bustling, vibrant and noisy without being intimidating, where serenely smiling ladies in cerise and maroon silk went hither and thither with trays of delicacies. Having neither the teatime takeaway association of the Chinese nor the 'after the pub and fourteen pints of Wifebeater' ones of Indian food, Thai food seems to have become the default ethnic cuisine of Middle England. You can see why. Fragrant, delicious and a bit exclusive, it has a cachet that vindaloo and chow mein have long since lost. I had tam ka soup, Malaysian fruit curry and a side dish of cashew nut and cauliflower. The staff were delightful and the Singha beer was crisp and cold. At some point during the salt and pepper aubergine, I thought I was going to cry. In between exquisite mouthfuls, with the Slaughters still in mind, I knew exactly why La Hurley and La Winslet and Messrs James and Cameron and Barker came here, even if their silly yellow corduroy trousers were still a mystery.

Back in Meriden, there was bad news disguised as progress. To be honest I'd had my doubts as soon as I'd glanced at the map and when I'd read that Meriden is not so called because of its position. It's nothing to do with 'meridian' or anything like that. It actually comes from the Middle English meaning 'the valley where merry-making occurs'. The Global Positioning System is no respecter of tradition and it seems that, armed with their tracking gear and distant satellites, the men from the Ordnance Survey have calculated that the centre of England is not Meriden but a muddy paddock in a field some eleven miles northeast on a farm in Leicestershire. Lindley Hill Farm, grid reference SP36373.66 96143.05, to be precise, and owned by a couple called, appropriately enough, Charles and Margaret Farmer, aged eighty-nine and eighty. When asked by BBC News Online, they said they were 'surprised' to learn their farm was special. 'Someone said we should build tea rooms here and possibly American tourists would come out, but I think we are a bit old for that.' In Meriden, they were philosophical. There were dogs to be walked and bikes to ride. And the Ordnance Survey themselves were conciliatory. Their spokesman Trevor Mouncey said, 'You'll never win an argument against tradition. It may be worth noting that cartography has come on a bit in five hundred years.'

But I had learned already that Middle England was nothing to do with satellites and co-ordinates, rulers and pincers and protractors. We are not a nation of bureaucrats and autobahn-builders. We are vague and romantic, a race of gentleman scientists chasing butterflies with silly nets. Middle England and deep Englishness cannot be defined by measurements. In his book *The English*, Jeremy Paxman lists some of his signifiers of Englishness including Elgar, Do-It-Yourself, punk, brass bands, Shakespeare, Cumberland sausages, double-decker buses, Vaughan Williams, gardening, Monty Python, the Beatles, Women's Institutes, fish and chips, curry, Christmas Eve at King's College, Cambridge, indifference to food, fell-running, ugly caravan sites on beautiful clifftops and crumpets. For me, too, this is how to go in search of Middle England. Not with a slide rule but with heightened senses.

It's about the food we eat and the music we listen to, the books we read and where we go on our days off, what makes us laugh and makes us scared. It's about village greens and craft fairs and smokers under gazebos, Sikh shops and Rastas in football tops and cycling memorials and Thai restaurants and Polish waitresses. You can't pinpoint that with your GPS. Besides, they can't move that monument in Meriden now. So on your bike, cold-hearted cartographer. I would look for Middle England through its fixations and foibles. And next I would test the water.

CHAPTER 2
Bathe of Glory

The English are dirty. Ask any Australian. One of their favourite derogatory terms for us, 'Pongo', refers to our lax and slovenly bathing habits. Complimenting us grudgingly on our swimming successes at the 2008 Beijing Olympics, the Australian swimming coach said it wasn't bad for a country with 'very few pools and not much soap'. Odd, then, how keen we are on spas. Not the ones where you can get Monster Munch and the *Daily Mirror* but the ones where, for hundreds of years, royalty, gentry and even oiks have come to disport themselves, to drink rank, sulphurous draughts to cure their lumbago and scrofula, to luxuriate in H_20, and most importantly, to gavotte, jig, minuet, gossip and conduct illicit assignations. There may have been no bombing or diving in the baths of Leamington and Buxton two hundred years ago. But there was plenty of petting, believe me.

Once upon a time, the spa was a place where the enfeebled or world-weary well-to-do could take what we might call the health of nature cure, a belief that immersion in or drinking of various weird, smelly liquids could rid one of sundry agues of the heart and mind. While still places of rest and recreation, the modern spa and the modern spa break is more likely to be enjoyed by a hen party in fluffy towelling robes or a small group of middle managers shuffling awkwardly towards the steam room in monogrammed Van Essen slippers after a morning on the mini golf course. The key concept here is 'pampering'.

Pampering is a very Middle English notion that reveals much about our national psyche, i.e., that essentially we expect life to be disappointing and unsatisfactory and that the smallest of treats – a sit down, a cup of tea, a Jammie Dodger, a leg wax – are what make it not only endurable but exciting. The Finns and the Germans do not do 'pampering'; they thrash themselves with birch branches and plunge into icy pools for their R&R. The French and the Italians, with their gorgeous climate, fine wines and plump cheeses, regard 'La Dolce Vita' as a birthright. They have no concept of pampering. Life is about pampering. These are not races who think of a digestive biscuit and a pouffe as a life-affirming experience.

Spas take their name, deflatingly, from a Belgian town near Liège called Spa. It's a spa, by the way. Continental Europe has tons of them, from the famous Baden Badens to the more cultish Hajdu Bihar of Hungary. We in Britain have a perfectly respectable eighteen. And perfectly respectable they all are. As a pub diversion, listing the eighteen spas of the British Isles will probably never replace naming the Magnificent Seven, the seven dwarves or the wonders of the ancient world. But there are some similarities. In the canon of English spas, Tenbury Wells and Droitwich are the Horst Buchholz, the Doc, the Lighthouse at Pharos. The ones everyone forgets.

By contrast, Buxton, Leamington and Bath are the Steve McQueens, the Dopeys and the Hanging Gardens of Babylon. According to a 2007 survey, only one per cent of Britons actually use spas – the natural sort, not the ones in hotels where hen parties hang out in fluffy towels getting their cuticles done – because of their 'perceived exclusivity', but this may be precisely what has made them so redolent of a genteel Middle Englandism, the sort of place where you have a lovely, refined weekend that ends with you looking enviously in estate agent's windows whilst eating an organic damson and juniper ice cream. While I'm on the subject, the best ice cream in England is to be found in a spa town. There's been a little wooden shack at British Camp in the Malverns probably since those industrious Iron-Agers built the camp on the adjoining hill. Go there soon and, eschewing the Lyons Maid on offer, ask the nice Goth girl for Rachel's home-made stuff. You won't regret it. I seem to remember that the elderflower and sloe gin is the best one. It's hard to say, though, especially when you're rolling around in the car park drooling. I'll remind you of it a little later.

The ices – to use the proper 1950s idiom – at the Henley Ice Cream Company are more famous and nearly as good. It's an attractive old timber-frame building housing a company established in 1934, and a much-loved and famed Sunday afternoon destination for West Midlanders for three generations. It's a tea room and gift shop now, with contented patrons slurping at their lemon meringue and strawberry double cones underneath a cheery logo of a cow jumping over the moon. As the nice ladies there will tell you – and if for some reason they won't, framed newspaper clippings on the wall tell the tale – the current owners took the company over eight years ago to stop this local institution falling into the rapacious hands of developers who care only for high-yields and buy-to-lets, and naught for cinder toffee ice cream 'with everything on it'. The various, bewildering flavours – all forty-one of them – are now made on farms in Staffordshire and Worcestershire.

Pleasant though Henley is, I'm only passing through on my way to one of England's most famous spa towns, and, for several years running at the turn of the twenty-first century, the most prosperous town in England. Royal Leamington Spa was a beacon and flagship of Central England's revival after the slump of its automotive industries, and thanks to improved rail links, the building of the M40 and the boom in communications technology. Leamington can make a good claim to be definitively Middle English, not just culturally but statistically. A 900-year-old tree called the Midland Oak, at Lillington, just northeast of the town centre, has a plaque claiming that it is the very centre of the country. At the time of going to press it is not known whether irate Meridens have uprooted it and borne it, Elgin Marbles and Stone of Scone-like, to a safe house. If you want more proof of its centrality, Leamington Spa is, according to recent socio-linguistic research, right on the very border of the north/south divide over the pronunciation of Bath, the 'a' being short as in 'bat' north of here and all languid and long as in 'bar' once you get south.

Geographically, Middle England led the country out of Major and Lamont's recession and right through Blair and Brown's fiscal prudence and into financial cosiness, for a while at least. Significantly, during the 2001 election, Tony Blair and his entourage made a beeline for Leamington, bringing chicken ciabattas, fizzy water and lollipops and crisps for the kiddies; this just before plump kids became the nation's bogeyman and we feared the coming of the twelve-stone toddler as we once feared nuclear attack. Blair's was a carefully choreographed visit to a scientifically selected target constituency in which, according to the *Independent*, 'Mr Blair mingled, for the benefit of the cameras, in the lavish tea room of the refurbished Royal Pump House and Baths ... Even the sun came out briefly to provide perfect lighting through the Georgian windows. The town's tea drinkers, supposedly a cross-section of residents, sounded suspiciously at times like they were reciting from a New Labour handbook. After the self-employed Kevin Finnan extolled the need to invest in public services, Mr Blair admitted with a self-conscious smile: "I couldn't have put it better myself."'

If Tony is here today I can't see him. He's certainly not enjoying a doner in the branch of Kebabish by the grand 1930s railway station. On arrival, Royal Leamington Spa (to give it its Sunday name), or Leamington if you prefer, or even 'Leam' as the racier locals have it, feels similar to the Yorkshire spa of Harrogate: knocked about a bit and suffering from some 1970s planning blight but still suffused with a certain old-world elegance to be felt along its Georgian crescents, in its grand hotels and amongst its abundant statuary, if not its pizza parlours and martial arts studios. In fact, idling by the river and wandering around the lovely Jephson Gardens, it feels distinctly superior to Harrogate, although of course that could be the embittered and begrudging Lancastrian in me.

The Jephson Gardens lie opposite the Pump Rooms on the river Leam which splits the town in two, Budapest style. The gardens were engulfed during Middle England's catastrophic floods of 1998 but have been restored and substantially improved with funding from the National Lottery. What would our parks and gardens do without the vain weekly hopes of the innumerate lower orders, eh? A panorama of bandstands, larches and strapping youngsters, many of them students at the University of Warwick, it all looks very sweet and terribly English. For a sudden surreal dash of exoticism then, seek out the other bank of the Leam on Priory Terrace, and a gentle slipway leading down to the river. This was built in the nineteenth century so that the circus elephants in their winter quarters in Leamington could be watered. I came across this astonishing fact in several sources on the internet and it is either a case of cyber Chinese whispers or a fact worthy of repetition over foaming ale whenever the name of Leamington is mentioned. They claim to have invented lawn tennis here as well but if I'm going to believe one bit of trivia about the town I'd prefer it to be the pachyderm-based one.

In 1612 John Speed wrote, 'At Leamington, so far from the sea/a spring of salt water boileth up.' Though this had been common knowledge since the Middle Ages, Leamington, like many of England's spa towns, was a rural hamlet until the 1780s when it became fashionable amongst well-to-do Georgians to take the saline waters. It burgeoned as a resort town, attracting queen-to-be Victoria herself in 1831. So impressed was she, possibly even amused, that she later granted it full regal accreditation and thus humble Leamington Priors became Royal Leamington Spa. Older residents will pointedly use this nomenclature when asking skateboarders to turn their music down or writing frothing letters to the local press. Leamington has long had a reputation as a retirees' dream town, which, coupled with its new popularity with students, gives it an interesting social mix.

One local resident though, in his blog Oliver's Poetry Garrett, is swooningly, flamboyant disparaging and captions a few fairly innocuous pictures of dustbins and the like with this: 'For a change I thought I'd show you the real Royal Leamington Spa – the side of this quaint, Regency town in quaint old middle England that visitors don't know exists. All the decay, tumbleweed and dereliction. The many bits of this tourist town that the council's vast income from tax, parking charges and other sources does not reach. The flaking paint, crumbling buildings, faded glory.' Clearly a sensitive soul. I hope the smelling salts were to hand, Oliver.

Speaking of which, going back a century and a half, the town boomed on health tourism and so great were the number of annual visitors that in 1814 a large new building, the Pump Rooms, was designed and built by C.S. Smith of Warwick. Leam prospered thus until the coming of the railways made seaside holidays fashionable amongst the wealthy and afford-able to the masses, and Leam's loss was Brighton, Blackpool and Bournemouth's gain. The resourceful Leamingtonians diversified into engineering and that too prospered until our manufacturing base crumbled, but the town still does quite nicely thank you via light industry, communications and the video game industry. If you know your MMRPGs and your shoot-em-ups, your Quakes, Mysts and Grand Theft Autos, you will maybe know the names of bleeding-edge games developers like Blitz, bigBig Studios, FreeStyle, Supersonic Software, Aqua Pacific, Codemasters, CustomPlay Games and fishinabottle. All are either based in or close to the town.

But the hi-tech attractions of Leamington's first commercial heyday were more lavatorial. The handsome Jephson Gardens commemorate Dr Henry Jephson, one of the leading figures in establishing Leamington as a health resort. In the newly restored Pump Rooms, a museum complex now gives a flavour and a whiff – metaphorical if not actual, perhaps thankfully – of the glory days of Leamington as a spa.

Leamington's doctors were aggressively propagandist about the virtues of the town's waters, not just for bathing but, even less appetising, for drinking. There were three types available on draught, as it were: saline (salt), chalybeate (iron) and sulphurous (er, sulphur), and they were said to cure everything from 'stiffness of the tendons', 'rigidity of the joints', and 'the effects of gout and rheumatism and various paralytic conditions'. 'Imagine drinking the yellow-green sulphurous waters,' asks a thought-provoking sign. 'They were said to be mildly laxative.' That doesn't surprise me; just the thought seems to have the desired effect.

As if to prove this, there is a picture of one of the town's evangelising docs, Dr John Hitchman, in a display case. Portraits of civic benefactors tend naturally towards the flattering and obsequious. Bucking this trend entertainingly, Hitchman here looks totally mental, like Einstein morphed with Ken Dodd on an amyl nitrate binge. Benjamin Satchwell, the enterprising local cobbler, postman and poet who saw the commercial possibilities of the town, doesn't get his portrait hung here but gives his name to a pub in the town where altogether more palatable restorative liquids can be purchased.

The good doctor Jephson set out some general rules for those who, burdened with a variety of ills, were planning to take the saline cures. There was a 'season' lasting from May till October. To get the best from the spa, patients were supposed to stay at least a month, drinking the spa waters and bathing in them two or three times a week. A recommended day would begin with a pint of the nauseating water followed by a constitutional around the town (a shaky one, I'll wager) and then breakfast. It's worth noting what Dr Jephson had to say on the matter of diet, which is salutary, and might warn us against taking the pronouncements of self-appointed experts too seriously. He, like our cheerless modern hamster-faced diet gurus, felt a good diet was crucial to health, and advocated stale bread, plain meat, plenty of sherry, black tea and butter and positively no fruit or veg. No five-a-day for Old Jephson unless it was five schooners of Harvey's Bristol Cream or a quintet of lamb chops. Maybe that's why Hitchman looks like he does in his portrait: happy but unhinged.

Let us now consider the nicer element of spa life: luxuriating in hot water till prune-like. But again, if you expected spas of old to have the flavour of those darkened, aromatic basements in boutique hotels, full of the scents of sandalwood and jasmine, lit by flickering candles and populated by Stepford-ish creatures from Debenham's perfume counter gliding serenely from massage chair to towel rack, think again. Spas of old were about bracing invigoration, not pampering. Here at the heart of Leamington's Pump Rooms are various menacing-looking baths and an array of slings and stretchers. I was shocked at how disturbingly medicalised the whole process was, although an elderly Brummie lady nearby did look admiringly at the stand-up metal needle shower in its forbidding wire cage and say, 'I could do with one of them at home.'

The Zotofoam bath cured obesity, it was claimed, by increasing the user's temperature and metabolic rate, which burned calories. An accompanying picture dating from the early twentieth century shows a ribald and rosy-looking fellow up to his head in billowing foam. An equally cheery and shockingly thin attendant looks on. Perhaps he too has immersed himself in the miracle waters. Or perhaps he's drunk a pint or two of them. There are also vichy douches and alternating douches. But I didn't like to ask.

On the way out I dropped into the art gallery. Stanley Spencer's wonderful, heavily symbolic *Cookham Rise* is here for reasons that are not explained beyond that it was presented by Alderman Holt in 1938. As someone who usually thinks of aldermen as fat blokes with watch fobs who stop the Sex Pistols coming to Wigan, I say, well done, Mr Holt. There's also a very good Ivan Hitchens, a nice Leamington 1940s snow scene by Steven Bone and Sir Terry Frost's *Madrigal* inspired by Auden's poem of the same name, which he first came across in Leamington library. The town seems to attract artists, and I pause by a selection from new resident Jean-Pierre Kunzler. Jean-Pierre describes himself, depressingly, as 'searching for the inner truths in human existence'. I'd have preferred it if he'd said he was interested in getting off with girls, drinking absinthe and mucking about in a smock.

I quite liked the exhibition of folk art (a trade-union banner from the railway workers' union, some graffiti, a few paintings of pigs by an unknown rural artist found in a barn and some photos of a girls' night out) and would have stayed longer but the curator was by now looking at me and my note-book suspiciously as if to say no one can be this interested in pigs, trade-union banners or, for that matter, Royal Leamington Spa. Well, I was. And I quite liked Leam.

I liked Buxton better, though. Maybe because I came to it in a lovely frame of mind, one gently nurtured by the hypnotic rhythms of the 10.37 from Manchester Piccadilly, the unfold-ing views of the Peak District foothills and the tide of fine towns that laps up against them: New Mills, Furness Vale, Whaley Bridge with its quaint, honeyed houses under the hill. You get the sense that this is where the austere grandeur of the northern lands meets the gentle warmth of Middle England. The fact that Vernon Elliot's delicate, musty music from Oliver Postgate's *Pogles Wood* and *Ivor the Engine* was playing on my iPod as the train pulled into Buxton made the arrival even nicer.

Buxton feels like LA after Whaley Bridge but it's still very pleasant indeed. The sort of place where – if, like me, you grew up in a dark factory town in a smoky hollow in the Lancashire plain – you would drive out to on Sunday trips and maybe would have moved to if Dad had won the pools. Stepping down from the train, you stand beneath 'The Huge Fan Window' as the plaque calls it. This is a somewhat literal description for what is, yes, a huge window in the shape of a fan. But you can see why Buxton is proud of it, not least because it was designed by Joseph Paxton, creator of Crystal Palace. That's the splendid glass artefact not the undistinguished Sarf Landan football team.

At just over a thousand feet above sea level, Buxton is the highest market town in England. Alston in Cumbria disputes this but it doesn't have a regular market so, come on, Alston, do the math, as our American cousins say. In any case, Buxton is surely the highest spa. Get down off that Manchester or Sheffield train in January and it will feel like it too, high on a plain where shale, gritstone and limestone meet, hard and cold but high and mighty. Unlike Leamington Spa, it was the coming of the railway in 1863 that ushered in Buxton's boom years, not its decline. Easy transportation made it extremely popular in the late Victorian era and the town's finest houses and civic architecture date from this period. The mineral waters have been famous since Johnny Roman, a sucker for a long soak and a salty drink, called the place Aquae Arnemetiae. The Elizabethans were just as keen too and Mary Queen of Scots took the waters here while she was a prisoner at nearby Chatsworth. The 5th Duke of Devonshire had the commercial acumen to properly develop St Ann's mineral springs in the 1780s by building the Assembly Rooms and Crescent, modelled on Bath's famous royal one, in an attempt to lure the glitterati of the day away from the Cotswolds to hilly Derbyshire.

After the Victorian boom, twentieth-century poshos tired of spas in favour of perhaps Noël Coward, cocaine and the Black Bottom, and Buxton settled into being what it is today: a high, handsome town popular with both northern commuters and those seeking to escape the urban rat race but not wanting to be completely out in the sticks. As an article in the *Independent*, wearily titled 'Spas In Their Eyes', had it, 'Buxton conjures up images of grand buildings, ornamental gardens, quaint tea rooms and its eponymous bottled water. But the little spa town, a natural gateway to the beautiful Peak District national park, has been quietly broadening its appeal over recent years.' What this means is that whilst Buxton remains refined and pretty, it isn't fusty. It's genteel and comfortable but with just enough rock and grit to 'keep it real', as the town's huge gangster rap and hip-hop community would say. Actually I've made that up. But famous Buxtonians do include Vera Brittain, mum of Shirley Williams and author of *Testament of Youth*, and Tim Brooke-Taylor, slightly subversive Middle England comedy icon and thoroughly nice man. The family business, Brooke-Taylor's solicitors, is one of the first things you see on the left bank of the curving street that leads to the town proper. It's a mean street too if like me you skipped breakfast: Simply Thai, Pizza Express and the Indian Palace. In the Trisha vernacular I might say it was doing my head in. In which case, the Buxton Health Practice offering crani-sacral therapy and metamorphic techniques might come in handy.

The town's museum is a former Museum of the Year award-winner. This surprises me. Not because it's rubbish; far from it. But it is old-school in a way that I would have thought put off awards committees – neat and quirky and defiantly non-interactive. There are no buttons to press and no breath-less exhortations to 'Imagine what it must have been like to live in a Bronze Age settlement/attempt to broker a lasting peace at the interminable Versailles negotiations/have your shop windows broken during Kristallnacht/slaughter, rape and generally lay waste to great swathes of Central Europe as one of Genghis Khan's Mongol Hordes!!!!'

Not all history can be reduced to the level of a 'Wiggles 'n' Giggles' nursery-school play activity. Nor should it be. There should be mystery and awe and maybe a little fear too. I'm sure more kids have been turned into natural historians by that huge, forbidding dinosaur skeleton in London's Natural History Museum than by any amount of flashing lights and touch pads. As I sometimes think I'm on my crotchety, prehistoric own about this, I was heartened to read Waldemar Januszczak on the mixed blessing of free museums in *The Times* of 27 April 2008: 'Why is Halle Berry's bikini in the Imperial War Museum ...? Bond and his Aston Martin have nothing to do with the terrible realities of war when our young men are having their legs blown away in Iraq and Afghanistan ... Pop along to the V&A on a Saturday afternoon and you won't see gangs of newly interested teens from Peckham or bands of Asian youths from Brick Lane but lots of middle-class mums using our museums as a free playground. Not only are our museums failing to oppose the infantilisation of Britain, the damn places are spearheading it.'

In the Buxton museum, there are curious things called Devensian Bone holes and tableaux showing how European reindeer hunters followed the migrant herds over here across ice and snow and fetched up in caves in the Peak District – pretty remarkable when you think about it. The exhibit marked 'The Wonder of the Peak' seemed to feature a disconcerting sound montage of someone having a massive, distressing bilious attack but actually turned out to be a recording of a bear.

The staff were lovely. Bright, personable, chatty ladies with specs on chains and ash-blonde hair and silk blouses. They told me genuinely interesting stuff about local fauna, geology and scandal, all of us trying to ignore the fact that a man in a cagoule and a neckerchief was looking at a representation of a boar hunt in the High Peak muttering 'But why? But why?' in a tone of anguished curiosity. Like libraries, museums in the daytime are still a great place to spot that dying English species, the unfathomable, inexplicable solo eccentric whom Larkin celebrated/bemoaned in 'Toads Revisited'.

I cross the road onto a large, raised mound that looks back over the snoozing town. This is called the Slopes and is really rather marvellous. There's a big Georgian civic building here all pumped up with Buxtonian pride, basking in autumn sun and looking out across to blue Peak District hills. The Opera House and Pavilion are down to my right but I decide to head the other way first, towards the market, here on Tuesdays and Saturdays. Pleasingly, it's a Tuesday.

By the time I emerge onto the big square behind the King's Head pub, where one imagines crowds of drinkers spill out on fine summer Saturdays, the market is quietening down with the distinct feel of a party that is breaking up in a desultory flurry of coats and taxis and Portishead album tracks. It's a nice day, though, and to console myself I decide to have a hotdog. Whilst fully cognisant of the health risks and the fact that hot dog sausages are made from toxic waste and eyeballs and fibreglass, I find them hard to resist, especially from a van on a market square. It's the cheap, buttery, irresistible aroma of the frying onions, I guess. I have vegetarian friends who, wandering the streets after chucking-out time, will have just these succulent, mouthwatering, fatty onions on a bap with a jolt of ketchup, a kind of Hot Dog Manqué of Drunken Solidarity. The lady in Buxton who ladles on my onions hands the finished product to me and says, 'Now you enjoy that and you be a good lad.' Then she pauses and adds, 'No, don't. It's boring.'

It's delicious of course. But in the manner of these things it is also gone in a gobbled, messy instant and if it hadn't been that I thought someone was watching, I'd have tried the 'businessman's lunch deal' at the Big Panda Chinese restaurant. I liked the name a lot and I was keen to find out whether I'd chance upon Bill Gates, Alan Sugar and Richard Branson having spare ribs and pork balls in Buxton on a Tuesday afternoon.

Down the hill I find what I think qualifies as a 'little gem', one of those hidden delights in a town that make you wish you lived here and could kill an hour or two here when the daily round got too dull or stressful. It is Scrivener's Bookshop and Bookbinders, five rambling, creaky floors of volumes on every subject from sexual health to Sanskrit texts, children's collectables to military history.

I wandered around it in a kind of daze. There is, winningly, a 'self-service coffee area' consisting of a kettle, mugs, teapot, catering tins of Nescafé and Yorkshire Tea, mismatched spoons and a bowl of sugar. Around a corner awaits a harmonium with sheet music scattered about and bearing the invitation to 'competent players' to have a go, suggesting that the midday reverie is sometimes shattered by semi or possibly utterly incompetent harmoniumists rending the air with tortured wheezings.

No matter how bad your harmonium playing was, I imagine you'd be chastised rather gently and sweetly by the two ladies running the shop this Tuesday. One is owlishly, funkily hippy with greying hair and round glasses, while her younger colleague is chestnut-haired, white lab-coated and sits picking at her Tupperware box of hummus and salad. From the ink and glue stains on the white coat, I guess this must be 'Holly Serjeant, Bookbinder' as advertised in the literature. Both are quite charming. I wander into the tail end of the conversation they are having, full of dramatic shivers and whispered confessions about certain rooms in the shop they do not like to enter alone, particularly in a later afternoon dusk in November. They spot my interest immediately and tell me that several customers have reported a spectral man flitting between the shelves on the higher floors. I'm heading that way myself and they ask me, only half joking I note worriedly, to let them know if I see anything.

I did. I saw a man on the stairs. He blocked my way rather ominously, chuckling quietly to himself. He was quite real, though, if rather queer and disconcerting too, with his ragged yellow pullover and snickering little laugh, another of those unfathomable people you meet in the middle of the day whose back stories and hinterland you will never know. I push past him and onto the *Just William* first editions, all out of my price range. I content myself with a small, lovely edition of Housman's *A Shropshire Lad*.

By the time I get back downstairs, another man has appeared, a much more personable one, though, and he is regaling Holly and friend and a little gaggle of customers with a spooky tale about the house he is in the process of moving out of. It seems to be called Flash and all the locals know it. He's leaving because his wife can't stand the unexplained, distressing cries and whimpers.

'It used to be a children's home, you know,' says an old lady standing by the religious section. Apparently no one did. At least I'm guessing that from the quiet that fell in the little room at the foot of the shop, a silence broken by the tinkling of the bell as I leave. When you're next in Buxton, do pop into Scrivener's, whether you want a Richmal Crompton first edition, a book bound or just a scary little interlude.

I walked out into that lovely curious netherworld that is the middle of the day in residential England: the children at school, Mum and Dad at work, Granny snoozing in front of daytime TV or Radio 4's afternoon play, Granddad doing the odd spot of weeding and, even though you're a stranger, giving you a cheery wave from his domain across the privets and azaleas. The houses in this part of town are lovely and the occasional one is a B&B in a quiet nook. I walk in brilliant sunshine down deserted avenues that are almost completely silent, save for a stray voice or laugh from an opened window and the faintly eerie sound, getting louder, of a school on its lunch break, I imagine.

To my left, somewhere up a sweeping bank of russet trees and the rolling hilly countryside at the back of town, lies Poole's Cavern, once visited by Mary Queen of Scots. The

Poole in question was a fifteenth-century thief who was said to have used the caves as hideout and store for his stash. According to a leaflet acquired from the nice ladies at the museum, the cavern's usage by locals dates back far beyond Poole, however: 'Artefacts have been found from the Stone Age, Bronze Age, and Roman period. The caverns boast exceptional formations, including colourful blue and orange stalactites created by minerals leaching from the limestone roof of the caves.'

I wouldn't know. I never got there. I feel distinctly sheepish about this. Real travel writers, the ones with scars, big shorts, bandanas, trunks with exotic stickers, pith helmets, that kind of thing, would not get lost finding one of Buxton's most famous local landmarks and attractions. They can find a way through treacherous swamps, shark-infested waters, minefields, snipers' alleys and ruined cities using only the Great Bear and a needle in a glass of water. Ray Mears and Ranulph Fiennes can make a serviceable house – with patio, barbecue area and maybe double garage – out of some wool. They can live on birch sap and rancid yak milk for weeks.

With hindsight, I reckon I went wrong at the bottom of Bridge Street. The sign was a bit misleading and I think I had the leaflet the wrong way up. And I definitely followed the direction of that little silhouette walking man on the Public Footpath sign. Whatever, I realised after twenty minutes or so that I was wandering in a desultory sort of way around a big grassy area that turned out to be the playing field of Buxton Community School. Strange men wandering around school playing fields has probably never been a heartwarming image, certainly not compared to, say, a tin of shortbread, some milk-maids, or a kitten in a beer mug. But over recent years, any lone man spotted pretty much anywhere where children may have once been in the last calendar year now hints at unspeak-able wickedness. Whilst the statistics all agree that kids gener-ally come to harm through the cruelty, neglect and/or idiocy of their own parents or politicians, the notion of the shadowy child-molester at the school gates has got Middle (and certainly lower) England twitchy as hell and led to a severe shortage of amateur referees and scout masters. As someone who detested every one of the eighty or so minutes I was a scout, this doesn't unduly bother me. But it did occur to me that, on this mild autumn day in Buxton, I ought to get back onto the street before a sniper picked me off from the art room window or parents with pitchforks ran me out of town.

Waving a hastily constructed placard that read 'I'm Not A Pervert, Honest' I made my way as best I could back to the residential street where I had gone wrong. This took me right across the athletics track and right back to 1975. Suddenly I was a small boy again, adrift in a vast, largely hostile Catholic boys grammar school run by virginal sadists in frocks. The lanes of the running track, the discus circle, the long-jump pit, the rugby posts, the stinging hail on red exposed thighs, the bad haircuts, the mock exams, *Nationwide* with Michael Barrett, the gentle thought of suicide, it all came back to me as a Proustian saver single to the innermost circle of hell. This playing field, I have to say, nestling at the foot of a wooded hill, was much nicer a setting than most of the places where I spent my bleak midwinter Tuesday afternoons. If you are going to be bullied into running 800 metres in a hailstorm, what a nice setting. Now, let's get out of here.

Back in Buxton proper, the Sahara kebab house is closed down and so its whitewashed window has become a kind of parish pump cum Reuters Agency for the town's youth. Various attention-grabbing headlines and op-ed pieces have been smeared and daubed in and of the oily white stuff. 'Nicole Ray is fit' reads one. Similarly, 'Emily Crowther is fit' according to another correspondent. Less generously, though, someone asserts that 'Aby is a mong'.

I pass a violin shop called, with admirable lack of palaver, Buxton's Violin Shop. I suppose there is not much need to call it Lord of the Strings or Premier Violins since, and I could be wrong here but feel sure I am not, competition in its chosen field must be scant, if not non-existent, even in as nice a place as Buxton. How has it managed to stay in business, eschewing, one assumes from its name, even the cello and viola? I don't know but I'm very glad that it has, one of those rare and cheering examples of how quirkiness and independence and specialism can still exist in the era of one-stop shops that sell you nothing. I think of all this whilst standing on the pavement trying to resist the lure of both the Coach House Chippy and Thompson's Fish and Chip Shop. Both look saltily inviting but as it is only a couple of hours since that hastily consumed 'research' hot dog, I pass by with a sigh.

Returning to the town centre via the market, I see that it is still sleepy, with the mid-morning rush long behind it now. There are cheap fleeces and even cheaper air-conditioning units. A white-haired man in a fisherman's jersey sits gently dozing on a lawn chair in the back of his blue van clearly not selling many of his rugs and pot plants. And you will think I have made this up but behind him, visible in a single quick glance, is the richness and absurdity of English life: a man selling pigs' ears from a bucket in front of two internet cafés.

Not put off even by the proximity of porcine offcuts, I decide to have that cherishable Middle English interlude, 'a nice cup of tea and a sit down'. Beltane, the café I'd seen advertised in the gallery, looks rather sweet – the sort of place where the proprietor will be reading Harry Potter and wishing someone would write it here. 'Sorry. No food today,' reads a hastily posted sign. 'The chef is having a day off.' I can't make up my mind whether this is quintessentially Middle English in its half-bakedness or almost Latin American in its winning mañana lackadaisicalness.

I don't mind. I only want that nice cup of tea and a sit down. Or a frothy latte as it turns out, as inside Beltane is all scrubbed pine, Zero 7 album, scattered copies of the *Independent*, nice young men with manbags and bottled Staropramen. I feel very sure there will be live jazz at some point soon. If this sounds like I'm sneering, then be assured that I enjoyed my latte in these convivial surroundings. Next door is a shop called Columbine, who must hate the new and grisly associations of their name but can console themselves that they sit on Town Bank, which is described on an information placard nearby as 'an elegant rise of Georgian town houses'.

At the bottom of this rise and down from the Slope sits the famous Pavilion Gardens, with broad grassy lawns, gentle fountains, shady arbours and cute little bandstands. Like the market, the gardens are decidedly somnolent on this autumn Tuesday, making me wonder whether Buxton is now a commuter town for nearby Manchester and Sheffield. Whatever the reason, I very nearly have the place to myself and there is a pronounced lack of those public park staples, Goths and tramps. I feel rather sad about this. I can't claim to find odorous men swearing and throwing punches at imaginary foes whilst drinking Special Brew appealing, but I have always had a soft spot for Goths, a sympathy hugely increased by the horrific case of the murder in a Bacup park of a young Goth girl, brutally beaten to death by a pack of thugs simply for looking different. At the time, this was passed over by most of the media who were looking the other way at the sweet, sad features of a little blonde girl called Madeleine McCann. In their own way Goths are just as gentle and vulnerable, for all their forbidding appearance and predilection for black eyeliner and Hammer Horror chic. By the way, if you still aren't sure what a Goth is, the best description I can offer was coined by the journalist Mark Ellen. Drive north on the M6 and just north of Silverdale or Grange-over-Sands, somewhere around junction 35, turn off. Head for the nearest large-ish market town and time your arrival for about dusk. Once in the town centre or market square, look for the war memorial and there you will find three or four young people dressed in black drinking cider from a bottle. These are Goths.

Back in the Pavilion Gardens, a lovely realisation dawns. Brilliantly, a river runs through it. A real one, the river Wye gurgling and frothing through the park in a series of meanders and frothing waterfalls, rendered a little brown and sluggish by fallen leaves. Though nearly deserted, there are pockets of activity here and there among the gazebos and fountains and bandstands that give the place the feel of Chigley.

A man is taking a picture of some ladies at the worst conceivable angle, with him in a dip and them partially obscured by said bandstand. Is this incompetence or art? Who can say? The smallest baby I have ever seen is being introduced to the delights of the swings and his or her expression itself swings between abject terror and joy, sheer bliss and delirium. A lovely couple are eating an ice cream on a bench by the pool. 'We're playing hookie from the office. I expect you think we should be doing something more exciting.' Not at all. It's life's little stolen pleasures that are often the most profound. A white-haired gentleman is standing by what seems to be – oh joy, it is! – the platform of a miniature railway. I've never had a train set and I carry no torch for miniature railways either, to be honest. But just knowing they are still there, between Ravenglass and Eskdale or here in a Buxton Pavilion Gardens, makes me feel warm and reassured, like knowing that the ravens still inhabit the tower and the church clock stands at ten to three and there's honey still for tea. I ask the white-haired gentleman is there a train due, but he just laughs and walks off chuckling and tapping the ground with his brolly. Clearly he knows something I don't. Minutes pass without a hoot, a whoosh or a cloud of steam. Perhaps there's a Miniature National Rail strike or the line fell victim to Beeching's axe. In any event, after a while I walk off too.

The old spa is part of the Pavilion. Once so crucial to Buxton's prosperity, it now seems to be a swimming baths, judging by the steamed-up windows and the kids with rubber rings. Within the elegant glass façade, the Pavilion houses several eateries. The simpler offers a pensioners' special lamb curry, whilst in the more chichi restaurant ladies and gentlemen of a certain age are enjoying what seems to be, viewed sheepishly from the doorway, a fine late lunch. They're taking bookings for Xmas, offering, for starters, a thought-provoking spin on a traditional gambit in 'pearls of melon with a Thai infusion'. Then comes 'Pan-fried canon [sic] of turkey wrapped in bacon with traditional trimmings of honey-roasted parsnips and Brussels sprouts', then Christmas pud, which I've never understood the appeal of. Maybe they'd let me have cheesecake. Thirteen pounds fifty a person anyway, which seems the most astonishing bargain to me, a man who is regularly reduced to mute astonishment by the price of a mango smoothie. I stroll to the attractions board to see what I have missed this week: a lunchtime dance with Peter Rogers. A record fair. There's a farmers' market next Thursday. I might pop back then and pick up an ostrich burger. They're bound to be selling them.

The Opera House adjoins the Pavilion and is a noted jewel, designed by Frank Matcham, one of Britain's most celebrated theatre architects and the man responsible for the London Palladium. It opened, with great civic fanfare, on 1 June 1903, when the audience were treated to *Mrs Willoughby's Kiss* and *My Milliner's Bill*. For the next three decades the Opera House played host to touring Shakespeare companies, West End successes, ballets, concerts and musical comedy and whodunits. In 1925 the great Anna Pavlova, later to be immortalised as a strawberry tart, performed the 'Dance of the Dying Swan' here. When movies arrived, the Opera House simply adapted and turned itself into a cinema too. But the great Lilian Baylis of London's Old Vic continued to present live theatre and summer festivals in Buxton. If Beltane had been going back in the 1930s, you might have found yourself slurping a mochaccino next to Dame Sybil Thorndike, Robert Donat, Anthony Quayle, Robert Morley or Alec Guinness.

Through the 1950s, 1960s and 1970s, though, audiences declined and its future looked doubtful. It closed for a while during the mid-1970s but in the late 1990s was the subject of a massive renewal programme with both public and private money and the full support of the town. It came back grander than ever in the new millennium and luminaries as diverse as Elvis Costello, Steven Berkoff, Peter Kay, Prunella Scales, Bill Wyman, Ken Dodd and Jo Brand have trod the boards in recent years. The *Knutsford Guardian* has eulogised it thus: 'Frank Matcham's glorious Opera House at Buxton, with its warm and intimate design, always guarantees a night to remember for theatregoers,' whilst the *Manchester Evening News* ('a friend dropping in' according to the TV ads of my youth) says, 'There is no better place for a panto than this gilded fairy palace, especially filled with hundreds of clap-happy, singalong children.' It is the hub of the Buxton Festival Fringe, a sort of mini-Edinburgh festival with less mime and shortbread.

Did I mention that it looks gorgeous, even from the outside? Sort of fanciful in a nice way, a bit like an elaborate and undeniably toothsome gateau: twin cupolas, gilt lettering, rampant Edwardiana and a balcony from which Marie Lloyd might have waved. The coming and present attractions give you an instant flavour of the tastes of every generation of Middle Englander. Roald Dahl's *Danny the Champion of the World* and a stage production of *The Darling Buds of May*, a selection of Radio 4 stalwarts such as Marcus Brigstocke and Paul Merton, an audience with Peter Sallis ('thirteen and fifteen pounds') and Rick Wakeman's *Grumpy Old Picture Show* ('consistent star of TV's *Grumpy Old Men* and the creative genius of Yes wallowing in musical nostalgia. Let your essential grumpiness go free!!'). And then into the bar for a sweet sherry or pint of bitter or chardonnay or Bacardi Breezer of whatever your Middle England tipple of choice may be.

You leave Buxton with a mildly contented air, rather like the one the town itself has. Even with the lorries on the A5 rumbling to Leek and Congleton and Macclesfield, it feels peaceful and happy with its lot. Passing the Buxton campus of the University of Derby, which boasts amongst various achievements 'the largest unsupported dome in Britain', I think: what a great place to be a student. Nice pubs and caffs, a market, some great chippies, the fleshpots of Manchester only fifty minutes away, lots of outdoorsy stuff like walking and rock climbing in the surrounding hills of the Peak District and the largest unsupported dome in Europe? You'd be living the dream for three years.

Though it seems almost too perfect, on the road back to the station I find a proper old-fashioned sweet shop, with jars in the window and an array of pleasures from another age, the age of Marie Lloyd and Frank Matcham: bullseyes, Everton mints, liquorice laces, cough candy, cola cubes, rhubarb and custard, sherbet, and that stuff we used to call 'kayli' that made your head explode when eaten with dampened finger. The idyll is only spoiled by the world-weariness of the proprietor, who mildly mocks my enthusiasm for his wares.

'What do they come in?' I ask. 'Quarters?'

'One hundred and fourteen grams,' he replies.

'What's a 114 grams?' I ask innocently.

'A quarter,' he says morosely. Perhaps he longs for another life, far from the cheap childish allure of the Black Jacks and Refreshers. A cocktail bar in New York perhaps?

Back at the station and sucking thoughtfully on a gobstopper the size of my head which fully lives up to its name, I notice that the Huge Fan Window is a bit cracked. Buxton has its vandals, then, like everywhere. Shame. As I get on the train I spy a little window into the room where the train guys hang out, their green room or backstage, as it were. There's a Thermos in the window and a Tupperware box of butties and a line of Clive Cusslers and Sven Hassels and Stephen Kings that must have sustained through many a shift. Sweet, I think, as I rattle off back to Manchester with *Ivor the Engine* in my ears. It was good to have soaped up on niceness in the spas. Because the next safari in my hunt for Middle England promised to be disgusting.

CHAPTER 3
Green Ink and Pleasant Land

Royal Tunbridge Wells is unique. It is, as far as I can see, the only town in the world that is associated with an emotion. We know Blackpool for its tower, Eccles for its cakes and Ascot for its races. We know Chesterfield for its crooked spire and Stilton for its smelly cheese. But the only place that is famous, infamous even, for the supposed character of its natives is Tunbridge Wells.

And maybe they wouldn't mind so much if they were known for their generosity or licentiousness, their wit, bravery or their gregariousness. They probably wouldn't even mind if they were legendary for being generally scared, baffled or absent-minded. But no. The people of Tunbridge Wells have become a byword for small-minded provincial insularity, for hidebound conservatism, for dullness and bigotry and the eagerness to take offence. 'Disgusted of Tunbridge Wells' is as much a national emblem as John Bull or Boudicca, the spluttering, aggrieved counterpart to the happy few and happy breed that Shakespeare and Noël Coward extolled. Is this fair? Is this right? And if it is, is the world becoming more like Tunbridge Wells?

In 1993, the Australian cultural commentator Robert Hughes published his *Culture of Complaint*, a book which nailed pretty impressively a nasty contemporary malaise: the desire to blame someone else for everything. He based his theories on America but the phenomenon is a global one, and some people would diagnose it as a very British, even Middle English, disease. For though Hughes's book is in some ways an attack on political correctness, in which it might seem a rallying cry for disgruntled colonels, it is also a tirade against whingers. And where once stoicism and 'mustn't grumble' were the watchwords of Middle England, it now seems that whatever upsets us, even inconveniences us – from the weather to cold-callers to radio programmes we don't like – someone must be to blame. Teachers, the government, pop groups, footballers; someone somewhere should pay for the fact that the world is not just how we like it. Once we'd have done something about it. Maybe switched channels, maybe thought hard about stuff, maybe exercised a little patience or equanimity. Now we want someone else to do something about it and fast. Someone should be sacked, someone should be carpeted, someone should apologise. An apology we won't accept, of course, our arms folded, our ears closed.

If we call it grumpiness, we defuse it, render it harmless, even funny. Given the name of one of the seven dwarves, it sounds cuddly. It conjures up Rick Wakeman or Arthur Smith complaining about mobile phone ringtones or call centres, rather than reactionary cant about gay people or workers' rights or art we don't like or understand. We used to be the people who said, after the Luftwaffe had razed our street, after we'd lost a leg or a cup final and treated those impostors just the same, 'Mustn't grumble.' Now our motto is, 'Always grumble.' They should put it on the coins.

The soundtrack to our lives is becoming an unmusical chorus of whining, a babyish low-level whimper of disapproval dressed up as common sense. Like babies, too, we have become monstrously self-regarding. As Hughes puts it: 'The self is now the sacred cow ... self-esteem is sacrosanct.'

Is this Tunbridge Wells' gift to the world then? Surely not. I went to find out whether these people were really as disgusted as we all believe them to be. You'd have to say, at first sight anyway, they aren't. The girl sitting on the steps of the posh clothes shop didn't seem that disgusted. Pausing mid-smoothie, she smiled and merely said, 'Doesn't it mean that we're all old fuddy-duddies?' Something she signally was not in her 'bling' shades and diamante-encrusted jeans, sipping her exotic mango and lychee drink. Whenever I could, on my weekend in Royal Tunbridge Wells, population 56,000, twinned with Wiesbaden and sitting prettily on the north of the sandstone of the Kent Weald, I asked people whether they were in fact disgusted about anything at all. And, with a couple of spectacular exceptions, they seemed about as relaxed and contented and, well, whatever the opposite of disgusted is, as a townspeople can be. Though I have to say I didn't ask all 56,000.

According to Bamber Gascoigne's *Encyclopaedia of Britain*, 'Disgusted of Tunbridge Wells' is the 'hypothetical signature for any indignant anonymous letter to a newspaper, suggesting blimpish outrage. It is not known when or where the joke began, but it is not popular in Tunbridge Wells.' I like Bamber Gascoigne. *University Challenge* was a lot more intellectually rigorous under his benign, ginger tutelage. For me, Jeremy Paxman's abrasive and hectoring style is curiously at odds with the downright easy-peasiness of the questions these days. But here, I think, Bamber may be wrong. The Tunbridge Wellers – affluent, chilled, well turned out – didn't seem much to care about their appellation. Also, theories proliferate as to how it all began, this mass generalisation of 56,000 people, this ethnic besmirching of a whole, really rather nice town.

According to a website bearing the very name Disgusted of Tunbridge Wells, it was 'the nom de plume of a prolific writer of letters to the *Thunderer* – the London *Times* – during the first half of the 20th century. His alias became almost as widely known as the title of the Fleet Street newspaper itself, and was synonymous with diatribe. He delivered scathing attacks on organisations and individuals that came to his ultra-critical attention … He was self-opinionated and convinced of his own infallibility. He was the quintessential Englishman. But what marks him out in particular is that, despite being regularly published, he was never identified, and his real name remains a mystery to this day. He was simply "Disgusted of Tunbridge Wells".'

Like most of the opinions expressed in the website – a tiresome, splenetic and occasionally nasty mish-mash of bigotry and wrong-headedness – this is the veriest bollocks. It seems that the designation 'Disgusted of Tunbridge Wells' used for a mean-spirited, harrumphing bore gained popularity in the 1950s. Historian and former newspaper editor Frank Chapman attributes it to the staff of the former *Tunbridge Wells Advertiser*. The paper's then editor, alarmed at a lack of correspondence from readers to fill his letters page, forced his staff to pen a few fictitious ones, a merry practice that I and my colleagues happily indulged in at the *New Musical Express* some four decades later. One of the staff at the *Tunbridge Wells Advertiser* signed his simply 'Disgusted, Tunbridge Wells', and a cultural touchstone was born.

It seems, though, that long before the 1950s, Tunbridge Wells had enjoyed, if that's the word, a reputation for stuffiness and stultification. In E.M. Forster's *A Room With a View*, written in 1908, Miss Bartlett opines, 'I am used to Tunbridge Wells, where we are all hopelessly behind the times.' In *The County Books – Kent* in 1948, Richard Church wrote that 'many people sneer at Tunbridge Wells, calling it a stuffy Victorian relic, full of retired snobs and ex-professional people whose only amusement is to meet for morning coffee on Mount Pleasant and to be most unpleasant in their querulous frettings over their rheumatism and the disgusting habits of the younger generation … Nevertheless, I love it.'

There are apparently references to the town in works as diverse as the Sherlock Holmes adventure *The Valley of Fear* and Oscar Wilde's *The Importance of Being Earnest*, Thomas Pynchon's bamboozling post-modernist tour de force *Gravity's Rainbow* and Zadie Smith's *White Teeth*. In British cinema, it is mentioned with sly humour in David Lean's masterpiece

Lawrence of Arabia, when the titular character concludes that 'on the whole, I wish I'd stayed in Tunbridge Wells', and in the James Bond film *On Her Majesty's Secret Service* when the soon-to-be-bumped-off Mrs Bond says she looks forward to living as Mr and Mrs Bond in that most idyllically uneventful of addresses: Acacia Avenue, Tunbridge Wells.

Former Tory leader, beer monster and baseball-cap devotee William Hague chose Tunbridge Wells to launch his local election campaign in the late 1990s. Reporting at the time, the BBC said the place was redolent of 'Doilies, Women's Institute, semi-detached, cricket on the green, retired colonels, bone china, bridge evening ... a by-word for traditional, conservative England'. It is conservative with both small and large Cs, remaining resolutely and defiantly Tory even during the Labour landslide of 1997 and beyond, although the late Robin Cook did choose the town's register office to tie the knot with his second wife. Two bastions of Middle English sport have lived here: cricketing golden boy David Gower, and Virginia Wade, the last Briton to win a Wimbledon singles title. Ringletted shouter of The Who Roger Daltrey has a trout farm nearby – what is it with rock stars and trout? – and the town's marketing strapline promises 'Georgian elegance, natural beauty'. All of which meant it came as quite a surprise when some of the first things I encountered here were robbery, foul language and angry rows motivated by sexual jealousy. All in good time.

I had really wanted to stay at the Tunbridge Wells branch of the chichi chain Hotel Du Vin, not so much because Keira Knightley and Orlando Bloom have stayed there but because it was home for the last seven years of his life to the notorious 'hellraiser' (showbiz for 'drunkard') Richard Harris. Shortly before he died, he was taken out of the hotel by stretcher to a waiting ambulance and he remarked to some American tourists, 'It was the food that did for me.'

Well, anyway, it was fully booked. So I stayed instead in Pembury, a village on the outskirts of the town. Just past the Tesco. You can't miss it. It has a mini village green, a Chinese takeaway, a chemist and several pubs, one of which shares its name with a fashionable and edgy district of North London. You would hardly call its position rural, sitting alongside a busy arterial road, but it was sort of traditional and welcoming, all candles and stripped pine, and smiling and helpful staff.

I arrive late-ish and decide to put off exploring Tunbridge Wells itself till the next day and amble down to the bar for something to eat. There is a blackboard offering an over-whelmingly diverse choice of dishes. As I don't particularly like fish, I now acknowledge that my choice of fish soup as a starter was a strange one. When it arrives it is brown and mysterious and way, way fishier than I am prepared for. After a few mouthfuls it is pushed aside in preparation for my main course. Steak pudding is one of the great northern dishes, best consumed, I always found, in a white foam tray with chips and curry sauce in a bus shelter at half past ten. It helps if you're sixteen and slightly drunk too. I order it here on the outskirts of Tunbridge Wells out of a certain amused and cussed northern-ness, feeling that steak pudding is surely the least Tunbridge Wells main course imaginable. In this, though, I accept I could be wrong, as it was after all a favourite dish of John Mortimer's *Rumpole of the Bailey* and possibly a staple at Eton and Harrow. Anyway, it was very, very good.

The people at the next table didn't seem very Tunbridge Wells either. By my reckoning, it was forty-something Mum and Dad with son and girlfriend, and what surprised me was that they were very much a cut below. Dad lolled in his chair looking faintly pissed and the young blonde girlfriend, pretty in an obvious sort of way, started casually effing and blinding like a Clydeside docker, a practice then echoed by everyone around the table, including Mum, who wore an M&S cardie and sipped chenin blanc. They swore not in rage or excitement but calmly and prosaically, as if they were reading out a recipe or a crossword clue. I almost choked on my suet. I wondered if anyone else was shocked. At the table beyond was a scrawny fellow in a turquoise T-shirt. I glanced at him to see if he felt any kindred nonplussedness but he looked vaguely distracted, was shuffling agitatedly and muttering into his mobile phone.

I read a little about the hotel. It is two hundred years old and is available for funeral wakes, again something I associate with the west coast of Ireland rather than suburban Kent. According to one bit of blurb, it sits 'majestically' at the north side of the village, which seemed to be laying it on rather thick, but no matter, the steak pudding had made me feel very well disposed to the village and the pub. At another table, two middle-aged women sit chatting about work. One has just got back from a trip to Amsterdam. They laugh brightly and over-loudly about something and she catches my eye, a little embarrassed. She turns to get something from the back of her chair and her demeanour changes, from girlish sociability to consternation and then clearly distress.

The scrawny man in the blue T-shirt has gone. So has her handbag. The two events are not unconnected. Me and the sweary family all begin to offer condolences and vague, probably useless titbits of help, me in regular conversational English, theirs peppered, landmined even, with choice four-letter words.

'Fack me, you don't expect to get your facking bag nicked here. London, yes, maybe the West End, but not here. Facking cheeky bastard. I thought he looked shifty.' I can't help thinking that a bright turquoise T-shirt is not ideal sneak-thief garb. Unless, of course, it's some kind of genius double bluff. Whatever, it seems to have worked. I feel sorry for the woman who now faces the grim, joyless task of changing her locks and stopping all her credit cards via a series of Kafka-esque late-night phone calls to Bombay. I go to sleep that night thinking that, on first experience, Tunbridge Wells is not so much home of the quintessential bourgeois dullard as a nest of foul-mouthed thieves.

Breakfast has a vaguely, charmingly, provincial French feel. There are baguettes, brie, croissants, some cold ham and a fantastically idiosyncratic way of getting your boiled eggs. A large electrical tureen of boiling water sits gently steaming on a table. Nearby is a basket of eggs. You select your egg and then place it in a small numbered egg-sized basket attached to a long hook. You hook your basket over the edge of the tureen with it dangling in the boiling water. Then you take a little digital timer back to your table where you gut and fillet the *Sunday Times* and by the time you have got rid of the Travel, Business, Motoring, Lifestyle, Education, Health and Parenting sections, you note that your egg is ready and you go to retrieve it, sharing a joke with the other people at the tureen, all a little childishly giddy about the way boiling an egg here has been turned into a diverting little game. I was almost beside myself with glee when I saw there was a baguette guillotine. How much more jolly was all this than ladling some congealing beans kept warm under a 1000-watt bulb onto your plate?

The family who run the pub were milling about, half working, half communing on this bright Sunday morning. Mum and son discreetly oversee the smooth running of the egg tureen and baguette guillotine and daughter-in-law arrives with a little girl. They've been to ballet lessons and the tiny one is keen to show off what she's learned, pirouetting in the sunlight while the breakfasters look on, smiling indulgently. Ahh.

Breakfasted, I venture into Tunbridge Wells proper. The underground car park is as horrible as underground car parks the world over but this has a uniquely unpleasant feature in that the Pay and Display machine does bad impressions. As your ticket emerges from its innards, you get a nasty burst of Frank Bruno ('Know what I mean, Harry') or Del Boy ('Luvvly jubbly!'), suggesting that the machine has been here since 1986. How odd then that no one has set about reducing it to fragments with a lump hammer. As it is, the smartly dressed lady before me in the queue merely raises her eyebrows and turns on her Russell and Bromley heel.

Tunbridge Wells has a lot of such ladies, young and old. They roam the streets, the older ones swathed in Nicole Farhi, Hobbs and Monsoon, the younger ones slightly brittle-looking and blingish in designer sunglasses that probably cost the price of a second-hand car. Not that any of the ladies in town this Saturday afternoon here drives a second-hand car, I think, as another Mitsubishi 4x4 rolls by down the high street. Looking around at the townsfolk I am reminded of a remark the Dutch photographer and film director Anton Corbijn made about his first meeting with Joy Division. Coming over from Holland to Manchester in the late 1970s, what struck him about the young band was how pale and skinny they looked, their clothes thin, their complexions sallow, a stark contrast to the well-fed Dutch with their comfortable welfare and social provision and healthy economy. In Tunbridge Wells, the people seemed taller and healthier than their counterparts on the streets of Manchester, Birmingham or Wigan, three places I know well.

I'm not surprised. The town has a general air not of stifling conservatism but rather of handsome, confident prosperity. The streets are broad and rising, surprisingly steep for those of us who think that south of Birmingham Britain becomes a bowling green. At a table in Carluccio's window, a woman in big shades and elaborate jewellery picks at some olives and reads the *Telegraph*. A poodle, maybe hers, lies disconsolate and bored in the doorway, head on paws. The shops speak of discreet affluence: Bang and Olufsen, Russell and Bromley, Habitat. Sadly the Quirky Turkey appears to have closed down. Perhaps there is no call here for left-field poultry sandwiches. Absentmindedly I end up making a phone call outside a posh ladies' clothes shop and attract the attention of a posh and very nice lady coming out.

'Are you from the north?' she asks.

'Yes,' I answer a little hesitantly, worried that she might be about to ask me to dig her some coal. But no.

'I was born in Scarborough,' she replies. 'What's it like up there these days?'

I tell her that I can't vouch for Scarborough but the rest of us do nothing but go to the ballet and design websites and, gratifyingly, she laughs as she walks away down the sunlit street.

BBC Kent has its studios in the shopping arcade and, as is the fashion these days, you can see right in. As a radio presenter, I'm not keen on this. It's a workplace after all and I don't expect butchers, dressmakers or lathe turners to be on show in a goldfish bowl. Besides, what if I've got my feet up and am having a snooze during 'Stairway to Heaven'? Anyway, in the studios of BBC Kent this fine afternoon, two young guys are singing and thrashing furiously at guitars. Who knows? Maybe this will prove to be their big break. I pop into the museum, as is my wont, and am instantly confronted with the most disturbing thing I have ever seen in such a genteel place, a display cabinet filled, for surely no good reason other than to terrify, with really scary old dolls. Clearly dating from the early days of doll production and before they'd got the hang of it, it is a distressing parade of glassy eyes, shapeless bodies and grotesque distorted features. Nearby is a case containing the stuffed remains of Minnie the Lu Lu Terrier ('a much-loved pet'), another unpleasant encounter, and one that reminds me of the wisdom of the title of Alan Alda's autobiography, *Never Have Your Dog Stuffed*.

An Australian couple join me and look on with horror but are clearly too polite to say, 'What in God's name is this all about?' Instead, with the easy geniality of their tribe, they tell me they are staying at the Hotel Du Vin. 'How's the food?' I ask, in memoriam Richard Harris, but they haven't eaten there. 'One more week to go,' they say and seem genuinely sad to be leaving our funny damp little island. Predictably, the weather has been 'up and down … but we've had a seven-year drought at home so we could do with some of your rain.'

Back out on the streets, the elegant women come and go, the tall children, the Mitsubishi 4x4s, the poodles and the tourists, shopping and lounging in the town's ambience of sweet propriety, its shelves laden with brogues and hi-fis, its bistros overflowing with polenta.

And it is all a lie. For the real story of Tunbridge Wells is one of depravity and wickedness. Not for nothing was this town called 'the most debauched town in England' by the Puritan diarist Roger Morrice. For great swathes of its history, Royal Tunbridge Wells was certainly more disgusting than disgusted.

Take a stroll around the town and you'll notice a plethora of street and place names evoking the Bible. There's a Mount Pleasant and a Mount Ephraim (where the infamous Judge Jeffries of the Bloody Assizes once lived). But the reason they are so called is not to reflect the upstanding nature of the citizenry, but quite the opposite. It was to deflect and obscure the town's bad reputation, which is all tied up with its heyday as a spa.

One day in 1606, a young nobleman, Dudley, Lord North (why do posh people never have regular names?), was staying in the area and languishing in poor health due to the excessive and dissolute lifestyle and general overindulgence at the court of James I, of which he was an enthusiastic member. Riding along what is now Eridge Road, he noticed some funny Tango-coloured liquid coming up out of the ground, which he recognised as a chalybeate spring like those at the continental resort of Spa, famous for their supposed health-giving properties. He slurped a mouthful (obviously – I mean, who doesn't drink orange water coming out of the ground when they spot it?), began to do so regularly, was cured of all his ailments and started a fashion for the stuff.

A hundred years later and the place was in full swing as a hip resort, patronised by royalty (hence its full name) and popular with the early-eighteenth-century glitterati. One contemporary account talked of 'music playing all the time; and the ladies and gentlemen divert themselves with raffling, Hazard, drinking of tea and walking till two, when they go to dinner. In the afternoon there are the bowling-greens for those that love that diversion; and on those greens are balls four times a week for the young people; and where any gentleman may dance if he pleases. At night the company generally returns to the shops on the Walks, where is all manner of play till midnight.'

The town became the haunt of rakes and courtesans and scandal engulfed it. Like Bath and Epsom but more so, Tunbridge Wells became a spot where the beautiful people could hang out and let down their hair – as well as other things

– away from the constraints of London society. It had a curiously classless and liberal vibe. Daniel Defoe said of Tunbridge Wells, 'Here you may have all the liberty of conversation in the world, and any thing that looks like a gentleman, has an address agreeable, and behaves with decency and good manners, may single out whom he pleases, that does not appear engag'd, and may talk, rally, be merry, and say any decent thing to them; but all this makes no acquaintance, nor is it taken so, or understood to mean so.' As far as I can see, all of this is simply a seventeenth-century version of the old rock and roll maxim, 'What goes on tour, stays on tour.'

In much the same way that the opening of a new London members' club will lure away the idlers and rakes and courtesans of our era, so Brighton's rise led to a quietening down of life in Tunbridge Wells. But from time to time it lifts its petticoats still. When the UK publication of Nabokov's *Lolita* was held up for fear that publishers Weidenfeld and Nicolson would be convicted of obscenity, it continued to be freely available to the public at one place in Britain: the public library in Tunbridge Wells, which had simply ordered a copy three years earlier from Paris. It proved no rival to Edgar Wallace. Said the assistant librarian to a journalist at the time, 'Demand has never been particularly high … Our top favourites at present are *Doctor Zhivago*, Monty's memoirs and the life of King George VI.' These days, the town likes to remind you of its racy past as counterpoint to its supposed modern respectability. The town has even hosted, with a hint of the flirtatious, a Scandals at the Spa festival.

The biggest scandal I can see this sunny afternoon is that some barbarian of the 1960s dropped a pre-stressed concrete car park right in the middle of the town. In my trips across Middle England I was to recoil from several of these eyesores. Now I'm no Prince Charles, no knee-jerking enemy of modernism. The Nye Bevan International Pool in Skelmersdale new town is a squat, forbidding cube that sits perfectly well in the walkways and concrete ramparts of Skem, where a honey-stoned Georgian villa would look daft. But the car parks of towns like Bath and Tunbridge Wells smack of wilful architectural savagery, akin to Chairman Mao and the Red Guard sending all those ballerinas to work in paddy fields. I am cheered, though, by the sight of a great display in the window of a department store, where a selection of retro-portables is showing *The Herbs*, *Button Moon*, *Wombles*, *Sooty*, *Roobarb and Custard* and more.

I am headed for what I am told is Tunbridge Wells' best feature, a quarter called the Pantiles. 'Quarter' may be putting it grandly. The Pantiles is really a sort of street, a colonnaded walkway if you want to be accurate. But whatever we call it, it is quite delightful: Italianate, maybe Moorish, indubitably Georgian. Frankly I'm saying the first things that come into my head. But I'm not alone in feeling this way. A guide to the town from the late 1800s says that a visitor to the Pantiles might remark, 'How antique! How un-English! How foreign!'

Pantiles. I'd puzzled a little over the name earlier that day. Perhaps it was Pan-tee-lesh and referred to a covered market in medieval Constantinople. But no. Pantiles are tiles. Just a lot rarer than you get in Homebase or Topps Tiles, and unusual enough as a walkway surface to be enshrined in the area's name. The Pantiles has been a playground and fashion parade ever since the fashionable and funky of the day first came here for the spa waters. The Musick Gallery, a wrought-iron balcony known locally as the Dutch Oven, provided musical entertainments by strolling players, a sort of superclub, I guess. The 'season' ran from May to October and, in Tunbridge's Georgian heyday, the 'Walks' as they were then known were the place to see and be seen. There was a strict if informal protocol about parading along them: gentry on the colon-naded Upper Walks and hoi polloi on the Lower Walks. Richard Beau Nash, the dandy of the spa towns, who acted as kind of promoter cum MC here and in Bath, policed these protocols rigorously, as befitted his rather stodgy self-appointed role of 'Arbiter Elegantorium'.

Today, even polloi such as myself can walk along the colon-naded Upper Walk without fear of ejection by Dandy, though they still have sedan-chair races here on bank holidays. This siting seems entirely appropriate, more so than holding them in Moss Side anyway. There is a charming array of shops, bars and restaurants, and on the balcony above a somewhat rumpled-looking man, a sort of Dandy gone to seed, is stretched out in a chair and snoozing in the sun. There is a Secret Games Shop where I could have killed several hours looking for new experimental Cluedos and a replacement Howzat?! Trevor Mottram's kitchen shop is an Aladdin's cave crammed with gadgets and whatnots and, as is obligatory in good old-fashioned hardware stores, cannot be properly negotiated without banging one's head on colanders, trivets and spring balances. It also smells like a proper hardware shop should, though I'm never sure what that smell is. Flux, maybe, the mysterious stuff in a grey bottle that Mr Duckett would squirt sparingly on your prototype garden fork during metalwork. Brilliant though I was at metalwork, my choice of studies was to deny these islands another Isambard Kingdom Brunel, because my fancy turned to other things, like the verse plays of Christopher Fry. His big 1930s hit *The Lady's Not for Burning* is unfashionable now but was a real teenage favourite of mine and not just because I got to sit next to the hauntingly beautiful Anne O'Neil. So I've always hated that the play is now best known for being paraphrased into a self-aggrandising quip by one Margaret Thatcher and her speechwriter drones. Anyway, Fry was director of the Tunbridge Wells players and *The Lady's Not for Burning* was first performed here on the Pantiles in the Pump Room. I think of Chris Fry's opening night and the laughter and Anne O'Neil, and I walk on in pleasant reverie.

The Pantiles has lots of nice places to eat with nice-looking people lounging about at pavement tables sipping long tall glasses of nice-looking stuff and picking elegantly at dazzling salads glistening with olive oil and balsamic vinegar. If this is all a sales pitch, it works. I ask the Spanish proprietor of the most popular eatery if he has a table for later that evening. He thinks for a bit and pops inside and pops back out and exhales slightly whilst pulling the kind of face that tells you that, yes, you're going to get a table but he doesn't want to make it look too easy. 'Seven o'clock OK?' Perfect, I reply, and make a mental note to choose whatever the girl in the yellow dress is having, as she seems to be having the best time anyone has ever had since the invention of fun. Life is certainly good in RTW, as I have decided someone must call it.

Across the road is a fossil shop, whose continued existence is testament to the quirky tastes of the British shopper and the unquenchable optimism of the British shopkeeper. I pootle about, buy a few guides and try to look interested in fossils. Most on display are very small and I fancy that the ones I'd like – a complete preserved sabre-toothed tiger perhaps, or a Pterodactyl in amber – must be both pricey and hard to come by. I fall into genial conversation with the two gentlemen within, proprietor and friend, both in smart slacks and short-sleeved shirts, each with creases you could shave with. They are clearly proud of their town and eager to share its joys with me, if a little wistful. 'It has lost some of its glitz. I wouldn't call it a proper spa town any more. But do try the waters, though, while you're here.'

This very opportunity presents itself at the far end of the Pantiles, nearest the town itself. Here is the spot where Dudley spotted the trickle of discoloured water, found it good and later wrote: 'These waters youth in age renew/Strength to the weak and sickly add/Give the pale cheek a rosy hue/And cheerful spirits to the sad.'

Today it looks disconcertingly like a rusty hole in the ground or a latrine in a particularly downmarket Albanian provincial restaurant, but I am still determined. The Bath

House was built on this spot by one J.T. Groves in 1804 and did originally contain showers and baths but fell into disrepair in the middle of the nineteenth century and became a shop, possibly selling fossils. In 1987, the façade was restored and you can once again enjoy a cup of the fabled stuff, as dispensed by the 'dipper'.

Today's dipper is a young woman with smart, severe designer glasses somewhat at odds with her period garb of little floppy bonnet and petticoats. Spotting me, a lucrative potential customer – it's ten pence a shot after all – she puts down her fat sci-fi paperback and emerges from the Dipper's House. 'Can I tempt you, sir?' she smiles, getting into character a little shyly and, of course, she can. I hand over my ten pence in exchange for a little glass of the surprisingly clear water. On the town's web forum, one posting reads, 'Did you ever try drinking ink when you were a kid, just to see what it tasted like? Well, the chalybeate springs in the Pantiles taste exactly the same.' I can tell you that it is much nicer than that. Yes, it is metallic-tasting and a tad minerally – I have no idea if there is such a word, by the way, and the spell-check certainly doesn't like it – but it's not the green sulphurous stew I was fearing.

Energised, I decide to head up the Commons, the town's beauty spot. As I turn the corner I walk straight into a girl gamely trying to run in ludicrous heels with a plastic cape around her shoulders and dripping wet hair tressed up in bows of silver paper. Showering me with water, she starts to explain that she sat down to have her hair done without realising that she had no money and the hairdresser's credit card machine is on the blink but, really, you didn't need to be Sherlock Holmes to work this one out. I leave her clasping her soggy money, cross the busy road and head up the track to the Commons.

Long before scandalous spa swingers, disgusted letter writers and lunching ladies came to Tunbridge Wells, Mesolithic hunter-gatherers made camp on the sandstone outcrops of what are known as Tunbridge and Rusthall Commons. Down the years they played host to Saxon swineherds, then freeholders, becoming a renowned beauty spot during the Victorian era when substantial improvements were made, such as a lake and terraced walk, whilst maintaining the untamed feel which in Pelton's guidebook of 1871 was spoken of glowingly: 'To our modern taste its natural and wild condition renders it far more attractive than the artificial parks which it is the fashion to provide for the healthful recreation of the dwellers in large cities. The furze bushes and the brake are the most noticeable ornaments; but the whole expanse abounds with other plants and blossoms — ling and heath, chamomile and thyme, milkwort and wild violets, being among the most abundant. In April and May the golden bloom of the furze, which is unusually profuse in this spot, delights the eye, and its rich perfume scents the breeze.' As was the wont of sentimental Victorians they thought that the famous Toad rock, in fact produced by wind erosion during the Ice Age, was 'the remains of an ancient sphinx'. Pretty much every rock on the common was named according to a fancied resemblance to something or other: the Elephant, the Pulpit, the Fox's Hole, the Footsteps, the Cottage Loaf, the Parson's Face, the Cradle, the Bloodstain, the Lion, the Pig's

Head. Nowadays, we would doubtless have Pete Doherty Rock, the Mobile Phone Stone and the Giant Bacardi Breezer.

The 256 acres of the Commons, now under the stewardship of a group of conservators, have never been landscaped or cultivated and are loved by Tunbridge folk for their abundant wildlife and their suitability for many kinds of recreation, healthy and unhealthy, approved or otherwise. On the little climb up from the back of the Pantiles, you can see the tawdry little secrets of the town's fashionable drag, what Wilfred Owen might have called its 'wrongs hushed up': a KFC and a branch of Subway, each with requisite pimply youths on both sides of the counter. Feeling literally and philosophically more elevated, I climb the pleasant thickly wooded hill and spy a bench surrounded by primroses with the graffiti 'Stu' emblazoned on it. I see this as an omen and so I sit down to take in the view. Feeling devil-may-care, I take my jacket off, fold it into a pillow, stretch out and put it under my head, and instantly drop off.

I wake to the footfalls and panting and hissing iPod of an Amazonian blonde jogger and the scurrying of a terrier hot on the trail of a tennis ball. Clearly, Tunbridge Wells enjoys its Commons. There are limits to its permitted uses, though, as the bylaws board points out. 'No bird or animal is to be trapped or hunted', I'm glad to see, and there is to be 'No graffiti'. This is hard to read as, ironically, my namesake Stu has graffitied all over it.

Wandering back deliciously aimlessly into town and in the general direction of my hotel, I reflect on the fact that one website claims that RTW has a large and transient population of homeless people. I'm not doubting this but they aren't readily apparent in these wide streets where the shoppers go. What is in evidence though is lots of ice-cream cones and shorts and smiling faces on the first really nice day in months. The only wrong notes are sounded by a poster advertising an evening with Alan Mullery at the Cumberland Hotel (I've nothing against the former Spurs midfielder, it just seemed more Chadwell Heath than RTW) and, a clanging one this, an argument I witness in the car park of my hotel as I return there in the late afternoon (and again more Chadwell Heath fun-pub than Regency Spa). A couple in their late forties, smoking furiously, glinting with gold and leathery with tans that originate in Ibiza and are topped up at Tanfastic, are pacing to and fro between the bar-room door and a flashy Golf convertible. First one and then the other will make as if to drive off whilst the other affects to re-enter the bar and/or chase the other in their preferred direction. It is as choreographed as *The Nutcracker*. The libretto is somewhat different though.

She: Oy, I told you I was only facking talking to that old bloke.

He: I couldn't give a fack who you were talking to.

She (forte): What is your facking problem, Jeff?

He (fortissimo): You are my facking problem. Go and talk to your facking old geezer. I'm off!!

By the time Jeff does leave, in a roar of engine and a plume of exhaust fumes, I feel I should applaud, as I would in a box at La Scala. Instead I go to my room and lie on the bed watching the football results. I'd booked a taxi to take me back to the

Pantiles and dinner but it never came. When I told the hotel's owners, they were genuinely upset for me and angry at the rudeness of their fellow Tunbridgians. So much so that the head of the family, Publican Pere, as you might say, went straight out to the family BMW, took out his little granddaughter's car seat and gave me a lift into town. Given that he was driving me to a competitor to spend my money there rather than at the Camden Arms – the hell with it, they deserve a recommendation – I thought this was extraordinarily decent of him. We northerners often like to think that we have cornered the market in friendliness and have a narrow-minded tendency to characterise southerners as terrified and snobbish cold fish who hide behind their *Guardians* on the Tube. Well, this may be true of Londoners but it is not true of Kentish folk in my experience.

On the way into town, he told me with evident and understandable pride how he and his family had transformed the pub, and how he was doing the same with another in the area, how he was importing a £50,000 fish fryer from America, and how he was having to lose 50 per cent of the clientele thanks to a clampdown on drug trading under the former regime, another unexpected facet of Middle England pub life, as well as tankards and shove ha'penny.

At the Casa Vecchia, I have the steak with parmesan polenta, mussels and chorizo and listen to the tinkling laughter of the most well-behaved hen party I have ever encountered. Not a chocolate penis in sight, just some appreciative and girlish giggling over the yumminess of the brûlés, panna cottas and tiramisus. Taking a turn in the mild evening air, I remember the 1871 guidebook. The Pantiles by night feel even more distinctly un-English than they do in the day. Italian almost, with their promenading girls and boys taking their passeggiata along the colonnaded walkway. There is a clump of drunken lads on the bandstand but they are utterly unthreatening, if a little noisy. We are used to hearing that the Shires by night are now an orgiastic bonfire of car crime, drug taking, violence and alcopop-fuelled promiscuity. In reality, it's young people letting their nicely cut hair down a little. Peckham and Longsight it isn't.

On the return leg, my taxi driver was as punctual as the Chigley clock I felt I would find somewhere in Tunbridge Wells if I looked hard enough. He came from an Irish family in south London and moved here in the 1980s. 'It was tough for first week but then I got stuck into playing rugby.' He supported Crystal Palace and told me that most of the town supported London clubs, and I recalled the West Ham and Chelsea kits I'd seen in my hotel's beer garden, although the odd diehard followed Gillingham, Kent's only League club. 'And you see the odd Man U and Newcastle top,' he added with a sigh. He'd had three sons since moving here and he told me with delight they had just got in at Tunbridge Angels. I somehow felt that asking who Tunbridge Angels were would take the sheen unnecessarily off his paternal pride so I simply whistled in admiration. I told him that I'd found Tunbridge folk very accommodating and welcoming. He said, 'The further south you get from your part of the world and the closer to London, the unfriendlier people become. But then you pass London and go south and we get friendly again!' Sorry, Luton, Northampton and Watford. I didn't say it. Take it up with the nice taxi drivers and lunching ladies and genial pub landlords of Royal Tunbridge Wells.

The day I leave I come across the website of one Helena Frith Powell, *Tatler* and *Mail on Sunday* columnist, writer of the *Sunday Times* 'French Mistress' column and author of such august tomes on gender issues and identity as *To Hell in High Heels* and *Two Lipsticks and a Lover*. Admitting to some of her ingrained attitudes, she remarks, 'At the risk of sounding like the legendary "disgusted of Tunbridge Wells", I am just that. Although happily I don't live in Tunbridge Wells.'

No, Helena 'lives in the Languedoc region of France with her husband Rupert Wright and their three children Olivia, Bea and Leonardo and two stepchildren Hugo and Julia'. Taking in the implications of that lazy, sneering 'happily' in that sentence, it occurs to me that whilst the people of Royal Tunbridge Wells may have been disgusting and disgusted in their past, and whilst their taxi firms may sometimes let you down, they are not smug, aloof or condescending. Happily.

I don't always trust Channel Four. They did give Britain the culture-sapping cancer that is *Big Brother* after all (he said, sounding just like Disgusted him- or herself). So when they said that Tunbridge Wells was the third nicest place to live in Great Britain, I thought it was just another southern canard. Now I wonder where the two nicer places could possibly be, and whether they could fit me in for tournedos Rossini and parmesan polenta with mussels and chorizo at seven thirty. Middle England, it seemed to me, was marching towards a new sophistication. And it was marching on its stomach.

CHAPTER 4
Let Them Eat Twizzlers

Just before the 2005 G8 summit, French president Jacques Chirac incurred equal measures of wrath and amusement by cracking a 'joke' about the English to Russia's Vladimir Putin and Germany's Gerhard Schroeder. 'How can you trust a people whose food is so bad?' he joshed.

First, this isn't a joke in my book. The *Sun* headlined their riposte, 'Don't Talk Crepes, Jacques.' *That's* a joke. Secondly, though, the arthropod- and amphibian-munching leader of those whom Homer Simpson once styled as 'cheese-eating surrender monkeys' did have a kind of point. Or at least he had the weight of history and opinion on his side.

The American writer Martha Harrison once speculated that 'what motivated the British to colonize so much of the world is that they were just looking for a decent meal'. More recently, after the fall of Baghdad and Saddam Hussein, American talk-show humorist Conan O'Brien reported that 'today in Iraq, American and British troops handed out food to hundreds of Iraqis. But to no surprise the Iraqis handed the British food back.'

Once upon a time, English food was the bees knees.

Indeed, it probably even included the bees knees since our appetite for every part of a living thing and our 'nose to tail' approach to cooking was notorious. Back in the Middle Ages our national cuisine was colourful and vibrant, full of imaginative mixtures of sweet and savoury. Meat dishes were sweetened with honey and molasses, chickens were stewed in thick milk sauces. *Liber Cure Cocorum*, a cookbook of the medieval period, has recipes that would not look out of place in modern Thai cookery, *viz.*: 'Take good almond milk anon and look you mix it with amidon ... or with flour that is baked. Color it with saffron. Season it with powder of ginger, cinnamon, and galingale. Take partridges and chickens and seethe them well.' In the same book are recipes for hares in onion sauce, tench in gravy, fish blancmange and pork gruel; all original and thought-provoking if not exactly appetising.

In his polemical book *Beef and Liberty*, Ben Rogers speculates that our food gradually became synonymous with our character. He traces the relationship in the eighteenth century between the British figure of John Bull, the consumption of vast quantities of beef, and our animosity with the French. Our implicitly manly hearty stews and fatty puddings were a sort of calorific criticism of the French's effete and foppish cuisine. Rogers even suggests that British cuisine failed to develop because the ingredients were of too high a quality. In contrast, the French had to devise all manner of sauces and marinades to cover up their ropey, poor-quality ingredients. The upshot of this was, as Sicilian nobleman Domenico Caracciolo mocked, 'In England, there are sixty different religions and only one sauce.'

For whatever reason, though, English food didn't develop; in fact, it declined after the Industrial Revolution. Our economic progress was at the detriment of our dishes. Unlike other countries, by the mid-nineteenth century most English people had moved from rural isolation to urban centres. The new working classes had lost contact with the land and with the art of cooking tasty, fresh food. From this spartan existence comes the drab notion of 'meat and two veg': food at its dullest and most minimal, regardless of what traditionalists and granddads say. The war didn't help. As we stood alone against the dark tide of fascism, we did so on powdered egg, whale meat and a grisly tinned South African fish called snoek. This was a fish too far, the people curled their lip and Churchill backed down in a way he never considered with Hitler. (South Africans mildly resent the way we sneered at snoek, and apparently chef Grant Cullingworth of the Table Bay restaurant does a very passable snoek and sweetcorn frikadelle, served with carrot, dhania and cumin seed salad, apricot ice cream and sweet chilli and apricot confit.)

Though we were far healthier during rationing than we are now with our supermarket aisles of tartrazine and saturated fats, we were understandably bored. Virtue, in my experience, is often intensely tedious. Foreign holidays, immigration and the books of Elizabeth David did help during the 1950s and 1960s. Spag bol, sweet and sour pork and chicken tikka masala became staples of Middle England on a par with steak and kidney pie and jam roly poly, although we've had curry houses here since the Hindostanee opened in 1809 in London's

Portman Square. But our restaurant culture would still have made Chirac chuckle. (Though God knows how Schroeder had the gall to join in the laughter. Cabbage and battered veal for me, *mädchen*! Yummo!) In the 1970s, Berni Inns introduced a generation to the notion of eating out, even if it did introduce it quite badly and out of the corner of its mouth via prawn cocktail, steak Diane and black forest gateau. Generally we were still in the thrall of French cuisine to an absurd degree. Our most celebrated TV cook Fanny Cradock worshipped Escoffier and even claimed there was no such thing as English cuisine. 'Even Yorkshire pudding comes from Burgundy,' she sniffed during her last TV performance. (It wasn't meant to be her last, incidentally, but so haughty and sneering was she that she never appeared again.) Cradock would pepper her dauntingly severe recipes with patronising asides to camera like, 'This won't break you' or, 'Of course, if you can't stretch to butter, then dripping will do'. Thrift as much as creativity was at the heart of British cooking. I vividly remember watching the Yorkshire TV show *Farmhouse Kitchen* with my nan and even the dour Dorothy Sleightholme's stodgy yet somehow frugal repasts would cause Nan to roll her eyes, tutting at the sheer extravagance of a cheese flan as if it were roulade of penguin. Robert Courtine, for many years the respected restaurant critic of the French newspaper *Le Monde*, wrote that 'only the rich can eat well in London, and then only if they dine on French food'.

But even the jet set weren't doing much better. The Revolving Restaurant at the top of the GPO Tower – sometimes nicknamed the Revolting Restaurant – was the last word in trend-setting haute cuisine of the early 1970s. But even its menu was an uninspiring litany of bombastic French nosh: *suprême de volailles Van Put* – chicken stuffed with pâté – *avec les légumes*, a less than exciting array including *les choux de Bruxelles* (the Brussels sprouts) and *les pommes nouvelles* (the new potatoes). I found this out, by the way, when I made a TV documentary about the Tower – now closed to the public on entirely spurious grounds of safety – and leafed through a menu with Tony Benn. I remember he got very irritated with the Tower's PR man who tried to get him to call it the BT Tower. 'It doesn't belong to BT. It belongs to the people of Britain who paid for it with their taxes. Margaret Thatcher gave it to you and it wasn't hers to give.' Delicious. Unlike the food.

I imagine cod and chips on the Grunwick picket line was Tony's idea of a nice meal out. Probably just as well, as fish and chips was one of the few reliably good things on Britain's menu, along with some tasty new ethnic arrivals, for most of the 1960s and 1970s. Then, coyly at first but with increasing ardour, Middle England's love affair with food began. Nouvelle cuisine didn't travel much beyond Hampstead. As Clive James once said, 'Here was a cuisine where the price of the dishes was in direct proportion to the number of sides to the plates.' Insubstantial and dressed up to be something it wasn't, it was the Spandau Ballet of food. But London's next culinary innovation was to sweep the Shires like leylandii and Tesco.

In 1991, Mike Belben and David Eyre took charge of a pub called the Eagle on Farringdon Road and made it over with scuffed wooden floors, menus on blackboards, an open-plan kitchen and simple, high quality food. They called their ensuing revamp a gastropub, and the phrase and concept revolutionised British eating. For decades, pub grub in Britain had meant carpet underlay bread, rubbery cheese and some Branston pickle; emergency rations elevated to the status of food by being called a ploughman's lunch. Now, almost overnight, even the most basic boozer offered you flageolet beans and sea bream, pane rustica and oaky Rioja. This has been a velvet revolution and an almost entirely welcome one, though there has been the odd dissenting voice. Writing in the *Guardian* in 2006, Laura Barton grizzled, 'What I miss are those shabby pubs that smell of dirt and tobacco and stout, where you're as likely to get into a brawl as you are to find a packet of ready-salted Seabrooks crisps. Where old men hunch over a pint of mild and the only soundtrack is the put-put-put of a game of pool in the back room. No DJs, no Heal's sofas, no blackened salmon or pilaff or cous-cous. No gastronomy, just pub.' Having grown up in pubs like the ones Laura pines for, I can say that I don't miss them at all, largely because I don't miss getting glassed whilst drinking gaseous urine.

The *Observer*'s Jay Rayner shares my feelings. He has 'never found anything particularly attractive about sticky-carpeted rooms with fake horse brasses festering on the walls, and a cadre of elderly regulars propping up the bar waiting for last orders, or death, whichever might come first'. In the same piece in October 2007, he also points out how the gastropub, so beloved now of Middle England, may be an innovation but is Conservative with a large C, an economic invention driven by market forces rather than changing tastes. In the late 1980s the Monopolies and Mergers Commission decided it was anti-competitive for the breweries to own too many pubs and legislation was passed requiring them to sell off thousands of their properties cheaply. Young chefs found they could buy a pub and go it alone. As Rayner points out, many of the old-school boozer fans who loathe gastropubs can hate them with even more passion now they know these new-fangled foodie boozers are a child of Thatcherism.

As I say, I don't mind them, although the relentless tide of Thai fish cakes and lamb shanks across every village and town in Middle England is a bit deadening. But it is a vast improvement on the days when whole pubs would quiver with delight at the prospect of 'the prawn man' coming round with his tray of marine delicacies in plastic bags and the resident wag would ask him if he had crabs.

Gastropubs and the rise of the restaurant culture have caused a subtle and significant shift in the way Britain lives. I remember sitting with my dad in the almost deserted lounge bar of a working man's club in Wigan a few Christmases back and wondering where everyone was. 'This place would have been packed thirty years ago,' my dad mused. 'Then people came out and wanted entertainment: a singer or a comedian. Now people go out to eat. When I was your age, only posh people went out for meals. Working people came home and had their tea and then went out.' He's right. Even when I was a kid, going out to dinner was something only the Saint, played by Roger Moore, did, or at least Peter Bowles in *To the Manor Born*. Going out for a meal was reserved for special occasions. Now it is as quotidian as buying a newspaper.

And so we have gone from being a culinary laughing stock to a nation obsessed with food, where cookery programmes swamp the networks and celebrity chefs are the new gods. It began in Middle England with one Delia Smith, the winsome, wholesome goddess of English cookery. From her humble beginnings (an ex-hairdresser who contributed a recipe for kipper pâté to the *Daily Mirror*) she rose to become a woman who could make or break companies and cause runs on the stock market with a casual recommendation. Supermarkets would run out of limes, capers, cranberries, Maldon sea salt, omelette pans or pestles and mortars after a mention from Delia. When she was filmed, well dined herself, shouting, 'Where are ya, let's be having you!' at reticent supporters of her beloved Norwich City, the nation blanched. It was like seeing your mum chasing the dragon in a Camden boozer with Pete Doherty.

In the twenty-first century even Delia has been eclipsed by the rise of newer, hipper celebrity chefs. Gordon Ramsay continually does his bit to coarsen British culture and promulgate an entirely false, macho distortion of kitchen life (Ferran Adrià's kitchen in El Bulli, thought by many to be the world's greatest restaurant, is a temple of zen calm). Jamie Oliver seems likeable enough but I find his elevation to unelected national diet tsar vexing. In 2005, he launched a one-man vilification campaign against a convenience food called the turkey twizzler. As the name suggests, it is not haute cuisine or one of your five-a-day. It is quite fatty, though presumably very tasty, which would explain its popularity with kids. A diet comprising nothing but twizzlers would doubtless make you as fat as a fool, but the odd one is no more injurious to your health than an ice cream or glass of sherry, neither of which should comprise your total diet either.

Oliver demonised the twizzler during an impassioned, almost tearful tirade on a TV show. Face quivering with rage and hurt, he railed and accused in a volley of four-letter words and a manner more suited to a denunciation of Third World child prostitution or the tyrannical regime in Burma. Such was the tide of sanctimoniousness swelling from Britain's middle classes that I felt like starting to eat turkey twizzlers, perhaps on a bed of saturated fats, just to wind the smug so-and-sos up. Because food, like the environment, has become the bourgeoisie's political crusade of choice precisely because it doesn't involve doing anything uncomfortable like going on strike or getting truncheoned on a picket line. No, you can just make fun of poor people's diets and waistlines instead. This is done constantly on radio and TV and stage by one of a repertory company of interchangeable, cancerously unfunny Home Counties posh boy 'satirists' with plonking ironic deliveries. Pavlovian and drooling, their audiences snicker, just as they do to the endless references to George Bush, David Beckham and old people smelling of wee. It's hardly Jonathan Swift or *Beyond the Fringe*, is it?

It's apt that this national hand-wringing should concern a snack most enjoyed by kids since, fundamentally, one might argue, our attitude to food is essentially childish. We don't grow it, we don't know where it comes from, we don't really know what we're buying but, possibly from urban middle-class guilt, we have become obsessed with it. Secretly we wish we had a smallholding in Provence or Tuscany where we could spend our days holding lemons or figs up to the fierce light of the sun as we squinted knowledgeably through wrinkled, sagacious eyes, before wandering down to Francesco or Pierre's little place in the village for a glass of rough local red and some grilled locally caught sardines. This is how a section of Middle England believes the continent lives, and they may be right. Certainly grassroots civic muscle – and ingrained, ungrateful anti-Americanism – have kept the fried chicken chains and the burger behemoths at bay in France and Italy to a degree that seems unthinkable here. I suspect, however, that the average citizen of Bologna or Toulouse spends a goodly amount of time on the settee watching *Les Simpsons* and eating Benito et Geraldo's Praline Surprise from the tub.

But there is one gustatory arena where, if we do not lead the world, we are the special ones, bringing to the activity a nuanced, passionate, deep-seated national love and flair that is almost akin to Brazilian football culture. Or – to use another football analogy – just as the Dutch soccer maestros of the 1970s played a brand of dizzying, all-embracing game called Total Football, the English are the maestros of Total Drinking.

The Finns and the Russians may drink more intensely, more broodingly, from bottles of vodka in cramped and dingy Muscovite tower blocks or from stills of grain alcohol in moonlit woods whilst mired in existential angst. The French and Italians may drink more discerningly, muttering about 'terroir', sniffing, holding glasses up to the light and squinting. But we have embraced drinking as a national pastime, for better or worse, in sickness and in health, hammered or sober. Our love of booze runs deep; in Elizabethan England, the water was so noxious it wasn't generally thought fit to drink. Beer was the liquid staple of our diet, our cuppa. A particularly weak version, small beer, was brewed specifically for women and children, hence the expression for something trifling. In our drinking we are fundamentally northern, as in Arctic Circle rather than Accrington, and we drink accordingly: copiously, as warmth against the dark and as fuel for our berserkings. The pint of foaming ale and the small sherry, the tipple of the squire and the spinster, are pleasing and stolid evocations of our national thirst but we have always showed an enthusiasm for excess. Binge drinking is nothing new. When gin was popularised in the 1700s, it was said that half the nation was pissed at any one time. In 1727 England consumed roughly five million gallons of gin; that's a hell of a lot for only six million people. Drunkenness became so widespread and such a dire problem that the government passed the Gin Act, restricting the production of 'Mother's Ruin'. So we should see the current concern over binge drinking not as a sign of the times but as an old friend coming round again. Peter Haydon, author of *Beer and Britannia: An Inebriated History of Britain*, writes, 'The British are big drinkers, it has always been part of our culture. That is who we are and we shouldn't wring our hands and try to suppress that [but] nowadays 22-year-olds are drinking flavours no more challenging than what they were drinking at 12 ... Drinking alcohol is not a challenging experience for young people any more. I remember my first taste of alcohol was disgusting ...' He has a point. Most of us can remember that involuntary shudder after tasting Dad's scotch at Christmas. It passes, though, for most of us. It would have passed a lot quicker, I guess, if Dad's Scotch had been mango and lychee flavour, sticky and coloured blue.

For me the moral panic over drink is muddled at best and pernicious at worst. Again and again, the anti-alcohol lobby picks the softest targets for its rage, and targets don't come much softer than pregnant women. As I write, women are now being told by 'experts' – Middle England hates intellectuals but loves experts – that it is OK to have a couple of glasses of wine a week when pregnant. If I were a pregnant woman I'd be tempted to shout, 'Oh for flip's sake, make your expert flipping minds up,' whilst downing a pint of rum. Leaving aside the twists and turns of this debate ('experts' now admit that they plucked the eighteen weekly units of alcohol maximum for women out of the air), I don't seem to recall the babies of yesteryear growing up any stupider, weaker, less intelligent, less brave or gifted or lovely back when Mum was having a Harvey's Bristol Cream of an evening. In fact, quite the opposite.

Drinking too much makes you fat, unhealthy and may kill you. This is unarguable and it should be said. But everyone has the right to go to hell in the manner of their own choosing. Dylan Thomas will be remembered when sober saints are long forgotten. That, though, is not the point. The point surely should be that one of the most serious threats to health from alcohol consumption is being battered by a drunken husband, neglected by a drunken father or glassed by a drunken thug. Yet I never see campaigns against male alcohol-related violence. I see little else but scare stories in colour supplements about female office-worker binge drinking. As with pretty much everything, men are the problem but women get the blame. It's enough to have you reaching for the Lambrini.

Sorry. Back to turkey twizzlers. Schools took them off the menu and replaced them with rocket and caper risotto, to the horror of the kids. In a move of breathtaking arrogance, Sainsbury's took them off the shelves. Not cigarettes, though, which are undoubtedly worse for you than a few grams of saturated fat. The ironic postscript to all this is that it emerged this year that Jamie's own pasta sauces have twice as much salt as a turkey twizzler, which stand revealed as positively radish-like in comparison.

Middle England has always loved its food, whatever the quality. We take comfort in it, from shepherd's pie to spotted dick, bangers and mash to Bovril. On the Icons of Britain website, contributor Hugh Peaman nominates 'biscuits' as one of said icons – everything is 'iconic' nowadays but don't get me started on that – and sings their praises thus: 'Ginger nuts, custard creams, bourbons, garibaldis, malted milk, digestives, lincolns, jammie dodgers, rich tea, fig rolls … A panoply of delicious low-cost treats that are an intrinsic part of our national character, and a major indigenous industry.' So I take out my map and, dipping a custard cream into a mug of piping-hot brown tea, I look for some of the places that food has put on the map. My eye is drawn to Leicestershire, and a town synonymous with one of Middle England's lardiest, loveliest treats …

Even the teenage ticket clerk at Birmingham New Street says, 'That's where the pork pies come from,' as I buy my ticket for Melton Mowbray. Like Champagne, Parma and Eccles, Melton Mowbray is a place whose name is synonymous with a comestible, and one that instantly evokes the heartiness and geniality of Middle England. I share my train with a gang of rowdy, pimply but good-natured teenage Ipswich Town fans making their tortuous way across the East Midlands for a football match. England is a long thin country and yet journeys along its spine are a doddle compared to even relatively short cross-country jaunts. Judging from the empty cans of Fanta and crisp packets, the lads have been on this train for some time, but they are still in good spirits and chipper, as befits well-brought-up middle-class kids. 'One of my Facebook friends said I was a tramp cos she lives in Buckinghamshire. I think where we live is well nice,' asserts one, and I'm sure he is right. When any church comes into view, they shout excitedly, 'Ely Cathedral!', clearly a private joke created for this journey. Quite sweet when you think about it, ecclesiastical-landmark-recognition jokes being fairly rare amongst British youth today. At one point one lets slip a 'fuck' and the others redden and hang their heads because of the presence of two white-haired ladies on a shopping trip to Leicester. Sotto voce and touchingly, another says, 'Let's not swear, eh?' It is one of those moments that restores one's faith in the Middle English, I think, as we pull into what even I as a Wiganer must acknowledge is Britain's pie capital.

The raised or standing pie developed from the medieval habit of making robust pastry cases that could be filled and baked without need for a mould. The pastry case was not intended to be eaten, being merely a basic flour-and-water casing that was thrown away. Then realisation dawned that with a little tweaking of the recipe the pastry too would be tasty enough to eat and, lo, the pie was born. Picnics, wedding receptions and half-time at football matches would never be the same.

Why did the pork pies of Melton Mowbray become so famed? Various theories have been mooted. According to local piemaker Stephen Hallam, it was a by-product of the local cheese industry, whose surplus whey supported large herds of swine. Also, Leicestershire has long been hunting country and the cold pork pie was the ideal portable picnic snack for the aristocratic houndsman. In time developed the Melton Mowbray pie, an aristocrat itself of the pie world. Aficionados sing the praises of its crunchy pastry, distinctive shape and coarse chopped pork, seasoned but not brined as in generic mass-produced pork pies. The latter may well be comforting but they come at a price in hardened arteries and excess poundage. My friend Paul Rodgers works in radio, not in pies, but he is from Rotherham and so I have no reason to doubt the veracity of two fascinating items of pork-pie-related trivia he once told me. The first is that a generic mass-produced pork pie contains more fat than an equivalent-sized block of lard. The second is that whilst pork pie sales are on the increase, the numbers of people who say they eat pork pies is declining. In other words, we are a nation of secret pork-pie consumers. I imagine men in cagoules on rainy garage forecourts furtively wolfing down the forbidden treats before returning home to their wives, claiming shiftily they had a pot of tuna salad for lunch. If you are going to eat pork pies, then, they should be Melton Mowbray pork pies, on the grounds that forbidden pleasures should be of the finest quality.

When speaking of the town rather than the pies, call it Melton. This will make you sound like a local. If you want to, of course. I learn this from a woman at the station taxi rank, information she manages to impart between her lung-sapping drags on several cigarettes and bouts of hacking and wheezing. I ask her if my hotel is within walking distance and she answers, 'God, no,' with a kind of shudder. I let her get the first taxi, which she makes wait until she's finished her fag. My chivalry is rewarded when my taxi driver turns out to be cordial, chatty and very informative. He tells me that another great 'iconic' local product, Stilton cheese, has never been made in the Cambridgeshire village of Stilton and that, sadly, Melton Mowbray pork pies are part of the Ginsters empire, which turns out to be not strictly true, though some of the pie companies produce for Ginsters. He also uses the word 'obtuse' twice during our short journey and is good on the town's restaurants, warning me off one particular Italian with a sorrowful shake of the head. 'Absolute rubbish. The worst carbonara in Leicestershire ...'

From the restaurant patio of my hotel I can see across the

river Eye (or possibly Wreake, both run through the town) and over dull pastures and playing fields dotted with dog walkers to a distant vista of churches and houses. 'Very flat, Leicestershire,' says the female half of a middle-aged couple, she twinkly and smart, he starchy and red-faced. They have come for the Quorn Hunt, an activity they follow avidly. 'Isn't it illegal now?' I ask a little mischievously, and he harrumphs. Actually harrumphs. Actually makes the noise 'harrumph' as he shakes open his newspaper which is, inevitably, the *Daily Mail.* She says something about following a scented trail rather than a fox. I think it rather funny that the Quorn Hunt should now be making do with a meat substitute.

Pies and hunting occupy me on my afternoon tour of the town. They occupy Melton too. So much so that the tourist information centre has closed down and been replaced by a computer terminal and a leaflet stand in Dickinson and Morris, the oldest remaining makers of the Melton Mowbray Pork Pie in town. Since 1851, this revered establishment has been selling pork pies. Proper ones, with the shiny egg-glazed pastry that bows out like 'the purse of a medieval merchant' and the uncured, unminced pork which is therefore a dull grey not pink like the garage forecourt staples. It must be baked for a time at a high temperature, around 200 or 210 degrees centigrade, then for much longer at 40 or 50 degrees below that, and then the gelatinous stock, made with trotters and bones, is poured through a hole in the lid of the pie. It is a food rich in nostalgia. The serving suggestion should read, 'Best eaten wearing thigh-length leather boots in a coaching house whilst drinking from a pewter tankard with a busty serving wench on your knee.'

Dickinson and Morris recently won a ten-year battle to get 'Protected Geographical Status', which means only pork pie producers using a traditional recipe and in the vicinity of Melton can use the name Melton Mowbray Pork Pie. Thirty-four other British products are also protected under the scheme, such as Arbroath smokies, Cornish clotted cream and Welsh lamb. I mull all this, furtively munching, as I head past the ubiquitous Edinburgh Woollen Mill and the grim hangar-like Tubes night-club and Melton Theatre ('Coming attractions … Slam Wrestling and Allo Allo') to the rather snazzy glass-fronted museum.

It is, of course, fun: fun being the condition that all muse-ums must aspire to even when least appropriate. Something of that desperate cheeriness underpins exhibits such as 'Fun with Stilton wedges!', in which children are encouraged to rearrange large plastic slices of the famously pungent cheese into a slightly differently shaped cheese. To be honest, children and Stilton do not make good bedfellows anyway. Stilton with its distinctive aroma and taste of a forgotten sock discovered in an old gym bag is best enjoyed by slightly drunk middle-aged male rela-tives at Christmas – I'm a Roquefort man myself – whilst kids surely prefer Dairylea Dunkers with their tawny port.

A pub landlord from Stilton commissioned the cheese, hence the name, but my cabbie was right: it's never been made there. In fact, legally it cannot be made there, because of EU restrictions, and is only produced in eight dairies, one of which is in Melton Mowbray. But since the cheese's appeal came from its availability at the Bell Inn in Stilton on the main stage-coach route from London to the north, the cheese bears that village's name. Melton is clearly keen to stake its claim to the whiffy comestible.

Next to the fun-filled wedges is a display that begins, 'There are many kinds of saddle ...' which sends me straight to the next one. This, more entertainingly, is a mock-up of old local chemist Attenbury's, complete with laxative display. I'm intrigued, but at the same time it is hard to ignore the increasingly seductive background chatter of the two guides. 'It's my sister's wedding at the weekend... so that's a new frock and shoes I can justify ... yes, first marriage ... I know ... Oh, believe me, she's had plenty of men but she's never settled down ... My sister's always put adventure before convention ... plenty of men, oh yes.' All this goes on beneath a huge plastic model of the Biggest Pork Pie in the World.

A great deal of the exhibition circles warily and diplomatically around the topic of hunting. This is hunting country. In fact, Melton is known as the hunting capital of Britain. Given this, the museum is admirably even-handed in its tenor. There's a tableau devoted to the Hunt Saboteurs Association, for instance. And a panel beneath a large figure of a red-coated huntsman reads, 'How do you feel when you look at this figure? He's got too much time and money on his hands? Or he is supporting a centuries-old tradition?' Sadly there is no box marked, 'He is a pampered, chinless parasite and whilst I have no strong feelings about foxes I would love to screw up Tarquin here's social life.'

Sometimes, though, the mask slips. One display trots out a mildly partisan list of statistics which claims fox-hunting brought in sixty million pounds a year in income to Britain, which has the unmistakeable scent of utter tosh to me. Next to it is a glass case and inside there's a badger, a rabbit, a fox and a deer. It's marked 'Wildlife in Nature' rather than 'Things We Like to Kill'.

Before leaving the museum, I learn that the phrase 'painting the town red' meaning 'to go on the razzle and cause a commotion' has its origins in one of the best-known events in the history of Melton Mowbray. On the evening of Thursday 6 April 1837, following a day at the local Croxton Park races, the eccentric hunt-loving Marquis of Waterford and his friends were making their refreshed way home at around three in the morning by carriage when they found Thorpe End tollgate closed for repairs. Continuing on foot, they helped themselves to the red paint being used in the refurbishment and proceeded to paint anything in the town that took their fancy: pubs, houses, the carved stone swan on the Swan Inn and, in some versions, the unfortunate toll-keeper himself. No ASBOs for posh folk or indeed anyone back then so instead we commemorate their orgy of drunken vandalism as a bit of a jolly jape. I decide to see for myself how riotous modern-day Melton gets its kicks of a Saturday evening.

First, I need to eat. For a moment I consider seeing just how bad the worst carbonara in Leicestershire is, but then I weaken and, of course, go for a Thai.

I say 'of course' because you will remember my theory from Chipping Norton about Thai Cuisine and Middle

England. To recap; it's my considered contention that Thai food has become the staple cuisine of Middle England and for a variety of reasons. One, the food is great. Moreover, Thai people are beautiful and polite and wear lovely purple clothes and their establishments have nothing of the late-night lager, vomit and vindaloo session about them. They seem to be a cut above, and thus the Shires have embraced them. I actually came across a couple of Thai Shires on my voyages. Melton's is called the Thai Sabai, however, and I get the last free table. It's been open four and a half months, the friendly proprietor tells me, and is groaning with people: nice people, Middle England people, not especially rich but not poor. In a few months, they will find their mortgages rising and their house prices falling and maybe nights at Thai restaurants will become rarer. Just before I leave, a man weaves his way unsteadily by the window and looks in at the diners. He offers his chips to some ladies in the window tables and everyone laughs.

The Anne of Cleves pub is even fuller. It gets its name from the fact that it was the boozer of choice for local monks for three hundred years before being taken over by Henry VIII during the dissolution of the monasteries. He later gave it to Anne of Cleves as part of the divorce settlement. It is, of course, haunted. When the publican, a scouser in a chef's apron, tells me this, I smile and, sensing my scepticism, he pulls from beneath the bar a thick plastic wallet containing the detailed report of the Paranormal Society's investigation into the pub and an overnight vigil that ended at 5.45 a.m. 'Norman saw a headless woman,' he declares. Who am I to doubt him? I ask him what he's doing so far from home. 'I'm educating them,' he deadpans. And an education of sorts I've had, knowing a lot more about EU food restrictions and painting the town red and the right colour of cooked pork than I did before I came to Melton Mowbray.

They told me I'd know I was in Burton-on-Trent by the smell. And they were nearly right. There's certainly a heady, hoppy tang in the air, as there used to be at Manchester Victoria station thanks to the Boddingtons brewery next door. But all those former recommendations about holding your nose as you pass along the high street are exaggerations now. There's just a warm flavour of beer and Marmite in the air and, if anything, it's the huge pipeline running alongside the station platform that gives you the more obvious clue you're in the capital of British brewing.

They've brewed beer in Burton for a thousand years, ever since the monks at the local abbey of St Modwen first spotted that the subterranean water hereabouts had that indefinable something which made for great bitter. Actually, it's a quite definable something, namely sulphate in dissolved salts from the gypsum-rich surrounding hills, though of course the monks didn't know that back then. Chemist C.W. Vincent discovered much later that it was this chemical enrichment that brought out the best in the flavours of the hops. Burton possesses another liquid asset: the Grand Trunk canal, dug between 1766 and 1777 to link the Trent and Mersey rivers and neatly wedging Burton between two watercourses. This ease of access, coupled with the water, meant that Burton became a brewing mecca. Not that they go in much for pints of best bitter in downtown Mecca, but you take my point. The town flourished and brewing became big business, buoyed by demand for Burton's hoppy pale ales. There were nine breweries here by 1801, which by 1888 had increased to a startling thirty-one. Beer brought all kinds of related innovation and expansion as the breweries supported businesses like coopers and blacksmiths, the ancestors of Burton's current-day metalworking and manufacturing industries. Burton beers changed Englishmen's tastes. Previously, our tipple had been mainly stout or porter, heavy dark beers similar to Guinness, but Bass bitter and its famed India Pale Ale, lighter and hoppier, came to predominate.

I learn a lot of this from tall, willowy, pale blue-eyed Julia in the tourist information centre. Over the last few years, I've spent a great deal of time talking to nice ladies like Julia in tourist information centres the length and breadth of the land and it is always a delight. Always eager to explain, always generous and enthusiastic and knowledgeable and often twinkling with a little gentle self-mocking irony. Julia tells me that there are still six breweries in the town and begins to list them. After four or five, her memory fails her and I say airily that it isn't important.

'Oh no.' She smiles. 'It's a matter of tourist-information honour. I've committed myself to six now.'

You can sympathise with Julia. It's actually five. Buyouts, mergers and consolidations have meant that Burton is now a town dominated by big beer multinationals rather than feisty independent breweries. The brewers of Burton were once the aristocrats of the town, dominating its civic life. Many of them were ennobled for their patronage of political parties, and became known as the beerage. But even by 1927, the numbers of breweries in the town had shrunk to eight. Now it's just Coors, Marston, Burton Bridge Brewery (founded in 1982 by Geoff Mumford and Bruce Wilkinson), Tower Brewery, a new microbrewery, and Cottage Brewery, based in the Old Cottage Inn. The Bass Museum of Brewing, which was part of the Coors visitor centre, made its own beer till the centre closed in summer 2008 in no little controversy, not long after my visit.

With great delicacy back then, Julia tried to explain the political situation vis-a-vis Bass and Coors. Essentially, the US conglomerate Coors now owns the proud British brand Bass. This, everyone accepts, is the way of the world, but what's irritated some is the closing of the museum and what's been seen as an attempt to erase every trace of the former brand. Toni Parker from the Museum of London put it thus: 'As someone who was born in Burton-on-Trent and who is a museum professional I feel quite saddened … On recent trips back to my home town it seems that Coors have tried their best to eradicate all traces of the existence of Bass in the town – the brewing towers have been relabelled with the Coors title and buildings that have long had Bass inscribed on them have seen the inscriptions covered up with Coors signs.'

I notice this as I stroll past and it does feel at best incongruous and at worst bullying. Because Burton means Bass. And the famous red triangle is genuinely iconic in a way that the Coors logo – it says Coors in nice writing – will never be. Picasso and his fellow Cubist Juan Gris incorporated the Bass red triangle into many of their collages. Great children's illustrators from Arthur Rackham to Quentin Blake have used Bass bottles to convey beer to their young audience. It seems clumsy at best not to have let the red triangle flutter over Burton. In fact, we could all take it as a national affront. For Burton and Bass was not just our national beer – all those Battle of Britain heroes 'went for a Burton' not a Coors – but also one of our characteristic national spreads, loved and loathed in equal measure, queer, quirky and quintessentially English, though with Teutonic intellectual roots.

When a German scientist called Liebig discovered that brewer's yeast cells could be concentrated, bottled and eaten he had, to all intents and purposes, invented Marmite. Burton had a lot of yeast and thus the Marmite Food Extract Company was established in Burton in 1902, fed by excess yeast from the Bass Brewery. Though the exact recipe is a trade secret, it is still primarily yeast extract with a little added vegetable extract and spice. When vitamins were discovered just before the First World War, Marmite became what we might call today a 'superfood', and sales soared.

There were no websites back then. But go to Marmite's website now and you will see how adroitly the current marketing men are managing the brand by actively encouraging people to disagree about it. The site has two wings, one for those who love the stuff and one for those to whom it is a nasty mystery, as it was for Bill Bryson, who in *Notes from a Small Island* wrote,

'There are certain things that you have to be British, or at least older than me, or possibly both, to appreciate: skiffle music, salt-cellars with a single hole, [and] Marmite (an edible yeast extract with the visual properties of an industrial lubricant).'

Marmite has always had smart ad campaigns. Those first marketing men called it: 'The growing up spread you never grow out of.' During the 1980s, the spread was advertised with the slogan 'My mate, Marmite', chanted in television commercials by an army platoon, reflecting the fact that the spread had been a standard-issue vitamin supplement for British-based German POWs during the Second World War. This is almost too perfect to be true, combining two things at the very heart of Middle Englishness: funny little nostalgic foodstuffs and the defeat of the Third Reich.

A more recent plucky Brit prisoner, Paul Ridout, a back-packer kidnapped by Kashmiri separatists in 1994, asked for some Marmite on toast as soon as he was released. He said, 'It was pretty good. It's just one of those things – you get out of the country and it's all you can think about.' Marmite's new campaigns, a kind of anti-advertising where the brand's demerits are seen to be its strengths, are the bleeding edge of post-modernity. Central to it all is the taste, which is almost impossible to describe. If pushed, I'd say it was like eating Swarfega laced with iron filings and gravy browning. And yet as I sit and type these words, the craving for some of the stuff, smeared into the melting butter on a piece of hot toast, is almost unbearable. At least half of you are feeling the same deep longing too right now. I know. And I know that there will be some in the kitchen cupboard because no one ever runs out of Marmite. A little goes a very long way. Comedian Tim Vine has a good joke about it. 'I won a competition. The prize was a year's supply of Marmite. One jar.'

I remember Vine's joke as I take an afternoon promenade around Burton. It is not what you would call a pretty town; the huge cylinders and silos of the Coors brewery see to that and Chloe's restaurant – dwarfed by the huge steel containers – must suffer on Valentine's day as a result. But it is character-ful and has its moments. It is festooned with handsome build-ings in a variety of architectural styles, mismatched oddments that speak of a wealthy past. The queer, squat old police station and magistrates' court both look like wedding cakes. Pausing to admire them, I am almost run down by two adult men cycling down the pavement at breakneck speed. Adults who cycle on the pavement are one evolutionary step up from the carpet slipper in my moral ranking and I would introduce swift pavement-citizens' justice to eliminate them. In the absence of this, though, I merely curse the pair, one of them with the sallow, prematurely aged look of the career smoker, the other with a baseball cap, always a good indicator of dimness.

Everywhere there are reminders of Burton's brewing past. A rather nice ironmonger's has a plaque that reads, 'Charles Leeson's Brewery stood here 1753-1800'. Now it stands next door to Aldi. I have a cup of tea and a piece of toast in Peckish sandwich bar. They don't do Marmite. In fact, the girl serving there makes a face when I ask for it. You make it here, I tell her. 'We make ball bearings here and I don't eat them either.'

She laughs. 'I can do you cheese on toast,' she says amiably. That's nothing like Marmite, I protest. 'No, you're right, cheese on toast is nice.'

I tell her that uncooked spaghetti dipped in Marmite makes an excellent emergency substitute Twiglet. 'I'll bear that in mind when I next have a party.' She chuckles as she clears away the remnants of some old boy's baked potato.

Burton's high street is a mixture of the traditional and the bizarre and thus offers something of a snapshot of Middle England in 2008. There is, of course, a Thai restaurant, which I suspect may now be compulsory by law. There is a shop called Let's Party Let's Dance, which seems to sell tinsel, feather boas and other essential hen-night kit. There is a pawnshop next door to a shop offering everything I might need for 'predatory angling'. A girl of about twenty in a high-visibility tabard is sitting on a transparent plastic box by the pelican crossing. She wears headphones that run to the box, which is, in turn, cabled up to a camera wrapped in a plastic bag on top of the traffic lights. I nearly ask her what all this is about but don't want to risk a prosaic answer about traffic censuses or some such. I prefer to imagine she is Burton's Tracey Emin and this is her latest, unfathomable art installation. Looming over all of this is the Riverside Centre, which looks like it may once have been the place in Burton to have your wedding reception, where you would bump and boogie in your implausible flares and side-burns to Barry Blue's 'Dancing on a Saturday Night' or The Sweet's 'Blockbuster'. Now, burned out and boarded up, it looks like the Kabul branch of KwikFit exhausts.

And then suddenly I arrive at the Trent, broad and choppy and winding beneath a very fine, low arched stone bridge that has stood here for eight hundred years. It would be a lovely spot to while away an hour with a *Daily Mirror* and a Thermos, if it were not so bone-shudderingly cold. Two hoodies are making desultory havoc with a lifebelt. Sans *Daily Mirror* or Thermos I still sit and have a sojourn at a picnic table and admire a very prim and pretty blue and white wooden boathouse across the Trent.

Bench-sitting, idly watching the world go by from a piece of civic furniture, seems to me an intrinsically English pastime. But there is something to envy too. What with 24-hour culture and changing shift patterns and distance working and telecommuting, afternoon bench-sitting is no longer a definite and default indicator of fecklessness, joblessness or aimlessness. Sitting by a duck pond or a bandstand during the four days of the English summer, possibly eating an ice cream, watching people go by, is a charming diversion. It is where you will find us all at some point, the lonely old, the unhappy young, the illicit lovers and the chatty mums. Our cousins on the continent elevate this time-wasting to a philosophical endeavour and call it being a flaneur or a boulevardier. Bench-sitting is just as profound and worthwhile. We just haven't thought of a poncy word for it yet.

Almost immediately I am accosted by two policemen on bikes. At least I thought they were policemen, an easy mistake to make given the black padded vests and combat-style trousers. They in fact turn out to be Mormons, evidently from the paramilitary wing of the Church of the Latterday Saints.

They are pleasant enough in that vaguely sinister, deadened way that the evangelising often have. One hands me a business card that asks, 'What is the purpose of life? Where do we go after this life? What is the true nature of God? Answers to these and other questions can be found by visiting www.mormon.org.'

I give a low whistle. That's pretty impressive, I say.

'Would you like to know about the Church of Jesus Christ?' asks the younger one with a smile. Not really, I answer truthfully. 'Do you know anyone who would?' he persists. Try those, I say, indicating the hoodies by the lifebelt who are now sharing a can of Foster's.

Flags flutter over Burton as I leave. The ones at the brewery read 'Coors' and the ones at the church, perhaps defiantly, bear the Cross of St George. I cross the 'Viking' play area and see the two pavement cyclists from earlier. They are eating Quavers and playing on a child's swing. They present about the most pathetic picture of British manhood imaginable. You would have to say that their fellow cyclists, the two Mormon paramilitaries, at least have some sense of purpose and energy on their side. And optimism, I think, as I pass them again later, deep in conversation with two women taking home their shopping from Aldi, both of them, as indicated by the red bindi dot on their forehead, incontrovertibly Hindu.

In 1986, an Italian journalist called Carlo Petrini was horrified to see that a branch of McDonald's had opened up at the foot of the Spanish Steps. This was the final outrage, a crass symbol of cheap greasy commercialism in the heart of one of the world's great cities of food. Petrini set up the Slow Food movement, now a global if grassroots concern, encouraging us to care more about quality, tradition and pleasure in food. The movement has now expanded to take on other aspects of our crowded, pressurised, noisy lives. At a Slow Food festival in Orvieto, several mayors set into motion the Cittaslow project, a drive – a very slow, scenic drive – to make urban life healthier, more environmentally sustainable and more enriching. The world now has several Slow Towns, from Katoomba, City of Blue Mountains in Australia, to Sokndal in Rogaland, Norway. The very first designated Slow Town in the UK was already a gem: pretty, charming, civilised and with every corner crammed with the most delicious food and drink imaginable, from its bistros to its B&Bs, from its sausage shops to its saloon bars. John Betjeman called it either England's loveliest small town or finest small town or possibly the perfect small town. No one seems to quite agree what he actually said. But no matter, Ludlow may be all three.

Ludlow sits in a lazy bend of the river Teme in that quietly bustling – if that makes sense – chunk of Middle England that is practically Wales. It's a curiously, attractively enigmatic and independent bit of the country: the Marches, as it's known, once almost a devolved kingdom. Except they had lords, not kings, busily building garrisons and mottes and baileys and markets in the rolling landscape between the mountains of Wales and the gentler inclines and river valleys of Middle England.

Still, on any given day, Ludlow's intricate maze of little streets is crammed with vans bringing delicious quirky things to be arranged alluringly in the windows of one of a hundred small shops. Tucked away though it may be, Ludlow has always had stuff on its plate in every sense of the phrase. It's been said that more has been written about Ludlow's history than any other English town. Ludlow has history like Burton has yeast. If you could make a tasty spread out of excess and leftover history, Ludlow could have a Marmite of its own. It has featured in scores of folk tales and ballads, such as *Fulk Fitzwarin*, mooted sometimes as the source of the Robin Hood legend. It has castles and churches in one of which, St Laurence's, is buried the poet A.E. Housman. Housman mentioned Ludlow in many of the poems in *A Shropshire Lad*. One of them, 'When I Came Last To Ludlow', is pure Housman: chilly, nostalgic, achingly sad.

When I came last to Ludlow
Amidst the moonlight pale,
Two friends kept step beside me,
Two honest lads and hale.
Now Dick lies long in the churchyard,
And Ned lies long in jail,
And I come home to Ludlow
Amidst the moonlight pale.

Ludlow has five hundred listed buildings and, unlike many towns, knocks down its monstrosities rather than its treasures.

The ugly 1887 Market Hall was described by Nikolaus Pevsner as 'Ludlow's bad luck ... There is nothing that could be said in favour of its fiery brick or useless Elizabethan detail.' Ludlow agreed. It was demolished in 1986, and today they put their excellent market stalls there. You can't eat architecture or history, and I had come for the food, for a sybaritic dirty weekend of indulgence and sensual gratification in what has been called the gastronomic capital of England. The screaming red-faced chefs of NW1 and Soho's sizzling kitchens may disagree, but the very best of English food has moved out to the country, where it lives quietly in the heart of Middle England.

It started in the mid-1990s. Before this, according to food writer Graham Moss, if you were in Ludlow and wanted a really nice meal, 'you had two options: drive as far as, say, Cheltenham, or stay put and cook it yourself. The most popular restaurant in town was a fabulously old-fashioned place in Broad Street called de Greys, which rambled lengthily through the ground floor of one of Ludlow's fine Tudor houses ... Everything about de Greys was stuck in the 1950s. The waitresses wore black frocks and white pinnies; the plat du jour alternated Welsh rarebit with sardines on toast. It was forever teatime at de Greys. To go there was like taking up temporary residence inside a poem by John Betjeman.'

During my time in Ludlow, I dropped in at de Grey's and whether it was the iced fruit granita or the croque monsieur or possibly even the white pinnies and the black frocks I don't know, but I found it a lovely place to let Sunday's hangover evaporate whilst doing the Jimmy Porter *Look Back in Anger* routine of gutting and filleting the papers. But I take Moss's point. De Grey's may be charmingly recherché but it will wait a while for its Michelin star. And for most of the past decade Ludlow had more of those twinkling, lusted-after baubles than anywhere else in Britain.

Shaun Hill's first job was cooking in the café at London Zoo. He then worked at several London restaurants before taking a prestigious post at the Michelin-starred restaurant at the Gidleigh Park Hotel in Devon. When in 1994 he announced he was moving to rural Shropshire to open a new restaurant, foodies thought he was mad. The AA Guide even compared the move to a racing driver giving up Formula One to drive a bus. But it was the opening of Hill's little Ludlow restaurant that sparked the town's rise to gastronomic legend. The Merchant House was an old Jacobean building at the northern end of town in what was once the tanning district. It was small: only eight tables with Hill in the kitchen and wife Anya front of house. The feel was that of a domestic kitchen rather than first-class restaurant. Hill even did his own washing up. But first class it was. The charm and verve and lack of pretension, coupled with the dazzling food, had journalists drooling and raving. The Merchant House got its star in the very first year and put Ludlow on the culinary map.

The Merchant House was joined over the next few years by two other restaurants in what would become Ludlow's big three. Claude Bosi's Hibiscus was more classically French whilst Chris and Judy Bradley's Mr Underhill's at Dinham Weir was the only one to offer rooms. Unusually, all of them were friends. In fact, one visiting US writer was stunned to see Hill lunching at Hibiscus. Ludlow has that kind of cosiness. Two of the big three are now gone. Hill now runs the Walnut Tree in Abergavenny and is largely responsible for the Welsh town now rivalling Ludlow as gastro-capital UK. Bosi moved the Hibiscus to London although he still runs a pub, the Bell Inn, at nearby Leominster.

So I booked myself into Mr Underhill's, always the best appointed of the lot, nestling on the broad river Teme at Dinham Weir beneath the eleventh-century castle. Apparently it was like Fawlty Towers before the Bradleys got hold of it. It is nothing like that now. As I sit and sip my gin and tonic on the riverside terrace, I watch the smart black-clad staff come and go with their kir royales and chenin blancs, and the lady I take to be Judy Bradley, wife of chef Chris, benign and magisterial and overseeing. The crowd of people this weekend are nicely mixed. There are elegant country-set ladies, businessmen, starched-shirted boys meeting potential in-laws, a gay couple, what might be a very sophisticated hen party and a man who seems to be deliberately testing Ludlow's reputation for restaurant informality with his blue replica football top, scruffy jeans and unkempt rope of a ginger ponytail. If Judy disapproves, she is too polite to say so.

Still, I suppose you want to know about the food. It was extraordinary. First comes what looks like a tiny ice-cream cone containing not Mr Whippy but a soufflé of marinated salmon. I regard salmon, along with oysters and caviar, as possibly the most overrated food in the world, but this is exquisite. The next course is an architectural triumph. It comes in the form of a white, shallow, minimal dish. At its centre is a sort of inkwell and in that inkwell is a small puddle of game consommé to be eaten with the longest, thinnest spoon I have ever seen. It is no more than a sip. But what a sip.

The rest is equally delicious and what the Bradleys describe as modern Scottish, Anglo-Mediterranean and modern British: 'ingredient-driven and nothing too radical'. This means nothing to be inhaled, no bacon and egg ice cream or starters served on toothbrushes. It's not dull, though. The duck-liver custard with quince confit and five-spice glaze inhabits a strange, almost disturbing no-man's-land somewhere between offal and dessert and shouldn't work but, oh boy, it does. I didn't spot anything Scottish myself, though apparently the Highland parfait with shortbread is 'to die for'. That certainly goes for the roasted slow-cooked shoulder of Marches lamb with red-wine jus, mint oil and mustard-scented creamy celeriac. I can still taste it now. A woman at an adjoining table, however, merely picks and prods it and Judy sails over, radiating concern.

'Aren't you enjoying that, madam?' she asks, bending low and solicitous.

'It's rather undercooked for me,' says the diner.

Judy explains patiently that the lamb is served slightly pink at Mr Underhill's, as of course it should be everywhere in the world.

'Well, I don't really like meat,' adds the diner, making a prissy little face. Now at this point, for all I know, Judy would have loved to say, as I did, 'Well, why didn't you say so, you silly, fussy sod? Hang on, I'll see if we can do you a baked potato.' What she actually says is, 'Oh, you really should have mentioned it. The food is quite important to us here.' There is just the gentlest irony in the latter. Everyone else seems to be loving it. The man in the ponytail wears the look of a dog that has just eaten a pound of sausages in a comic: dazed, sated, slightly drugged.

Back in my little room across the road I sip a large, peaty whisky and muse, in my own slightly dazed and drugged state, on Middle England's new obsession with food. It's not all a good thing. Does the world need another celebrity chef? Only if they're less like Gordon Ramsay and more like Nigel Slater, whose recipe for a bacon sandwich includes the instruction, 'must be on white plastic bread with tomato ketchup. Best eaten whilst slightly drunk.'

The room has a fridge, a tacit acknowledgement by Mr Underhill's that while you're in Ludlow you will have become so food-crazed, so droolingly comestible-bamboozled, that you'll have trawled the town's delis as certain hollow-eyed men haunt Hamburg's Reeperbahn and Bangkok's Patpong district, and returned to your room not with Thai sticks and good-time girls but with goat's cheese and marinated olives.

There are four family-owned butchers each with their own specialities and all with tempting, defiantly non-vegetarian fare. There is game and fresh venison from the nearby Mortimer Forest, pork pies and pasties, black pudding and its even more disturbing cousin white pudding. And for those whose palates have become so jaded that regular animals will no longer do, you can buy meat from rare-breed animals, which is probably not as immoral as it sounds but makes me feel uncomfortable that they might sell you Javan rhinoburgers or unicorn pâté.

If you can live by bread alone, or even if you just fancy some fancy bread with your grilled ocelot, there are bakers by the dozen and nary a Mother's Pride loaf in sight. No, in Ludlow, it's more likely to be slow-rising sourdoughs, plaits or dark beer and walnut loaves made with Hobson's Old Henry. There's a dedicated cheese deli called the Mousetrap, a gourmet chocolate shop called, skilfully, the Chocolate Gourmet, and the Marches Little Beer Shoppe clinks with ciders and perries and porters that will make you feel, as you slip into oblivion, that you are not a drunk but an adventurer. It's a nice thought, one that encourages me to have, oh go on, another small one before slipping into the aforesaid and well-fed oblivion.

I rise the next day if not bright and early then bright and early enough by fifteen minutes. You can tell a lot about a traveller I think by the way he or she approaches the tricky subject of the hotel breakfast. Being a raffish man of the world I often eschew this repast altogether on the grounds that, if it's been a late night, fifteen minutes on the pillow or in the shower is worth all the croissants in the world. But when I do make it down for breakfast – and in somewhere like Mr Underhill's I certainly do – I make sure I arrive fifteen minutes before the cut-off. Any earlier is way too keen and too much like hard work, any later and you're being rude to the staff who have been up since six, will hate you and may put their finger in your egg yolk.

None of the smart, elegant young staff here would do this, I'm certain. Their manners and their sense of aesthetics would forbid it. Instead they bring me what is a masterpiece of culinary elegance and design itself: the full English breakfast. Like a little black dress or the London Tube map, the full English breakfast is unimprovable in its purest form, which, ideally, should involve the following at least:

A fried egg comprising a corona of pale white flesh crisped and gently brown at its outer rim and cradling at its centre an orb of gold which trembles like a molten teardrop awaiting the puncturing kiss of ...

A triangle or three of fried bread, crunchy but yielding and just greasy enough to smack of forbidden pleasures. Close by should be ...

A brace of mushrooms that have darkened and aged in smoking-hot butter until their fresh young skin has gained laughter lines and a creased W.H. Auden complexion ...

A disc of black pudding as thick and inviting as a stack of old vinyl singles ...

A plump, self-satisfied, glistening sausage flecked with green herbs ...

Two rashers of bacon, fat and pink and lolling against each like tongues in a lazy, post-coital French kiss and ...

Controversially, I know, a viscous dollop of baked beans, deep red and saltily oleaginous from having been sizzled in the corner of the pan where the bacon and sausage came from.

Somerset Maugham famously remarked, 'To eat well in England you should have breakfast three times a day.' This is normally cited as evidence by those seeking to malign English food. Perhaps innocently, I prefer to think of it as simply a tribute to what is maybe England's greatest culinary achievement. Eat breakfast thrice a day and you'll be well fed, if sluggish. An even more perceptive literary discussion of the FEB comes in Julian Barnes' *History of the World in 10½ Chapters.* The final chapter is a witty and poignant musing on the afterlife and, in particular, Heaven. A new arrival is learning to his delight that Heaven is a kind of holiday camp where you can have whatever you want and the choice is unlimited, from sexual partners to home furnishings to food. Feeling a little silly but childishly delighted, the new arrival picks his daily menu: full English breakfast for every meal. Heaven's representative notes this down impassively. 'Aren't you shocked?' asks the new guest. 'No,' replies Heaven's staff member. 'It's what everyone asks for.'

The full English breakfast is simply irresistible, either when rising bright-eyed and bushy-tailed to greet a busy day or when lurching into the morning with a dense throbbing magenta cloud of a hangover lingering like a storm front over the frontal lobe. Put it this way: have you ever heard anyone say, first thing in the morning, 'I could murder a continental breakfast'? The very smell of an FEB, sizzling in a sunlit kitchen on a bright, crisp morning, has been the undoing of many a vegetarian.

Well breakfasted, I prepare to leave Mr Underhill's. Though every seam of me, both flesh and fabric, is groaning, Judy Bradley offers me two home-made cookies with my bill: 'Just in case you get lost … you are going into Wales after all.'

Judy knows I am going into Wales – just – because I have asked her directions to my next destination. I guessed she would have heard of it. If you call your hotel Mr Underhill's (the pseudonym Bilbo Baggins uses when he goes adventuring in *The Hobbit*), I fancy you were once a cheeseclothy, hippyish sort of person who would have heard of the hill I was headed for and the 1970s concept album named after it. Moreover, the sort who would approve of pastoral lyricism, folk tunes, English romantic music, gentle psychedelia and the idyll of rural isolation and inspiration that has struck a chord in English musicians of every stamp from Elgar to Nick Drake, Vaughan Williams to Pink Floyd.

Food is the food of love in Ludlow. But music has been the food of love for Middle Englanders since a young Warwickshire buck called William Shakespeare first used that chiming phrase in *Twelfth Night*. It was time to pack our guitars and our cellos, our manuscripts and Rizla papers, and to start 'getting it together in the country'.

CHAPTER 5
The Land Without Music

Every nationality has its way of identifying, outfoxing and humiliating outsiders. With the French and the Chinese it's the food: things that sweat and smell, putting things on the menu that you find on the bottom of old plant pots and eating the bits of the animal that even the animal thinks are its worst features. With the Americans it's stupidly complicated sports rules, and with the Germans, traditionally, it's been completely unjustified military invasion.

With us, it's language. The only good reason to pronounce Worcester 'Wuster' is that it gives bar staff a chance to snigger at American tourists when they ask for the sauce in their tomato juice. We can be so insular and protective that we have even invented linguistic mantraps and trapdoors for lesser members of our own tribe. All those Featherstonehaughs (Fanshaws), Belvoirs (Beavers) and Cholmondleys (Chumleys) are really there to act as a kind of password into rarified social strata. If you know the pronunciation, you're in. It works the same way as saying 'I'm a friend of Big Dave's' in certain after-hours Bermondsey drinking clubs. The shutter slides shut, the bolt slides off and you're in.

Hergest Ridge is pronounced 'Hargest' with the 'g' hard as in garden. You'll find this out as soon as you ask for directions. The lady in the newsagent's will snigger, the paper boy will join in and you'll finger the cookies in your pocket that the nice lady in Ludlow gave you. You're lost, as she predicted, and in a foreign country.

Well, nearly. Hergest Ridge is a big, shapely, friendly hill that sprawls on the English-Welsh border. Certain long ways up begin in Wales, but whichever way you come, climb high enough and you'll end up in England as the summit lies there. From the top – a large green sward made for kiting or striding or lying on your back chewing grass and listening to the drone of light aircraft on summer afternoons – the view is sweeping and grand. East and south lies Wales, land of song, of trilling harps, of valleys ringing with the sweet upraised voices of sooty-faced coal miners singing of love and chapel and community and keeping a welcome in these hillsides. West and north, though, lies England. And silence.

That's what our old friends the Germans used to think anyway. In 1904 Oskar Adolf Hermann Schmitz published a book about England entitled *Das Land Ohne Musik*, or 'The Land Without Music'. Admittedly the years leading up to the First World War were not the most cordial for Anglo-German relations and the book was intended to pander to chauvinistic feelings in his homeland but the central premise – that England cares about music less and produces less music than all its European neighbours – had currency in general and specialist circles for centuries. The quote 'Das Land Ohne Musik' had first been used half a century earlier by the German music scholar Carl Engel, and Schmitz, in his book, goes on to try to diagnose our national tin-ear.

'I have asked myself what is missing from this nation. Kindness, love of people, humour or aesthetic sense? No, one can find all these attributes in England, some of them more noticeably than among ourselves. Finally I have found something which distinguishes English people from all other cultures to quite an astonishing degree, a lack which everybody acknowledges therefore nothing new but has not been emphasised enough. The English are the only cultured nation without its own music (except street music). This does not mean that they have less sensitive ears but that their life overall is much poorer for it. To be immersed in music, even ever so little, means being able to lose yourself.' Ralph Waldo Emerson also said in his *English Traits* of 1856: 'England has no music. It has never produced a first-rate composer and accepts only such music as has already decided to be good in Germany and Italy.'

The poet Heinrich Heine – guess what, another German! – even dissed our moves on the floor, alleging that: 'The sons of Albion are themselves the most awful of all dancers, and Strauss assures me there is not a single one among them who could keep time. He too fell sick unto death in the county of Middlesex when he saw Olde England dance. These people have no ear, neither for the beat nor indeed for music in any form, and their unnatural passion for piano-playing and singing is all the more disgusting.'

Which is a bit rum when you take into account The Beatles, The Rolling Stones, Vaughan Williams, Elgar, Bax,

Nick Drake, The Clash, Kate Bush, Harrison Birtwhistle, Delius, The Smiths, Paddy McAloon, The Human League and a thousand other rock and rollers, jazzers, rappers, composers, choirs and folk singers.

However, and however galling it might be, up until roughly the turn of the twentieth century these slurs and canards may have contained a goodly portion of truth. While Bach, Mozart, Beethoven, Verdi, Wagner et al were churning out masterpieces by the yard in Vienna, Leipzig, Salzburg, Bayreuth and Rome, we were quiet as church mice when we weren't hammering and welding and forging our way to industrial supremacy. We didn't have much in the way of opera or string quartets, true. What we did have, though, was a fabulously rich folk music tradition: drinking songs and working songs, songs from farms and mills and latterly factories, murder ballads and bawdy tales, songs about generals, rascals, cutpurses, children, lusty wenches and peevish masters and the whole panoply of life as it was lived in the raw by the ordinary people of England not the gods in Valhalla.

As has so often been the case, because this canon was the preserve of ordinary working people rather than the privileged classes, it was dismissed. The parlours and drawing rooms of middle-class England tinkled to the sound of prim gavottes and mazurkas written in Paris and Prague whilst outside the window, a gardener whistled 'Barbara Allen' or 'Dives and Lazarus' or 'Lovely Joan'; beautiful old melodies worth in a few bars the whole tedious cabbagey length of *The Ring,* ja.

Then around the start of the twentieth century, a handful of enlightened individuals began to see the worth in our indigenous music. First came Cecil Sharp, a light composer who chanced upon some Morris dancers in an Oxfordshire quarry and fell in love with English traditional music. Sharp was something of a prude – he bowdlerised many of the songs to remove their erotic allusions – and he was rather prescriptive about what counted as folk music, dismissing much Lancastrian music because it originated in factory and mills and wasn't 'rural' enough. But he was crucial in a sea-change in the way we saw and heard our own music. Inspired by Sharp, a young composer called Vaughan Williams began to travel across Middle England, collecting and transcribing the folk melodies he found in pubs and farmers' fields and village squares. Other like-minded individuals took up the cause and soon a kind of English music revival was under way, spearheaded by Vaughan Williams, Bax, Ireland, Moeran, Butterworth and more, who unashamedly took as their wellspring the deep traditions of English music. Later they would become misunderstood and mocked for this. Vaughan Williams in particular, the greatest English composer ever, I'd say, was unjustly looked down on for years. His work was dismissed as 'cowpat music' by Elizabeth Lutyens, a dry intellectual of the serial music school that dominated in the 1950s, and Constant Lambert, another vastly inferior composer, said sneeringly of his wonderful *Pastoral Symphony* that it was the musical equivalent of a cow looking over a gate. Recently his transcendently lovely and radiant *The Lark Ascending* was voted the nation's favourite piece of classical music in one of the polls that appears every day in modern Britain. The music critic of *The Scotsman*, Ken Walton – not to be confused with the former all-in wrestling commentator Kent Walton – sniffed that it was 'a very safe choice … it's fair to say that he is loved by middle England'.

There is real snobbery here, not just about music but about Middle England itself. Lutyens' arid, forgettable music was written in the style of the Second Viennese School of Schoenberg, Webern and Berg. If Vaughan Williams' is the cowpat, it may be that hers is the squeaky gate at the corner of the field. Implicit in her comment is the notion that music rooted in the verdant, rich and passionate soul of England cannot be worth our serious attention, merely a pretty diversion, an amusement. She was wrong. Vaughan Williams was right. And in some ways, in their insistence that popular song, the songs of the people, the tunes whistled and danced to and loved to and wept to by the great mass of us were as worthy as grand opera, Vaughan Williams and Cecil Sharp were the forefathers of English pop and all its glories. That, as the title of the late music scholar Ian MacDonald's book reflects, truly is the People's Music.

All of which is sort of why I'm here on Hergest Ridge on this fine and windy day. It's a name you may know from the sleeve of a battered vinyl album reeking of patchouli oil and perhaps bearing the distinct brown stains that tell of having been used in the construction of aromatic recreational cigarettes at some point in the past. For the Middle English countryside has not just been a touchstone and mother lode for classical musicians. When they decamped from swinging London to a remote Berkshire cottage in 1967, the rock band Traffic pioneered what was to become a rock cliché: 'getting it together in the country'.

Singer Steve Winwood of the band told *Q* magazine: 'We were staying in a house in London and whenever we wanted to play, the neighbours would be banging on the walls. We wanted somewhere where we could just play whenever we wanted. We found this cottage in the Berkshire Downs. It was a big estate with a sort of hovel for the gamekeeper, which was what we rented ... Actually, it was a beautiful place and we set up a sort of mud stage where we could just play in the open air. It was very cut off with no road to it, just a track, and there were only about three weeks in the year when you could get a car up there. The rest of the time it was just a quagmire.'

'I think we endeared ourselves to our contemporaries,' added Traffic's drummer the late Jim Capaldi. 'People would come and hang out with us – Bonzo, Leon Russell, Stephen Stills, Ginger Baker, Pete Townshend, Eric Clapton – the hours would just drift into days. I suppose, looking back on it, they were all in cities in hotel rooms, going to the Bag O' Nails and all those clubs and getting out to the country was a nice break for them. You'd call it a hippy commune now, but at the time it was just a practical thing, but very inspirational. When I hear Traffic records and look back on those years, I don't really think of festivals and clubs and rock 'n' roll, I think of tracks on the Berkshire Downs, crows over a coppice. It was a very powerful experience.'

Not far from where Traffic were getting it together in their gamekeeper's hovel, in the Reading suburb of Tilehurst, a young man called Mike Oldfield was taking his first footling steps in the music industry, playing with his sister in local folk clubs and the bass with English eccentric Kevin Ayers. Oldfield's was a traumatic childhood, dominated by his mother's struggles with alcoholism and mental illness. He sought refuge in music, in the countryside and in particular in the creation of a long, purely instrumental piece that married folk, classical and progressive rock into a unique whole. He hawked a tape around various record companies to absolutely no interest and was looking for the address of the Soviet embassy, having heard that the state there supported musicians, when the phone rang. It was someone called Richard Branson.

It's amazing, bizarre even, to think that without that troubled kid from Reading and his unsaleable magnum opus, there would be no Virgin trains, no Virgin airlines, no Virgin pensions, no Virgin broadband. Without Mike Oldfield's forty-odd minutes of defiantly uncommercial music, you wouldn't be able to use your Virgin mobile to tell someone that your Virgin train would be late due to signal failure at Leighton Buzzard, and there'd be no Virgin cola to put in your Virgin vodka as you quietly fumed. Mike Oldfield's *Tubular Bells*, the music no one wanted, was the first release on the fledgling Virgin Records label, a mail-order business set up by beardy, youthful, public-school entrepreneur Richard Branson. It turned out that lots of people wanted it, were enchanted by its haunting, plaintive, complex melody, and bought it in their droves. Branson and Oldfield, both barely twenty, became world-famous and multi-millionaires. One of them didn't handle it very well.

Never the most emotionally robust of individuals, Oldfield found the overnight success of *Tubular Bells* (it stayed on the chart for five years and sold 17 million copies around the world) brought its own stresses. 'If it had happened ten years later, after I'd been through the therapy and the psychological training, then probably I could have been the person that

Richard wanted me to be: "OK, I'll go out and flog my album to death, talk to everyone you want me to talk to, play concerts all over the world." But there I was instead, hunkered down among the sheep on Hergest Ridge, terrified of life, completely ill-equipped to do the things he wanted. Mental torture, let me tell you.'

As it was, Oldfield fled. To here, this lovely corner of Herefordshire and the splendid bracing uplands of Hergest Ridge. He bought a property called the Beacon, now a B&B, and set about building a multi-track studio there so he could avoid even going back to Virgin's Manor Studios in leafy Oxfordshire and hardly an urban jungle itself. He disconnected the phones. He flew model gliders and he bought a sheepdog called Bootleg, both of which feature, along with the hill itself, on the cover of Hergest Ridge. He made local friends like William Murray and Les Penning and got drunk with them in the local pubs. Recently I was speaking to Kevin Ayers, the dissolute, dishevelled ladies man and songwriter who employed Oldfield as a bassist, and I told him I'd visited Hergest Ridge. 'Oh yes, I went up there to see Mike at the time. We …' and then he either said 'had some lagers' or 'flew some gliders'. It could have been both. Kevin had had a late night.

Oldfield also took flying lessons from Martin Griffiths of nearby hotel Penrhos Court, and his kids sang on a subsequent recording, 'On Horseback', which is perilously close to being twee but does offer an insight into Oldfield's bucolic bliss. 'I like beer and I like cheese,' he offers, Hobbit-like, in one verse and concludes, 'If you feel a little glum, to Hergest Ridge you should come.' He pronounces it wrongly, suggesting he hadn't gone entirely native. Speaking to the *Sunday Times* in 2008, Oldfield admits that he is very much a product of 1950s Britain. His love of Middle England and its ways even extends to sounding like a *Daily Mail* reader sometimes. 'I don't know what the hell went wrong with our country. There's a culture of thuggishness that I can't help but blame on punk-rock music. I know it's fashionable to think it was a great advance, but it also inspired two generations of young people to think that being rude, aggressive and violent is cool – and it's very much not cool. I felt less and less safe in the UK. You could no longer walk around the local town – I won't say which it was – while all the pubs had been taken over by chains and turned into places with loud music and no chairs, designed for people to get plastered in and to start fighting. That's not the country I grew up in. The Britain I love is disappearing.'

Clearly he hasn't visited the Welsh Marches in a while. Here you get the feeling that if time has not quite stood still, it is moving forward more slowly, like the river Arrow at its most midsummer sluggish. Staunton on Arrow is simply beautiful and the border lands hereabout are strewn with converted churches, old rectories and public schools. Near the village of Lucton, I spot a hand-painted sign for, of all things, a coracle regatta. Pembridge is the most attractively higgledy-piggledy half-timbered chocolate box of a village I have ever set eyes on. 'The Bootomics are back!!' declares a blackboard outside the local pub.

The bunting is out in Kington; not for me, I'm sure. Perhaps it's always out. Whatever the reason, it made the town look awfully nice, although friends of mine from nearby

Leominster said it can be rough. That could just be local rivalry though. Leominster, by the way, is another of those linguistic traps for the unwary. It's pronounced 'Lemster'. But Kington is just Kington, and on the Sunday morning I was there, it was gearing up for a medieval festival so there were lots of chain-mailed dummies in crusader garb anachronistically grinning out from the window of the local Spar. On the bench outside the police station, which looked shut, a young girl in her Primark finery was languorously texting from her pink Nokia, her face a picture of exquisite boredom. I don't ask her whether she's heard of Mike Oldfield. I think I know the answer. In a tiny village at the foot of the hills, a brisk, genial man in his fifties with a small boy in tow – young granddad maybe or second family – is collecting his *Sunday Telegraph* from the large plastic honesty box. I doubt if anyone has ever pinched one. He's heard of Mike Oldfield ('*Tubular Bells*, yes? Popular with the students, wasn't it?') but wasn't aware that the large, steep hillside behind him was the inspiration for *Tubular Bells*' sequel.

A cheery woman walker with poles and a map case passes me as I climb the whaleback of the ridge. Apart from those accoutrements, she could be dressed for dinner at the Ivy. All is bracken and fern and lush grass, there are squirrels, rabbits and sheep and the view is a delight. In the distance lies a favourite local hill, Twympa or, as it is better known, Lord Hereford's Knob. Better known as this since obviously it is much funnier to say that you can see Lord Hereford's Knob from here, that you spotted some people larking about on Lord Hereford's Knob, etc etc.

Only one thing spoils the view and that is the sight of a

huge SUV 4x4 parked right on the summit. Middle England's love affair with these wretched things is a blight on all of us. To drive them at all is pathetic, but to drive them to the top of hills which should be the preserve of walkers and birdsong should see you in the stocks. The door is open and the driver is lying back with his eyes closed. He may have been asleep but I entertained the pleasing notion that he was dead.

Returning to the village via a lovely little muddy pool crowded with dragonflies I pass a young lad in cricket whites who lifts his bat in greeting. It really is too perfect. However, as I drive past the bilingual sign near Burlingjobb I notice that the English has been crudely painted out, leaving only the Welsh, suggesting that something might simmer beneath this tranquil exterior.

Hergest Ridge was hugely successful, by the way, and, in a pleasing irony, was the album that knocked *Tubular Bells* off the top of the chart. The critical response was frosty, most dismissing it as son of *Tubular Bells*. I like it a lot. You can hear in it the rolling hills, the wind on moor grass and a sense of old, deep peace, as Oldfield himself commented to *Melody Maker* on the album's release. 'There are no Tube trains, very few car doors, lots of open countryside, smooth hills, a general feeling of smoothness and well-being and non-hysteria, just a much nicer environment ... It was really like Herefordshire ... There's lots of things hidden, things that may seem meaningless, but they do have a meaning, a musical meaning. And just the general texture is so comforting.'

That sense of comfort and security is often mistaken for smugness. The critics of *Hergest Ridge* misread it, just as those who sneered at Vaughan Williams' *Pastoral Symphony* assumed that the landscapes evoked were stolid vistas of ploughed fields and hay bales in the Home Counties. They weren't. They were inspired by the fields of France that Vaughan Williams saw during the catastrophic and bloody conflict of the years 1914 to 1918.

The First World War haunts English music and culture for long passages of the twentieth century. This national wound may be at the core of the ineffable, indefinable sadness and loss beneath the loveliness of so much of Middle England's music and poetry. It is a cliché to talk of a lost pre-war idyll and such. But it is also true. A generation was lost, amongst it writers like Wilfred Owen and composers like George Butterworth. For those who saw the bloodshed of Ypres and the Somme, the tranquil beauty of the Shires would forever after contain that sense of deep melancholy that the end of a late summer evening has, ripe with the sweet ache of mortality. It's become a motif, a meme, of English art. And before we leave pop music, we should say that pop has not been immune to this Middle English melancholy, embodied in two lost talents whose stories echo those of Butterworth and Owen and the rest. These two young men didn't go to war. But they did go missing in action.

To reach the grave you take the curving path around the church and into the quiet wooded section to the rear. A very English vista opens up: mixed woodland and rich Warwickshire pasture land stretching towards the horizon where a line of comfortable houses stand. To the right of the path stands a fine oak tree and, below it, the family grave of the Drake family, who lived in nearby Far Leys House. It's a late spring Saturday evening, the sun is slanting through the branches and glinting on the stained glass of St Mary Magdalene. The evening is golden but a chill is creeping into the sunlit air. There is no one here but me. It is, in a melancholy and very English way, perfect.

The headstone tells you that here lies Rodney and Molly Drake and their son Nick. But more telling is the sign attached to the oak tree: 'Fans are requested to pay their respects by leaving only small tokens or flowers.' By and large, they have done that. There is no gruesome cairn of tat like the one at Jim Morrison's grave in Père Lachaise, Paris, just a few Rizla papers and a couple of plectrums. Nothing much to suggest that Tanworth-in-Arden is a place of pilgrimage.

Nick Drake could not have been a more different kind of pop star than Jim Morrison. Morrison of The Doors swaggered about in ludicrous leather trousers, was prone to getting his penis out on stage and partial to the odd armful of heroin or cocktail of narcotics. He sang about wanting to sleep with his mother, violent revolution and other very 1960s Californian notions and fronted a full-on psychedelic assault that made him a very rich and famous man.

Nick Drake, on the other hand, was a quiet, bookish acoustic guitarist who sang plaintive, muted, lyrical songs about fruit trees, rivers, loneliness and lives quietly wasted. He studied at Cambridge but opted for a failed career as a musician. He sold few records, certainly far fewer than his talent deserved, and that fact only deepened his existing sense of depression and isolation. Nick Drake died when he was twenty-six, Morrison when he was twenty-seven, both deaths the result of drug use. Except Morrison died coughing up blood after a fix of heroin in a Paris bathroom and Nick Drake passed out in his parents' house in a sleepy Warwickshire village after what may have been an accidental overdose of Triptizol, an antidepressant.

Drake died in the winter of 1974. At that time his music was at best a coterie enthusiasm, largely ignored. Part of Drake's problem was to have been an introspective balladeer at a time when rock music was at its loudest, most physical and most communal. In the intervening years, however, his cachet has grown to the extent that Brad Pitt, Jennifer Aniston and the late Heath Ledger have queued up to eulogise him. Documentaries and front covers abound now, a bitter irony given that one of Drake's saddest songs 'Fruit Tree' concerns lack of recognition during life, concluding, 'Safe in your place deep in the earth/ That's when they'll know what you were really worth.'

Phil, the husband of the churchwarden at St Mary Magdalene's, is standing in the sunlit doorway of the Bell Inn sipping his pint and looking contentedly at the sunset over his village church. He has much to be contented about. Tanworth feels like a delightful place to live, but it has seen the same changes that many of the villages of Middle England have. Once it would have been a self-contained community with its little shop, its blacksmith's, its cluster of surrounding farms, possibly even its paternalist squire. You'd have worked here, in field or forge or mill or workshop. Now you probably work in Birmingham, and Tanworth, smarter than it once was, is a dormer village, a commuter's dream, just half an hour from central Brum by performance car or 'ultimate driving machine'.

Inevitably, then, the older villagers, the farmers and such, drink elsewhere. Though not in the bar of the Crossroads Motel. For many years Tanworth played the village of Kings Oak in that long-running and much-mocked Midlands soap opera, and it's odd to think that while Noele Gordon et al were hamming it up criminally for a film crew on the village green, Nick Drake may have been hunkered in his room just some yards away, writing the beautiful, stately songs that no one would listen to till after he was dead. In the graveyard, coincidentally, there lies another son of Middle England: the nine-times motorcycle champion Mike Hailwood, who drove his car into the path of an oncoming lorry one dark winter's night taking his daughter to the chip shop. Phil tells me this as he sips his pint thoughtfully on the pub's threshold.

Inside the doorway is a sign proclaiming that this is one of the fifty best pubs in England and by it hangs a picture of Nick Drake. It is a typical picture, the handsome young man with his thatch of modish 1970s hair and his inscrutable, wry, slightly pained half smile. Inside, the restaurant is bustling and the bar is full of tanned, smart, new locals in smart casuals from Boden and Next. Is this Middle England? I ask one. 'Oh yes, absolutely, and the best place on earth too. God's own country,' he says, draining half his pricey continental lager at a pull. He is wearing an aftershave full of woody top notes, wearing a Hugo Boss shirt and the keys to a top-marque German car are on the bar by him.

Not everyone agrees with him. Some locals feel that the gentrification of the village has gone too far. 'Overpriced food and beer obviously appeal to the wealthy villagers living behind their electronic gates' is one comment on a local internet forum, whilst another reads, 'I got the feeling that proper local villagers would only be welcome if they had suitable cool and trendy clothes on that would blend in with the modern surroundings. It is interesting to wonder (had he lived) what Nick Drake would have made of his new-look local.'

I don't know if Nick Drake went in for pubs much actually. I somehow can't see him sinking a pint of Grolsch while watching Chelsea on the big-screen telly or engaging in ribaldry with the barmaid before putting money in the quiz machine. The church across the way is somehow more in his line. Phil is taking the choir to the Royal Albert Hall tomorrow for a competition. He shows me around. There's a brass organ stop in memory of Nick, paid for by Rodney and Molly, and the visitors' book is full of tributes to Nick from pilgrims from all around the world. They have come from Albuquerque and Athens, from Milan and Moscow. They leave sweet messages and quote his lyrics. Once a year what began as the organist playing a recital of his music has blossomed into a small, very Middle English festival. They come from far and wide, in BMWs and camper vans, pitching tents in the local farmers' fields. They don't, as a rule, stay at the Bell. When Rodney and Molly were alive, they'd let them in, make them copies of Nick's home recordings, let them be photographed in his room. The new owners are, understandably, a bit less welcoming of these zealous strangers camping on their doorstep and hammering at their door.

'We do get older people, the sort who might have bought Nick's music the first time round, but it's mainly younger ones. They're often ...' here Phil chooses his words delicately – 'they're often a bit lost, I think ... a bit unsure of themselves. A bit like Nick really.'

This Saturday evening, a young girl who fits the above description rather well is sitting in the church porch on the bench below the parish notices. She is pale and thin, smoking furtively and reading from a battered paperback novel. When she sees me, she smiles and even gives a little wave but scuttles away before I can talk to her. I decide she's a local girl getting out of the house for a crafty fag rather than an acolyte come from afar. But even so, it seems an apt image: a lost young woman in a twilit English graveyard where one of Middle England's lost young men lies asleep.

Syd Barrett was asleep, lost, even dead you might say, for three decades before his actual death. Like Drake, he was a well-brought-up son of Middle England. Like Drake, he spent his formative years in Cambridge and, like Drake, he was a delicate, attractive youth whose promise was lost due to mental fragility. In Barrett's case, though, the former front man and initial genius of Pink Floyd was seemingly waylaid and devastated by a cataclysm brought on by hallucinogenic drug use in the late 1960s. Barrett's music, both his solo work and that with Pink Floyd, teems with images of childhood and innocence and, lurking behind it, menace: scarecrows, gnomes, wonky bicycles.

For me, Nick Drake and Pink Floyd are as much the sound of England, indeed the sound of Middle England, as 'Greensleeves' and the *'Enigma' Variations*. Though they fall loosely under the auspices of rock music – very loosely in

Drake's case – their sound and their mien are literal and metaphorical miles from The Clash or Oasis or even The Rolling Stones. Mick and Keith are good suburban Kent boys rather than the plantation-owning piratical pimp hustler drag-queen romantic poets they would have you believe, but nothing in their work echoes Middle England like Drake or Floyd, with Barrett or after.

With Nick Drake, it's in the actual sound. The finger-picked acoustic guitar with its hint of minstrelsy and the delicate pastoral arrangements provided by his Cambridge friend Robert Kirby. No synthesizers or searing electric guitar solos here, but the plaintiveness of oboes and cellos, the sweetness of celesta and chamber strings. Drake's voice too – deep, refined, thoughtful – is more Keats than Keith Richard and more given to regretful reveries than sexual braggadocio.

Pink Floyd, especially after Barrett's departure, evolved into a rock behemoth, massively amplified, hugely successful. But at the heart of their work is a comparable melancholy. On their magnum opus *The Dark Side of the Moon* they actually sing of 'plans that either come to naught or half a page of scribbled lines' and 'hanging on in quiet desperation is the English way'. You don't come across 'naught' in many Bon Jovi or Guns N' Roses lyrics. And even though their music is self-evidently rock, it is full of evocations of otherness, a very Middle English otherness: the tolling of bells, the ticking of clocks, murmured conversations. It is an eerie world, reminiscent of Lear or Belloc, and dates back to Barrett's earliest work with the group.

'His old bike went for fifteen grand, you know. Just a rackety old thing that he used to cycle down to Budgens on.'

Marcus Barraclough vaguely remembers Barrett from his youth when Marcus's dad gave the young Syd, or Roger as he was then, extra tuition in maths. Marcus is giving me a lift to the station after a few days in Cambridge for the folk festival. As we drive along the Cherry Hinton Road, he tells me that Barrett was a fairly common sight around town, shopping, cycling, largely undisturbed by locals if occasionally hounded by door-stepping journalists and fans. Pictures of him from this time show a bald, overweight, middle-aged man in dowdy T-shirts and shorts. Whenever a new one of these saw the light of day, taken without his consent or approval by some tittle-tattler or hack, the ensuing commentary would revolve around how terrible he looked. In truth, he doesn't look that terrible. He looks depressingly like quite a lot of fifty-odd-year-old blokes in modern England. No, the problem is that he doesn't look like Syd Barrett, the dark-eyed lysergic romantic of the summer of love. 'He were a good-looking lad, alright, if you look at his old pictures,' says the chatty, amiable lady in the very Budgens where Syd bought his provisions (milk, pota-toes, cheese, eggs, nothing fancy). 'Such a shame. That's drugs for you,' she says sadly, standing in front of her rows of Blue WKD, Smirnoff Ice and Marlboro Lites.

Barrett had lived here, quietly, reclusively even, since his withdrawal from the world of rock and roll. The story is well known in the world of rock and a paraphrase will suffice here. Having been the presiding genius behind Pink Floyd's first album, that high-water mark of British psychedelia *Piper at the Gates of Dawn*, Barrett's behaviour became increasingly erratic. At live shows he would play one chord for hours, detune his guitar, stand immobile, rub Brylcreem and crushed-up Mandrax pills into his hair and generally right royally piss off his band mates. An old schoolfriend, David Gilmour, was recruited to cover for Barrett's unreliability and for a while both were in the band. According to Gilmour, on the way to a show at Southampton University, one band member in the car said, 'Shall we pick Syd up?' and another replied, 'Let's not bother.' That was the end of Barrett's time in Pink Floyd.

How much Barrett's problems were clinical and psychiatric and how much drug-induced is hard to say. There are lurid tales of unscrupulous dealers and hangers-on keeping him a prisoner in a cupboard and feeding him massive doses of LSD. Whatever, after his departure from Pink Floyd and an intermittent attempt at a solo career, Barrett came home in 1981 to 6 St Margaret's Square, Cambridge, and stayed there for the rest of his life.

It's a tidy if nondescript bay-windowed little house in a quiet suburb of Cambridge, or as the estate agents put it when it went up for sale in 2007, 'occupying an outstanding position in a highly regarded cul-de-sac to the south of the city centre'. I like the idea of a highly regarded cul-de-sac. I myself have never come across one. However, it may be the cul-de-sac's top-notch reputation amongst suburban mews devotees in addition to the Syd connection that brought in a hundred viewings. In the end it was bought by a French couple who hadn't a clue that the lost genius of English rock had lived there. The new owners are not in evidence today. Then again, what was I expecting? Onions? Stripy T-shirts? Gallic shrugging and Gauloises? I don't hang about as the place used to get its fair share of creeps and gawpers back in Syd's day and I don't wish to be lumped in with either category or chased off by one of the famously (and rightly) protective neighbours.

Instead I find a wi-fi hotspot by a town centre café, watch the students cycle by, order a latte and find various news items relating to the sale of 6 St Margaret's Square after Syd Barrett's death from pancreatic cancer on Friday 7 July 2006. The items are largely in the plonking, quite charming but largely uninformative style of the local teatime magazine show. It's a little curious hearing Barrett, creator of 'Interstellar Overdrive' and doomed angelic avatar of British progressive rock talked of in the same jolly, RANDOMLY emphasised delivery usually employed for sheep who wear iPods or a retired dinner lady who has made a flan in the shape of Prince Charles.

'These are the bizarre yet banal belongings of one of Britain's true eccentrics,' says the jaunty lady on the voiceover whilst the camera pans across examples of Syd's botched DIY in the form of a couple of slanting shelves straight out of *The Cabinet of Doctor Caligari* and a useless-looking toilet-roll holder. Then we move on to Syd's belongings being prepared for auctions. A blue anglepoise lamp is labelled, breathtakingly, '£70', and there are two 'sit up and beg' bikes, one in red and one in blue. Just as Syd sang in the madcap classic 'Bike', they both have 'a basket, a bell that rings and things to make it look good'. It's this resonance with the 1967 song that means the bikes will eventually go for that reported cool fifteen grand. In all, Syd's funny, touching collection of knickknacks and arty-crafty things fetches a hundred thousand pounds.

I finish my latte and take a cab to the outskirts of town

where there's a Floydian landmark I want to see before I leave. The band were all very rooted in this university town, its cloistered cool, its sense of academe and reverie as well as hi-jinks and 'games for May'. After Syd had gone, they made an album called *Umma Gumma*, apparently Fenland slang for sexual intercourse, and on this album was a track called 'Grantchester Meadows'.

I'm walking through those meadows now. Cambridge is a fine town in terms of history and architecture and the famous 'Backs' are a nice spot for a punt but really first-rate scenery is at a premium. Flat and swampy make for evocative but not for romance. So generations of Cambridgians have come to frolic here, in these wild acres of riverside meadows. You can reach them by punt naturally – allow about three hours, you can hire one in the city – or via a long-ish walk from town via the path known as the Grantchester Grind, which gave its name to one of those comic novels by Tom Sharpe that I never found as funny as everyone else did. Or you can cheat and get a taxi and nip behind the Red Lion and the Green Man – you may even get distracted temporarily here – and down to the riverside from the village path. Curiously, I meet a lady in a cerise pashmina with diamante filigree struggling to contain a high-spirited cocker spaniel. 'He once found half a pound of sausages here so he thinks it's going to happen every time,' she explained, as Benjy leaped and jumped and strained at his leash, the memory of his previous feast still very much alive in his mind.

I don't ask why his owner is so fabulously overdressed for Benjy's daily constitutional. Perhaps she is an eccentric academic, an absent-minded astro-physicist or maverick poet. This is entirely possible since this outlying village of Cambridge is said to have a greater concentration of Nobel Prize winners than anywhere else in the world and, Pink Floyd aside, there are at least two other reasons for coming here if you're searching for the soul of Middle England. That's for later though. For the moment I stop and, slightly self-consciously as the day isn't really good enough to merit sunbathing, I stretch out in the long grass on the sloping bank between the pubs of the villages and the lazy meandering river and take out my iPod, scroll to the Pink Floyd section and play the two songs I associate with this tranquil but slightly eerie spot.

Appropriately the songs are tranquil and slightly eerie. One is 'Cirrus Minor', which may or may not be about Grantchester but I've always associated it with this kind of landscape in this flat, still part of England. It begins in a cloudy noonday haze of birdsong and unfolds into a gently bleak evocation of river, churchyard and willows, always trembling somewhere between reverie and nightmare ('laughing in the grasses and the graves') and eventually dissolving into what seems an acid-drenched fantasy backed by organ chorale ('On a trip to Cirrus Minor/saw a crater in the sun, a thousand miles of moonlight later'). I've loved it since I first heard it on the copy of *Relics* I borrowed from John Howarth – he'd coloured in the Heath Robinson machines on the cover in felt-tip, bless him – in my first year at grammar school. Here, amongst the ripples and the reeds, it is creepily perfect.

The other song is, of course, 'Grantchester Meadows'. You don't have to be Sherlock Holmes or a crack musicologist to work that out. Many visitors to the place come because of the song, perhaps a favourite once smoked along to in bedsit and crashpad, and the lyrics are framed in the nearby museum. 'Basking in the sunshine of a bygone afternoon ... and a river of green is sliding beneath the trees/laughing as it passes through the endless summer making for the sea.'

In the distance I can hear Benjy barking, the sun comes out and warms my face and a light aircraft drones overhead. It is just gone noon and, in some mystical sense that feels a little embarrassing to recall, I am at the very centre of Middle England with the universe gently wheeling around me.

'You total arse, Greg.'

Ah well, it was good while it lasted. I am pulled back from the edge of slumber by the sounds coming from a punt in the distance. Two boys and a girl, the boys clearly showing off for the girl's benefit. She's got soaking wet and it's stopped being funny. They think it is, though, and they laugh exaggeratedly and theatrically as they pass between them a bottle of pinkish plonk. One day, they may be called upon to take out your liver or discover a new star. Let them have their fun for now. The serious stuff comes soon enough.

Vaughan Williams was a high-spirited student once too, and not a very diligent one either. His grades were middling at the Royal College of Music and he later said that he learned more from his fellow students than he did from the traditional teaching of his tutors, which sounds suspiciously like a post-hoc justification for mucking about to me. No wonder I like him so much. Later he became a student again, studying orchestration under Ravel in Paris and acquiring a 'little French polish', and he bloomed into the finest English composer of his age – and a very English one.

You'd be hard pushed to find a more English spot than Down Ampney, Gloucestershire, where the composer was born. It sits just inside the Cotswolds and near the Wiltshire border, not far from Cricklade and five miles from the flesh-pots of the urban jungle that is Cirencester. It has a handsome church, a village green, an annual scarecrow trail and a classic Giles Gilbert Scott K6 design 'Jubilee' red telephone box commissioned by the GPO to mark King George V's Silver Jubilee of 1935. At the time of writing its football team languishes in tenth place in the Cirencester and District Football League between Avonvale United and Golden Farm. The reserves have withdrawn from Division Two for mysteri-ous and unexplained reasons.

In contrast to Stratford or Haworth it wears its pride lightly. There is no giant animatronic Vaughan Williams to welcome you to the village. There is no Lark Ascending roller-coaster or Sea Symphony log flume. There isn't even a Tallis Fantasia tea rooms, just a shy addition to the road sign: 'Welcome To Down Ampney, Birthplace of the composer Vaughan Williams.' Even that wasn't there when I first came here about ten years ago, soon after I'd fallen in love with his music. Then there was just a modest display of photos in All Saints' church where his father was the vicar. As I wandered around it, 'in awkward reverence' as Philip Larkin puts it in his wonderful poem 'Church Going', a smiling lady swept the pews and arranged the flowers. 'We're very proud of him,' she said, 'though he really didn't stay here very long. Went to London. He didn't like the countryside much. Too smelly.'

Since then the village has got a little less bashful about their favourite son. In May 2008 they staged a Vaughan Williams day with celebrations of his music and, for twenty pounds, lunch and a guided tour of Pilgrims, his childhood home. Later a tenor sang songs in the church. According to the village website, 'Celebrities attending included Sir Bernard Lovell, of Jodderell (sic) bank fame, and Bill Turnbull, Newscaster, whom some of you may recognise as one of the celebrities in Strictly Come Dancing.' A rapacious and venal cash-in it is not.

Down Ampney's Vaughan Williams connection lives on in a musical way too. Though a lifelong agnostic and pinkish lefty – another aspect of the man the caricatures ignore – the composer was fond of setting his own hymn tunes. One of the most famous is 'Come Down O Love Divine', or as it is now known in honour of Vaughan Williams' birthplace, 'Down Ampney'. The hymn tunes are never going to be my favourites of his work, not even the lovely ones like 'Rhosymedre'. 'Down Ampney', with its plonking changes, melodies designed for lusty unsophisticated singing and dreary resolutions at the end of every verse, reeks to me of draughty church halls and inter-minable services, wondering how much of this stuff is there left and will it still be light enough to play football in the park.

Some people love it though. Look how many people watch *Songs of Praise*. And this is from a web forum called *Ship of Fools*, where contributors can excoriate the most hated kinds of people they know and condemn them to eternal damnation:

'I call to Hell all those who take it upon themselves to lengthen the minim (half-note) at the halfway mark in Vaughan Williams' fabulous tune "Down Ampney". This includes the editors of the latest Anglican Church of Canada hymn-book (Comic Praise), but also the musicians on BBC Choral Evensong broadcast recently from St Endellion in Cornwall. It deflates the whole feeling of movement ... Bring back the Inquisition, I say ...'

There is something of the very soul of Middle England in this too, I feel. The feeling that despite the stolidity and stoicism of gentle people you can push them thus far and no further. You can bomb us, flood us, throw us out of work, but muck about with our salad cream or phone boxes or the minims in our hymn tunes and you'll see that we 'can go from a Chamberlain to a Churchill in a New York minute', as an American I once met observed.

If they are still a little coy in Down Ampney, by contrast the Malverns come over as a cross between Saatchi and Saatchi, Rio Tinto-Zinc and Max Hastings, a drooling publicity-hungry raptor that will stop at nothing to sell, sell, sell. And what they are selling is a piano tuner's son from Worcestershire who used to be the bandmaster at the Worcester lunatic asylum.

For ex-pats, spinsters and *Telegraph* readers, Edward Elgar embodies Middle Englishness in music. Whereas Vaughan Williams was a big dishevelled bear of a man in a landslide of ill-fitting suit who made Patrick Moore look like Audrey Hepburn, Elgar even looks the part. With his neat centre parting, extravagant moustache, high starched collars and prim, stiff-backed expression, you can just imagine him saying, 'This is going to hurt me more than it hurts you, my boy.' Even his local paper the *Worcester News* recently admitted his image was that of a dull old country gent with a huge moustache. Like Vaughan Williams' music, Elgar's is richly romantic, often nostalgic and unashamedly tuneful. But with the intense exception of the *Cello Concerto*, there is little of VW's darkness or strangeness or experiment in Elgar's work. Which is why I guess I don't like it half as much. Millions do, though, and the good burghers of the Malverns – or, as they call it, Elgar Country – know it well. If you've got him, flaunt him.

The house in Great Malvern where he was born in 1856 was once called the Firs. Now it is the Birthplace Cottage. There are two museums. There's a major festival so well established it has spawned its own fringe. There's an Elgar motoring route – look for the violin signs – and any number of Elgar trails taking in significant, and sometimes pretty minor, landmarks in his life in the area. There's a grand statue of him in the middle of Great Malvern. You can buy books on Elgar the Cyclist, celebrating his bike trips around the hills immortalised in Ken Russell's fine black and white documentary from the 1960s. (Don't worry, Elgar fans, it's no *Music Lovers* and there's no naked romping with Glenda Jackson.) This, in turn, has led to the development of Elgar bike trails and an Elgar charity bike ride. There is an Elgar housing association and an Elgar school of music in nearby Worcester and an Elgar foods limited, one of the region's high flyers in the world of 'cake, muffin and doughnut injectable fillings'.

At the top of quaint Church Street, the Blue Bird tea

rooms trades on the fact that Ed was a regular customer in the 1920s and 1930s and 'would certainly still feel at home here in this quintessential English tea room'. There's even an Elgar mature cheese, a concept some might find wryly apt. It adds a certain humour to the programme note for a performance of his *Dream of Gerontius* in Germany in 1908. 'Edward Elgar – a man who has done his best work living quietly in the Malvern Hills, remote from commercial distraction and the strife of commercialism.' And now his face gazes out at us from the back of the twenty-pound note.

But the folks of the various Malverns (Link, Wells, Hills, Great) are right to be proud of him. He led the revival in British music during the early twentieth century and he remained fiercely loyal to his Middle England roots. I was speaking to Robert Plant once, singer with another local music legend, Led Zeppelin, and he described a certain piece of music as 'Elgar on acid'. (Anyone who uses the phrase 'on acid' should, of course, be horsewhipped but, hey, this was Robert Plant.) 'Are you an Elgar fan?' I asked. Of course, he replied. 'He was a Wolves supporter like me.'

So he was. He's believed to have gone to his first match in 1895 with Dora Penny, the teenage daughter of the rector of Wolverhampton, who later wrote about her first meeting with the composer: 'I quickly found out that music was the last thing he wanted to talk about. I think we talked about football. He wanted to know if I ever saw the Wolverhampton Wanderers play and when he heard that our house was a stone's throw from their ground he was quite excited.'

In 1898, he was so taken with a phrase in a newspaper

report, which said forward Billy Malpass had 'banged the leather for goal', that he set it to music. In other words, he created what is claimed to be the first football chant. These days, the team often emerge to the strains of Elgar and it's even claimed that the Wolves diehards sometimes chant the *'Enigma' Variations*, which seems implausible, although of course his 'Pomp and Circumstance No 1' ('Land of Hope and Glory') has often rung out from the terraces as 'We hate Nottingham Forest'.

Elgar was far, far from pomp or circumstance himself. He left school at fifteen with few qualifications, ran the afore-mentioned lunatic asylum band and struggled to make a living for most of his young manhood. He was a devout Catholic, which made him something of an outsider in established Middle English society. After an abortive attempt to establish himself in London with his wife, an ex-pupil, he came back to his beloved Malverns and took inspiration there for the rest of his life. He didn't achieve real artistic and national recognition until in his forties. He skied, flew kites, betted on the horses and went on a 1,000-mile Amazon voyage in his sixties. He was fascinated and excited by technology, opened Abbey Rd studios and would have loved iPods and downloads. Cathy Sloan, curator of the Elgar Birthplace Museum, put it like this: 'Elgar had such a wide range of enthusiasms and, far from being stuffy, he had a tremendous sense of fun. He also learned how to use his fame to his advantage by endorsing various products – in many ways he was the David Beckham of the early 20th century.'

He wasn't posh then. But he was Becks. And more than bikes, kites, cigars or Wolves, he loved the Malvern Hills. You can see them from pretty much any high vantage point in the Midlands. A three-pronged fin like the one on the back of a Stegosaurus, they run north to south for eight lovely undulating miles from Worcestershire to Herefordshire. For decades, they've been a playground for Brummies and Black Country folk of every hue and class, from hearty hikers and alcopopping youngsters to Tolkien and Auden, who both knew and loved these hills, Tolkien taking the Malverns as inspiration for the White Hills of Gondor.

Auden taught in Colwall, just to the west of the ridge, where there's a nice squat hotel that does brilliant things with the local beef and such. The snug fills up with locals and tourists and, the night I was there, the young Latino bar man disappeared upstairs after his shift and came down in the kind of outfit that Liberace might have regarded as showy. Details are scant – I should have written it down but it seemed unnecessarily anthropological in full view – but I seem to remember something alarmingly snug possibly in PVC and a studded denim cap. The locals, red-faced men drinking cider at the end of a hard day doing unspeakable things to pigs, I'll wager, grunted and chuckled indulgently while Claudio waved his hands around, sipped his sticky drink and announced he was going into Birmingham 'to find some fun'. I hope he was successful. I love how Middle England's hotels are now entirely staffed by the hardworking young people of four or five continents, all bringing flamboyance, exotic accents and pale almond eyes to the snug bars and breakfast tables of the Shires.

Near the southern end of the hills is the Herefordshire Beacon, or 'British Camp' as everyone calls it, after the ramparts and defensive ditches at its summit which date back to the Iron Age. The Briton in question was Caractacus who, according to legend, defended the fortress against the invading Roman army, inspiring Elgar to write his cantata 'Caractacus' after visiting his mother who was staying in Colwall. Looking across at the earthworks of British Camp, Ann Elgar said, 'Can't we write some tale about it?' They did, with his neighbour A.C. Acworth writing some words and adding a spurious love interest and Elgar knocking off a rousing arrangement which savvily responded to the patriotic fervour of Victoria's Silver Jubilee.

You can get up to British Camp in fifteen minutes from the road, and everyone does, the grannies, the aunties, the backpackers, the kids, the dogs, the courting couples. For me, though, the pass below British Camp is a place of pilgrimage for reasons that are nothing to do with patriotism or antiquarian ramparts. Just by the car park is a wooden kiosk that has been there for many years and where, come rain or shine, a smiling Goth girl with multicoloured hair and woollies will sell you a polystyrene cup of steaming tea, a bacon sandwich and the best ice cream you will ever taste in your life. Rachel Hicks from a nearby farm in Ledbury makes ice cream that is so far removed from the tasteless ice blocks of the mass market or the unvarying homogenised scoops of even the luxury ones that it deserves a different name. It comes in luscious, drool-inducing flavours that reflect the country around it: gooseberry and elderflower, damson and sloe gin, brown bread, honeycomb, treacle toffee. On a hot summer's day – if one should ever occur again in England – they transcend a mere ice cream and become a religious experience. Incredibly, you can get them mail order too, delivered overnight in a casket filled with dry ice. She advises you to open it wearing gloves. I'd be too impatient to find the gloves. And it's worth losing a hand for anyway.

Sit with your ice cream, then, up at the toposcope on the Worcestershire Beacon, the northern counterpart to the Worcestershire Beacon higher up the ridge, where it's said that you can see sixteen counties and think of Elgar whizzing up and down the lanes and the bridlepaths with his head full of melodies. Look at the people thronging around here in their cagoules and tweeds and high heels, their Goretex and Primark and DKNY, kissing and strolling and throwing sticks for bounding dogs and then consider that this was the sight that inspired William Langland to write 'I saw a fair field full of folk', the opening line of *Piers Plowman*, one of the first masterpieces in English, written in the dialect of the Midlands. These fair fields full of folk, these sixteen counties, are not just full of song but teem with words. Tolkien and Auden wandered here, and all across these Shires words and music go together in a very English way. Local songwriter Clifford T. Ward wrote a bookish, heartbreaking love song called 'Home Thoughts From Abroad', which echoed Browning and asked, 'How is Worcestershire? Is it still the same between us /Do I still occupy your mind?' in a delicately, agonisingly English outpouring of thwarted love. When Pink Floyd were choosing a title for their first album, at a time when the rock world was celebrating its psychedelic head liberation with *Trout Mask Replicas* and *Surrealistic Pillows*, the Cambridge boys named their debut disc *The Piper at the Gates of Dawn*.

It wasn't a new variety of blotter acid but one of the chapters in Kenneth Grahame's *Wind in the Willows*, a tale of moles and toads and 'messing about in boats'.

All things considered, it was time to curl up with a good book.

CHAPTER 6
Ex Libris

It is late in the evening and, like nearly everybody else in the world at this moment I guess, I am watching something on YouTube. In my case, it's a clip that has been viewed roughly a quarter of a million times before. Now I grant you that that is nowhere near as many times as people have watched the video for Avril Lavigne's 'Girlfriend' or something called 'The Evolution of Dance' – it's a bloke dancing – or 'HaHaHa', which is a Swedish baby laughing for an unutterably cutesy and tedious one minute and forty seconds while his doting dad makes a noise like a berk. But it is impressive given that all I'm watching is a bloke in an olden-days shirt mucking about in a pond.

It's possible that you don't know what YouTube is but I bet you do. Jane Austen quite definitely wouldn't have, though, since she died some 213 years before it was invented. In fact, Jane missed out on a whole lot of technical advances, such as cement, fridges and photography. When Jane was alive, cutting-edge technology was the miner's safety lamp and the kaleidoscope. This then makes it all the more remarkable that in our world of MP3, wi-fi, sat nav and Blu-ray, JA should be CEO and MD of RomCom, and more popular than at any time since her death. The bloke in the pond I'm watching, by the way, is Colin Firth and his brooding, dampened Mr Darcy in the BBC adaptation of *Pride and Prejudice* is just one of the reasons why the gentle fever of Janemania is epidemic in the land, three centuries on from the premature death of his creator.

There are any number of both pen portraits and elephantine biographies of Austen around so I shan't add another. Let's just say that she was an interesting woman: the daughter of a clergyman, something of a tomboy, with little in the way of romantic incident in her own life (we think), who died barely into her forties leaving behind six novels. These were largely ignored in her own lifetime, then taken up by academics and intellectuals, and finally in the twentieth century embraced by both the mass reading public and the literary establishment. There are Janeites everywhere now, behind the podiums of our universities and the checkouts of our supermarkets.

But it has only been in the last decade or so that Austen has not merely been revived but seemingly revealed as the high priestess of Middle English chick-lit. In an age where Francis Fukuyama declared that history had ended, where we are apparently post-feminism and where war, poverty and disease are far less prevalent or frightening than bad hair days, counting calories or ticking biological clocks, Austen has become more relevant than Marx or Mailer, a mania amongst modern women, and even a few men.

For a well-brought-up middle-class girl, Jane causes more

than a little contention. Her devotees love her for her light wit, shrewd social observation and, of course, for the sheer romance of her novels. Long before *Bridget Jones's Diary*, Austen was amusing and delighting the reading public of the day with her tales of personable young women, flighty and grave and lovelorn, their desires and their quest for happiness and security. For some, though, this is not enough.

Celia Brayfield, lecturer at Brunel University and a fine writer herself, has criticised Austen for her lack of any real social engagement or insight. 'I think she betrays her time and I'm always gobsmacked by what she ignored ... She focused on such a narrow strain of human reality. Correct me if I'm wrong but wasn't the Napoleonic War going on at the time when she was writing; she doesn't mention it ... There is no poverty in her novels, no corruption, ambition, wickedness or war. Yes her wit is enchanting and her human observations enduringly accurate, but the world she writes about is so tiny. I find it claustrophobic.'

Similarly, the columnist Zoe Williams, by no means a humourless stick, scorns Austen's essential frivolity. 'It's all too graceful and lacks guts ... I'm not crazy for Austen. The Brontës' novels are so overheated, so female, you have to look them in the eye when you read them ... Austen's popular because everyone likes a good costume drama and with Austen you know what you're getting. You're guaranteed a manor house, daughters, dresses and weddings. You're not with authors like Gaskell and Dickens, their stories are not so pretty.'

It's a girl thing. That's the theory anyway. The young and

cute Brit actor James McAvoy made modern bosoms heave as the romantic interest in the recent Austen biopic *Becoming Jane*. But he made blood boil too when he declared to one interviewer that Austen's *Northanger Abbey* was 'one of the worst books I've ever read in my life, full of badly written giggly girls'.

Here he is in good, venerable and blokeish company. In his travel diary *Following the Equator*, Mark Twain described the library on his ship thus: 'Jane Austen's books ... are absent from this library. Just that one omission alone would make a fairly good library out of a library that hadn't a book in it.' More pithily, if less wittily, Joseph Conrad asked in a letter to H.G. Wells in 1901, 'What is all this about Jane Austen? What is there in her? What is it all about?'

Her supporters amongst the literary elite, though, from famed don F.R. Leavis to contemporary Oxford professor Richard Jenkyns, point to the fact that her novels are as much about class, commerce, convention and social status as they are about romance; as much about hard cash as heaving bosoms. Jenkyns insists that 'people who want Regency-type escapism can get it elsewhere ... I think [Austen's] appeal is that she was the first modern novelist and it is her recognition of human life and the strength of the plots [that people enjoy]. The plots are fairly timeless stories about human interaction which are familiar to us.'

She was no naïf. She was conversant with the ways of the boardroom if not the bedroom. 'A large income is the best recipe for happiness I ever heard of,' she writes in *Mansfield Park*, and *Pride and Prejudice* begins with a famous and waspish social aperçu: 'It is a truth universally acknowledged, that a single man in possession of a good fortune, must be in want of a wife.'

But Jane condemns herself to slightness when she writes, 'Let other pens dwell on guilt and misery. I quit such odious subjects as soon as I can, impatient to restore everybody, not greatly in fault themselves, to tolerable comfort and to have done with all the rest.' Guilt and misery may be inconvenient but they are part of our human lot too. They can make for a rattling good yarn or movie or song.

I like to think of myself as one of the girls; or as much of one as a hairy straight man from Lancashire can be. I like Abba. I like clothes. I like dancing. I like gossip. I don't like cars or golf or shouting in pubs or rugby union. I moisturise. I've been known to exfoliate. But I still don't really get Jane Austen. Like P.G. Wodehouse, she seems to me an acute social satirist, but like Wodehouse mildly superficial, a minor if undoubted talent. But I could be wrong of course. And I'm increasingly aware that we may be living in a Jane Austen universe, one where gossip and chatter are the prevalent discourse of modern life, conducted against a backdrop of remote foreign wars, economic uncertainty and an obsession with doing the right thing, property prices and the lives of a pampered elite.

Jane Austen lived in Bath for five years. She came here after her family left the rural Hampshire parsonage where she grew up till the age of eight, and set two of her novels here. During her time in this charmed and charming city she may have owned a kaleidoscope and possibly even a miner's safety lamp, but she definitely didn't have an iPod. I do, and as I wander the lovely, lambent streets of Jane's old stamping ground, I am listening to a podcast entitled 'Jane Austen's Bath', another striking, crazy example of how she endures.

This is the ancient shrine of Sulis, county borough of Somerset, World Heritage site and a very, very easy city to fall in love with, as I am finding out. Before you even arrive, you're a bit smitten. As you drive in on the A6, she reclines below you, like a Regency beauty on a chaise longue, demure and gorgeous. You get a little closer, thinking she won't be as pretty as this up close. But when your sat nav's abrupt teutonic voice instructs you to turn right onto Great Pulteney Street, you will give a low murmur of appreciation at her easy elegance and style, especially if you're a boy from the cramped streets of Lancashire. And you will think, wow, she's probably out of my league. But what the hell?

That was last night: a Friday in early summer, the sunset filling the broad street with caramel light and long shadows, the town sighing and chattering as the working week falls from its well-dressed shoulders. There was just time to throw the bags into the hotel room before the curry. Bath, as you'd imagine, has no shortage of chic eateries where the balsamic vinegar flows and the polenta is always drizzled. But a) I really fancied a curry and b) I'd heard good things about one on Bridge Street. Checking out its website I'd been intrigued by its litany of celebrity endorsements, which were nothing if not eclectic. Some were straightforward ('The best' – Rolf Harris, 'Terrific' – David Essex, 'Thank you for the good food' – Keith

Floyd). Some were conventionally and believably cheesy ('Great hot stuff!!' – Lionel Blair, 'The band are good but the meal was great!!' – Des O'Connor). Some were portentous ('I will return' – Ken Livingstone, MP). Others reveal a bizarre and eclectic range of diners ('Lamb tikka amazing' – Peter Gabriel, 'Yum!!' – Brooke Shields, 'Excellent as ever' – Roland Orzabal, and 'Five Star' – Ravi Shankar). And some were simply baffling ('Now I know what Joana of Avenger felt like' – Gareth Hunt).

Appetite and curiosity naturally whetted, I booked a table. While I yield to no man in my admiration for Roland Orzabal and Gareth Hunt, I have to say that it was just OK. Perhaps it's a result of spending a lot of time in the West Midlands over the last decade or so but when you have gorged on the pillowy naans, fiery jalfrezis, sweet, creamy pasandas and piquant pathias of Ladywood and Smethwick, learned to distinguish the Kashmiri from the Goan, the Hyderabadi from the Bengali, you can become spoiled, blasé and immensely fat if you don't watch it. Interesting again though how the cuisine of the subcontinent has become a staple of Middle England. The average bank manager probably knows what a dupiaza is but not a posset or syllabub. When J.K. Rowling's boy wizard Harry Potter reacts thus to a magical banquet, 'He had never seen so many things he liked to eat on one table: roast beef, roast chicken, pork chops and lamb chops, Yorkshire pudding, peas, carrots, gravy, ketchup and, for some strange reason, mint humbugs', it rings entirely false and of pure nostalgia for Jennings and *Just William* books. British children today salivate over bolognese, sweet and sour and tikka masala, not chops and suet.

The Cobra was good, though, and after a couple of pints of it, a nocturnal tour of the town seemed appropriate. To those who sit cowering behind bolted doors gleaning their view of the world from the *Daily Express* and 24-hour news, Middle England is a jungle by night, where drunken youths pause in their fornication and vomiting only long enough to stab each other, lit by the searchlights of the police helicopter whirring above. It's nothing of the sort, of course. Bath was lively in an attractive way, its pavements crowded with young folk showing off for each other in much the same way they've been doing since the dawn of time. The girls have got a little shriller and louder maybe, even here, but then so has everyone and everything. I peer over the parapet of Great Pulteney Bridge and down at the great semi-circular weir and the fast-flowing river and watch the equally fast-flowing tide of humanity alongside it. A boy is stretched out comatose on a bench, his girlfriend kneeling alongside him trying to rouse him. Even at this distance I gather that he is called Jimmy. Every now and then he groans and rolls over and flaps his arms as if swatting imaginary flies. She gently persists in her ministrations and smoothes his fringe out of his eyes. It is quite a touching tableau really. And if you are going to drink yourself into a deathly stupor, what nicer place to do it than under the three great arches of a handsome bridge by the swift and murmuring Avon on a mild June night?

Pulteney Bridge is thronged by a different crowd the next

day. There are smiling Japanese girls looking at maps. There are Sikh families taking pictures of each other. A big beaming American man with an unruly ginger beard is fussing over his West Highland terrier, which is called Peanut. The Japanese girls, giggling and putting their hands over their mouths excitably, are very taken with Peanut. It would be hard not to be.

Pulteney Bridge, built in the Palladian style by Robert Adam for local bigwig Frances Pulteney, was a brand new and striking addition to the Bath cityscape when Jane Austen was around. It is one of only three bridges in the world to be lined with shops. You come across this fact everywhere, but it's harder to find out what the other two are. (One's the Ponte Vecchio in Florence actually.) The shops are a bit of a mixed bag in truth. There's a clothes shop with a huge picture of Judi Dench in the window which positively screams, albeit in a smooth well-modulated scream, 'Middle England'. There are some tacky and incongruous souvenir shops selling teddy bears and postcards of punks with green Mohicans. There is a coin shop and an antique map shop, the first antique map shop I have ever seen that hasn't closed down.

Over the bridge and you are in Bath proper. The gorgeousness just keeps on coming. Everywhere you turn there's some crenulated doo-dah or tiny delightful wotsit or balcony thingy to die for. Then there's the abbey where fans of ecclesiastical architecture coo and swoon and sketch and where I had an ice cream, which is often my considered response to an overpowering amount of lovely stuff in the same afternoon. I'm not sure whether I'd put Lawrence Tinnal's millennium sculpture in that particular category. His risen Christ seems to be swathed in bandages and newspaper and experimenting with Michael Heseltine's haircut. But it is certainly different. Standing just by it, a lisping podgy young man is pouring his heart out to a pale, worried-looking girl: 'I simply wouldn't make a good finance director any more than you would make a good history teacher, Susan.'

All of this is but a preamble to Bath's main attraction, its raison d'être. It isn't called Market or Bridge after all, charming though those features are. It's named after its big draw, the reason that the Romans came and stayed, not for its wealth or strategic power, not to make a road or a garrison, but purely for hot, steamy fun.

The story goes that a millennium or so before Christ, there was a Prince called (unattractively, I think) Bladud, the son of Lud Hudibras, King of the Britons. Young Bladud liked to travel but unfortunately somewhere in foreign parts contracted leprosy. His tribe banished him and he was reduced to working as a casual swineherd in the Avon valley. Then his pigs became infected and diseased and it looked like he and they might starve. A kindly farmer advised him – from a distance, one imagines – to look for acorns on the far side of the river around Stainswick. He did just that whilst his pigs wallowed in the hot mud of the swamp, as pigs are wont to do. When his porcine pals emerged, he scraped them clean and found their skin was cleansed and cured. So he jumped in too and, you've guessed it, emerged to find his skin clear and his disease healed. Bladud returned to the tribe where he later became King. (I'd have been tempted to burn their huts down, shouting, 'Who's a leper now, you heartless bastards!') In due course, he sent his servants to Bath to establish a settlement, building a temple by the hot springs. Bladud became the ninth king of the Britons and supposed father of King Lear.

All of which sounds pretty far-fetched to me but what is indisputable is that Bath has a thermal spring – the only one in Britain – and the Celts knew and loved it. They believed that deities and ancestors could be contacted via the conduits of hot springs (which makes as much sense as tea leaves, I suppose) and worshipped the goddess Sul as the guardian to this gateway. When the Romans got here in AD43 they developed it as, essentially, a resort: a place devoted to fun, frolics and relaxation. They built a bath complex called Aquae Sulis, and soon it was attracting visitors from across Europe in search of all three. A little of this air of genteel licentiousness clings to Bath to this day.

The bath complex was a remarkable feat of engineering and a superb example of Roman art and architecture. It housed healing hot baths, swimming pools, cold rooms and sweat rooms heated by an ingenious plumbing system. Sadly, the temple was eventually flooded by the rising water levels of the river Avon and fell into disuse after the Romans left, becoming a civic dump and then a Saxon burial ground. General stuff accrued on the site and the Roman baths were forgotten about until rediscovered at the end of the nineteenth century; Jane Austen would have known nothing about them.

She'd have known about the spa waters, though. They made Bath popular throughout the Georgian era, which saw the building of the Pump Room and the Royal Mineral Water Hospital under the auspices of William Oliver, a Cornish physician and inventor of the famous and tasteless Bath Oliver biscuit.

At the turn of the century the Roman baths were uncovered again and in the early 1900s the spa water was bottled and sold as Sulis Water, promising relief from rheumatism, gout, lumbago, sciatica and neuritis. Following the First World War wounded soldiers recuperated here, and after the setting up of the NHS, the health authorities of Bath provided water-cure treatments on prescription. Then in 1978 a girl swimming in the restored Roman bath swallowed some of the source water, and died five days later from a rare form of amoebic meningitis. Tests showed that the *Naegleria fowlerii* bug was in the water and the pool was closed for public use.

However, there was a groundswell of support for the notion of redeveloping the Roman baths as a tourist attraction. National Lottery funding was acquired but the project was dogged by problems. The paint peeled off the new pool as soon as it went on. Then the pool started leaking. The architect blamed the contractor, who in turn blamed the council for ordering cheap materials. All 274 windows had to be replaced. So did the water-filtering system. When the baths did eventually reopen, it was years late and £30 million over budget.

And it was worth every day and every penny. Let pettifoggers cavil and harrumph. The Roman Baths at Bath may be the best tourist attraction of its kind in Britain. Other councils and historic sites take note: this is how to do it. Crucially there is none of the silly and faintly desperate dressing up and trivialising of the past that ruins nearly every other museum and exhibition these days. Kids get their own tour and their own little headset thingies. Adults get an intelligent, insightful and well-written tour presented by Stephen Fry and Tamsin Greig, two paragons of Middle English wit and erudition. Plus there's a sort of additional commentary with a personal flavour by Bill Bryson.

What all this means is that the past is conjured up with genuine flair and mystery rather than buried beneath a landslide of pointless blather, boring games, the trying on of tunics and such. The large central pool with its terrace of statues is lined with forty-five sheets of lead and filled with hot spa water and once stood in an imposing hall over a hundred feet high but now stands open to the sky. For many Roman visitors, it may have been the biggest building they had ever entered in their life. The commentary reveals it as a place of daily activity: in one corner off-duty soldiers play dice, on a bench two business men make a deal as they might on a modern golf course and, in the shadow of the colonnades, a couple conduct an illicit flirtation.

I like this. Not only does it make the place 'come alive' in a way that some cash-strapped actors in a toga could never do, but it strengthens our Austen connection and shows that Bath was a city rich in social manoeuvrings and elaborate choreographed dances of status and hierarchy over half a millennium before *Northanger Abbey* and *Persuasion*. Bath feels even now like a town where gossip, flirtation and intrigue can flourish.

Of course, there may be a downside to this. My friend Lucy was a student here; she said it could be snobbish and small-minded and I have no reason to doubt her. Jane Austen seems to have felt the same. But if you have to come up against snobbery and small-mindedness, rather here amongst colonnades and courtyards than behind the net curtains and pampas grass of suburbia.

Bill Bryson explains that the Gorgon's Head – found lying about by workmen in 1982 – is a stunning combination of Celtic and classical deities, a real religious hybrid, and has a strangely and touchingly human look about it. At the heart of the complex is the Sacred Spring where hot water at a temperature of 460°C rises at the rate of 1.17 million litres a day. This was a holy spot and, peeking into its shadowy, sulphurous, subterranean depths, you get a distinct shiver of the other-worldly. The natural phenomenon of the spa, the hot water bubbling up through a crack in the earth, having gained pressure and heat on its journey from the rainy Mendip hills, was beyond the Romans' comprehension and they believed it to be the work of the gods. It looks like magic to me too.

I spent a good hour and a half in the baths and could easily have spent more. It really is fabulous. As I leave I overhear a snatch of conversation between two young women guides, clearly very posh local students doing some part-time work. 'It wasn't even a borderline first. It was a proper first,' one is saying while the other looks on enviously. At the side of the baths is the Pump Room, a watering hole of renown in Austen's day thanks to the tireless promotion of our old friend Richard

'Beau' Nash. Fifty pence will still buy you a cup of the hot waters which Charles Dickens famously described as tasting of 'warmed flat irons'.

But we should say a cautionary word about our other literary friend here. Whisper it to the Janeites who come in hordes and charabancs from all over the world, but Jane Austen didn't actually like Bath that much. Some say she hated it and used to cry in the carriage when she had to come here, others that she merely didn't much like it as a place to live, which is not quite the same. She once wrote that she found the 'hot white glare' of the city stifling. She did have Catherine Morland in *Northanger Abbey* proclaim, 'Oh, who can ever be tired of Bath?' But in the same book Henry Tilney ripostes, 'For six weeks it is pleasant enough but beyond that it is the most tiresome place in the world.'

What a berk Henry must have been, I think as I stroll along the shady Gravel Walk as featured in a romantic episode in *Northanger Abbey* – much nicer than its name, maybe gravel was a cool new thing in Jane Austen's day – and up to the sloping green lawn that leads down from the Royal Crescent to the ha ha. There cannot be a better address or a des-er res in the whole of England, a great sweeping curve of a Georgian terrace comprising thirty or so houses and possibly the great 'ta dah' moment of world housing. Nowadays it's hotels and flats so even we mere mortals can stay there. The lawn is full today with picnickers and Frisbee throwers, and I take my place among them, lying back on the grass. Sitting near me on a tartan rug, a young American girl explains her internship and independent study course loudly to her two British companions – 'You don't have to go like every day and you have mini lessons and they give you a bunch of stuff' – before launching into an even louder denunciation of hip-hop culture and the concept of 'bling'. 'They say they're from the ghetto but don't they know that those diamonds they wear have been mined by slave kids in Africa?' She is undoubtedly right but the strained smiles on the faces of her friends say, quite clearly, that they want to stab her through the heart with a fork.

I roll over and look up again at the Royal Crescent. It does make you wonder about the strategic nous of the Luftwaffe that they would flatten Coventry – possibly thinking it was Stratford – but ignore Bath, at least initially. Whatever Henry Thingy thought about the place, the blow to local and national morale of seeing the Royal Crescent in flames would surely have been devastating. The admiralty's entire warship design operation was based here; another fact the Nazis seem to have overlooked. When it did get the odd bomb, they had generally been aiming for Bristol. Up until April 1942, that is, when as an act of revenge for the Allied bombing of Lübeck, they bombed Bath for two nights and killed four hundred people.

You would never know. Bath quietly and skilfully rebuilt itself and now the only eyesore is the horrible City of Bath College and the nearby excavation of yet more Roman remains. A passing street cleaner did tell me what this was all about but I confess to not really taking it in. I was just delighted to find a road sweeper with an interest in Roman archaeology and with an accent as rich and gooey as a Somerset cream tea.

I didn't manage one of those but that night I climbed the steep hill to the Olive Tree restaurant and ate a piece of fillet beef that I can still remember. The staff were discreet and stylish and knowledgeable and one of them pointed me in the direction of a couple of dessert wines that almost reduced me to silent tears of joy. I pulled myself together, though, and I silently toasted Jane Austen, the lady who had brought me here, and I made myself two promises: one, to come back to Bath and, two, to have another go at *Northanger Abbey*.

People who don't like Jane Austen will often quite like Mrs Gaskell. Don't be put off by the name. It makes her sound dreadfully severe and fusty and schoolmarmish. In fact, by all accounts Elizabeth Cleghorn Gaskell was witty, principled and something of a rebel, although in the one picture I have seen of her she really ought to have done something different with her hair.

She lived into the age of photography – just – and in books such as *Mary Barton* and *North and South* she displays something Jane Austen barely touches upon, an awareness of the economic structures around her and political issues of the day. *Mary Barton* has been compared to the work of Engels in its unflinching critique of the conditions endured by Manchester's Victorian working class, and *North and South* views the industrial conflicts of the north-west through the eyes of a sensitive woman from the south. The latter was originally serialised in Charles Dickens' magazine *Household Words*. She must often have been late with her copy as Chas once said of her in exasperation, 'Oh Mrs Gaskell. If I were Mr G, O how I would beat her.'

In between these two social tracts is a very different book, a sweet almost Austenish thing about the genteel if disadvantaged folk of Middle England. It was too sweet for Virginia Woolf: 'too great a refinement gives *Cranford* that prettiness which is the weakest thing about it, making it, superficially at least, the favourite copy for gentle writers who have hired rooms over the village post-office'. Not everyone was as sniffy; *Cranford* is many people's favourite of all Mrs G's oeuvre. Just as in *North and South* Milton stands for Manchester, so Mrs G modelled her Cranford on a real Cheshire town, one waiting sleepily and nervously and a little snobbishly for the coming of the railways. Nowadays you're more likely to come across a premiership footballer in designer sunglasses here than Judi Dench in a bonnet. But Knutsford is still genteel. Hardly disadvantaged, though, unless you count not changing the Lamborghini this year as an index of poverty.

Around the north-west, Knutsford has always been thought of as a cut above, not least by Knutsford itself. It lies contented and secure, at least pre-credit crunch, in the rich fat Shires of Cheshire stockbroker land now colonised by a different kind of highflier, the Dimitars, Cristianos and, er, Waynes who comprise football's global elite. They play half an hour up the road – less, if you're driving a Lamborghini – at Old Trafford. In less privileged parts of the north-west – you'll know this if, like me, you grew up there – Knutsford has always been spoken of as having a certain sophistication and class.

Moving there was a sign of rocketing social mobility. Not that anyone I knew ever did. A 'comedy' punk band called The Macc Lads have a song called 'Knutsford Scabby Women' sung lewdly to the tune of 'Nutbush City Limits' but this is clearly just the raging inferiority complex inherent in coming from nearby Macclesfield.

For Elizabeth Gaskell, Knutsford was 'the little, straggling town close to the entrance lodge of a great park'. She grew up here at Heathwaite House, situated on what is now Gaskell Avenue, married here and liked it enough to set her sunniest novel *Cranford* here. As the late Miles Kington pointed out: 'She came up with a damned good name for a fictional town. "Cranford." It sounds just right. It sounds real. It sounds a lot more real than real-life Knutsford. "Knutsford" sounds like an uneasy mixture of Danish (Cnuts) and Saxon (ford).' Which is precisely what it is, the place where King Cnut forded the river, possibly as training for not holding back the waves.

Writing of *Cranford*, Mrs G talked of its 'elegant economy!' How naturally one falls back into the phraseology of *Cranford*! There, economy was always 'elegant', and money-spending always 'vulgar and ostentatious'. Things have changed a little. The oldest of the old money here may think it vulgar but Knutsford quietly flaunts its healthy bank balance. Walking down from the railway station past the civic centre ('Coming soon! Rory Bremner! Elaine Delmar! A Laughology workshop!'), I notice that even the chip shop is the most gleaming, spotless, high-tech one of its kind I have ever seen, comprised of sleek, steel cylinders rather than the normal glass counters where you can watch pies congeal and burn your forehead on the red-hot metal strip.

Turn into one of Knutsford's innumerable and cute little alleyways and the sense of quiet opulence becomes even headier. There are Zapatos designer shoes; the Via Via deli where finely dressed, slightly severe ladies of a certain age are indicating with impeccably manicured hands the cuts of serrano ham and the varieties of marinated olives they would like to take home. In the Loch Fyne oyster bar, a man in Armani taps listlessly at his Blackberry. In Est Est Est, smiling families tear at their Tuscan bread topped with vine tomatoes and garlic.

It gets prettier as you turn into one of the two parallel curving main streets. Knutsford's streets are narrow and crammed with cars and Cheshire's distinctive black and white timbered buildings. Completely belying its name, King Street seems to have been invented for women and clearly they have become more trend-conscious than in the days of Mrs Gaskell, who wrote, '[The Cranford ladies'] dress is very independent of fashion'. I mean, how many bespoke contemporary jewellers can one small Cheshire town need? Black Rose, Aphrodite, Innovation; as I note down these alluring names, I see the owner of the sandwich bar, a sandy-haired lady of about forty, smiling at me from the doorway. 'Pricing a special present?' she asks, wiping baguette crumbs from her apron, which features a stylised cartoon of a rabbit holding a bouquet of flowers. 'I've often thought about taking out a mortgage on one of those drop earrings myself ... if trade picks up I'll go back for the other one.' I don't know if it's the Gaskell influence but even the sandwich-shop owners of Knutsford are adroit satirists.

People in Knutsford and beyond are talking about Mrs Gaskell's *Cranford* again because of a recent, sumptuous and much-acclaimed BBC adaptation of it. It has been an Emmy-nominated hit in America, thanks to PBS Masterpiece theatre. In interviews there, its star, the emblematic Dame Judi Dench, has perceptively outlined part of the story's appeal. 'We have lost that feeling of a community all being together, and of course irritatingly wanting to know what everyone else's business is.' So *Cranford* is big at the Heritage Tapestry Centre Knutsford, DVDs and illustrated editions to the fore in its windows. Actually, not quite as to the fore as the wooden sculpture in the yard outside, a terrifying sort of tree wraith or pagan Pan figure, his arms made of ribbons and his jagged beard made of splinters. More genial is the flutter of bunting and Union Jacks and *Cranford* DVDs. There is a Spanish class in progress and in between little flurries of tinkling laughter I hear Mediterranean verbs being declined in accents of Cheshire crystal. In Knutsford, I assume, a smattering of conversational Spanish will come in handy when ordering your serrano ham and Rioja.

Maybe it was the Union Jacks but there was a vaguely patriotic feel to this corner of the affluent north-west. The Zizzi chain may serve Italian food but its doorway is flanked by one of Giles Gilbert Scott's old red phone boxes and a GPO red pillar box, as if to say this place may sizzle with extra virgin and reek of basil and garlic, but you are in the heart of

Middle England. Next to the restaurant is a wonderfully pretty little pink and white alley called Marble Arch, which is much much smaller and much much nicer than the one in London.

At the top of Tatton Street, there is an unassuming way in to the famous Tatton Park, the 'great lodge' Mrs Gaskell mentions and a much-loved local beauty spot. When I was a child I'd come here with my family on bank holiday trips, though I'd have preferred to go on the slot machines on Blackpool Pier. For old times' sake, I did spend an hour or two strolling its handsome and refined gardens and great tracts of parkland but have little to report except that as I was leaving and brushing a little pathside dirt from my shoes, I heard a teasing woman's voice behind me ask, 'Who's going straight into a lovely hot bath as soon as I get him home?' Turning round, I was actually a little disappointed to see that she was addressing her Jack Russell.

Just alongside the park, though, stands a slightly bizarre but not unattractive Italianate hotch-potch of a building called the Ruskin Rooms. There's a Laura Ashley shop nearby, a gorgeous little terrace called Hillside and, apart from a distracted old man who nearly reverses over me in his mobility scooter, a general lack of incident. But it has not always been this way. Sixty odd years ago, this corner of Knutsford may have heard the kind of language you won't find in *Cranford*, language so ripe and lewd and filthy that even Hollywood had to tone it down when they put the words into George C. Scott's mouth and won him an Oscar.

We don't know for certain that the famous speech that

General George Patton gave to members of the Third Army on 5 June 1944 was delivered in Knutsford, but it may well have been, since hereabouts was where the infamous Blood and Guts general had his operational base at the end of the Second World War. Patton himself stayed at the Ruskin Rooms and he frequented local pubs in Peover and nearby Mobberley. But if he did give the speech in these parts, a bowdlerised version of which opens the 1970 movie *Patton*, then there's a lovely irony in this charming and prosperous Cheshire town ringing with phrases like:

> *This individual heroic stuff is a lot of crap. The bilious bastards who wrote that kind of stuff for the* Saturday Evening Post *don't know any more about real fighting, under fire, than they do about fucking.*

And:

> *Don't forget, you don't know I'm here. No word of the fact is to be mentioned in any letters. The world is not supposed to know what the hell became of me. I'm not supposed to be commanding this Army. I'm not even supposed to be in England. Let the first bastards to find out be the goddamn Germans. Someday I want them to raise up on their hind legs and howl, 'Jesus Christ, it's the goddamn Third Army and that son-of-a-bitch Patton again.'*

Patton was indeed not supposed to be in Knutsford, although word soon got around, which, of course, was just what such a theatrical man wanted. Some say he was sent here because the top brass thought him an attention-seeking, foul-mouthed nuisance. Even in sleepy Cheshire he managed to get himself into hot water and nearly ruin his career. The so-called Knutsford Incident was a speech in which he appeared to ignore the Russian contribution to the war effort. Most witnesses say he actually did mention them but it was misreported, perhaps deliberately. Patton's promotion to the permanent rank of general was placed on hold and Eisenhower scolded him in a fiery letter: 'I am thoroughly weary of your failure to control your tongue and have begun to doubt your all-round judgment, so essential in high military position.' Nevertheless, old Blood and Guts lived to fight another day and Knutsford gained another little bit of history.

I wander down George Street where several windows sport posters for *Wanted One Body!*, a new production at the Little Theatre on the corner of the street. Lavish big-budget productions like the BBC's *Cranford* have their smaller brethren in the amateur dramatics productions that play in church halls, little theatres and schools all across Middle England. In fact, they may have something of the soul of Middle England about them, all those productions of *Hobson's Choice* and *The Importance of Being Earnest* and *Grease* and *Sleuth* played by bank managers and dentists, bakers and florists and retired policemen.

I happily confess to a fondness for the world of Am Dram. I used to do a bit of it myself, although back in Skelmersdale we were a bunch of scallies and dole-ites and lecturers and such. Still, I like to think they still talk with awe of my Macbeth in parts of Lancashire, an ambitious modern-dress production in which I played the titular despot as Derek Hatton. If nothing else, Am Dram provided me with a fund of funny stories, of which one shall suffice here since it seems to have something sweetly Middle England about it. We were playing a benefit for the Walsall branch of Amnesty International and, at the fall of the curtain, a nice bank-manager type came on, said some complimentary things about the production and made a serious announcement. 'As you know,' he began gravely, 'every branch of Amnesty International has its own prisoner who we campaign for, write to and support. Well, unfortunately …' and here his pause quietened the room – 'ours has been released.'

Saying the right thing and a desperate, nervous, slightly absurd obsession with propriety and appearance is at the heart of Mrs Gaskell's observations of Knutsford, as transmogrified into demure and dithery *Cranford*. Then they were worried about the coming of the railway and what these grimy behemoths would bring to their genteel lives. Who knows what they are anxious about today. The credit crunch? Negative equity? Polish plumbers? Whatever, Mrs Gaskell would probably still smile at the ambience of the town, even if she never bought a pair of designer sunglasses.

Appropriately, while Knutsford is aware and alert to its Gaskell associations, it could hardly be said to be ruthlessly exploiting them. That would be rather vulgar and – *Hollyoaks* and Wilmslow WAGS notwithstanding – not very Cheshire really. The literary heritage industry that has turned Haworth into a museum exhibit and Stratford into a theme park has not quite taken root here. There is a leaflet promising 'A Cranford Walk Around Knutsford' produced by the Gaskell Society and sold for 80p, which hardly seems slaveringly mercenary. There are a few books and some civic nods: Gaskell and Cranford Avenues, Elizabeth Gaskell Court, the Gaskell Memorial Tower. The Cranford and Matty pharmacies and the Cranford Cake Shop have gone. But, happily for a thirsty and footsore me, there is a Cranford Sandwich Bar.

As I sit there sipping my latte, I wonder about a few matters. I wonder what the sandwich bar was called a year ago and what it will be called a year hence. I wonder who will win the nearby Crewe and Nantwich by-election, emblazoned in the window of the local Tory party offices though less loudly than the Knutsford Amateur Operatics Society new production of *No, No, Nanette*. The society, by the way, rejoices in the acronym KAOS, the very same name as the legendary Los Angeles hardcore punk band. I wonder if they ever get confusion over tickets. And I wonder if two hundred and fifty years ago, Knutsford/Cranford was even then a nice place for gently idle young blonde women to loll in cafés in that delicious, no-man's-land between teenage dreams and the responsibilities of adulthood and wonder what cake to try. The ones at the next table to me in the spring of 2008 plumped for the carrot and walnut. It was, they told me, to die for.

*

Rather like the chips at Fryways, Nuneaton. Although I imagine the clientele here don't much use that particular expression. In much the same way that this particular chip shop, unlike the Cranford Sandwich Bar, isn't trading on its local literary lady icon and hasn't called itself the Mill on the Cod or the Battered Sausage on the Floss.

I don't know if anyone eating here today has read any George Eliot. There are a few people engrossed in literature as they eat but it's the *Sun* rather than *Silas Marner* or *Middlemarch*. No matter. The chips are fabulous and the girl behind the counter every bit as magnetic as Dorothea Brooke and much less likely to saddle herself with a dry old vicar like Edward Casaubon. The girl in Fryways was a Middle English rose, I guess. Just not the typical sort. She wore an Umbro top, whose replica I couldn't discern, but she gave me a cone of sweet golden chips for a pound and in an accent that I guess Shakespeare and George Eliot spoke in said words just as sweet as I lingered in the doorway. 'Come in quick, it was raining right hard before and it might do it again. One cone of chips? That's just a pound, sweetheart, salt and vinegar and all your sauces there.' After the niceties of Knutsford and Bath this may seem poor fare. But I was hungry and it was miserable and Nuneaton and the world seemed under a cloud. Drizzle fell on the window, steam rose from the fat fryer, but the chips were good and the welcome was warm.

My arrival in the town had been less than auspicious. I'd seen a man with the most grotesquely tattooed face imaginable, like a Maori warrior after a messy nervous breakdown, clutching a Special Brew as he sat with a terrifyingly ugly dog at a table outside a pub. The pub was promising, at eight thirty, 'Krazy Legz', whatever that may be. Across the road was some grim unfathomable traffic system and a bus station, the first thing you see when you leave the railway station. Whatever the practicalities, towns that do this are committing aesthetic suicide. The first thing you see when you leave Liverpool's Lime Street station is the staggering neo-classical splendour of St George's Hall. It's no accident but an act of quite deliberate civic swagger. Leaving Nuneaton station you see a bus station and an amusement arcade. And the most terrifying dog-man combo in Warwickshire, though that, I appreciate, is not a permanent fixture. Crossing the road (sharpish, obviously), I'd almost been run over by a bus. The bus bore the legend 'The George Eliot Shuttle Bus', which was appropriate enough since I had indeed come in search of Georgie Girl.

George was really Mary. Mary Ann Evans, a local farmer's daughter of lively mind and penetrating intelligence, a religious radical in a scandalous open marriage, who became one of the most important novelists in the language, not under her own name but the assumed name of a man. The irony here is that after George Eliot, no other woman writer would need to bother with such clumsy subterfuge.

She was no looker, at least according to her supposed chum Henry James, who wrote of her somewhat ungallantly in a letter to his dad: 'She had a low forehead, a dull grey eye, a vast pendulous nose, a huge mouth full of uneven teeth …

She is magnificently ugly – deliciously hideous … in this vast ugliness resides a most powerful beauty which, in a very few minutes steals forth and charms the mind, so that you end as I ended, in falling in love with her.' So it turns into a compliment eventually. And she has had no shortage of them from illustrious peers and successors. Virginia Woolf called *Middlemarch* 'the first novel for grown-up people', and D.H. Lawrence said of her psychological insights: 'You see, it was really George Eliot who started it all … It was she who started putting all the action inside.'

I stole *Middlemarch* from a store cupboard at my grammar school when I was twelve, partly because I knew I ought to be getting to grips with this stuff, and partly because the tiny, yellow compact edition, chunky as a Bible, was a thing of beauty in itself. I still have it. It is years since I read it and if anything the bonnets and bosoms adaptations, splendid as they are, may have turned me against it. I must revisit it. It is a great novel but it is not a romantic one in the conventional sense. It is not about boy meets girl. It's about Woman meets World. And is really disappointed by it.

For idealistic and essentially nuts reasons, the bright and inquisitive Dorothea Brooke marries Edward Casaubon, a boring scholar engaged on a huge and wrong-headed work of religious scholarship. This and several contrapuntal plots are played out in the provincial Midlands in the years leading up to the Great Reform Bill of 1832, which tried to wrest political power out of the hands of wealthy landowners in the teeth of opposition from the Tories. It's a big book about a great many subjects – politics, marriage, education, women, honour – but at its heart is poor Dorothea's dutiful, doomed and bloodless marriage.

In the end it is not because the Rev. Casaubon is plain or fusty or crap in bed that renders him inadequate. It's a lack of virility of the mind. He is dull, pompous, plodding. But the sex is bad too, it seems. Eliot hints at this rather than illustrates it – it was 1870 after all – but the hints are sometimes unsubtle, as in when Dorothea is found 'sobbing bitterly' on honeymoon and when even Casaubon bemoans that what he thought would be 'the stream of feeling' turns out to be 'an exceedingly shallow rill'.

Nuneaton has other famous sons and daughters as well as George Eliot. An interesting bunch too, from camp comic Larry Grayson to left-wing film director Ken Loach and censorious housewife Mary Whitehouse. But none have got their own hospital or shuttle bus or indeed immortalised the town in the way George – or rather Mary – did, as Milby in *Scenes of Clerical Life* (nearby neighbour Coventry is the model for Middlemarch itself).

There's a 'Nuneaton George Eliot' walk on the web, which is actually just a handful of itinerary points, such as the hospital, so I end up wandering around in an aimless way through the pedestrianised streets that clasp the town centre like a friendly octopus. In this way I find the world's tiniest Debenhams and next to it the Barracuda Bar, closed down. In its shabby, litter-strewn doorway, a woman of about seventy in gold strappy shoes is having a crafty fag. In the town square, a lady of about the same age in a vibrant pink jacket stops and asks me the time. In these days of information overload I would generally think this a preamble to being mugged. But not by this nice lady in pink, I fancy. They seem a law-abiding folk. Every litter bin has a tiny cairn of cigarette butts atop it. And their accent is curious and homely: 'It dunt luk very nahce, dus it?' says a lady aloud, watching the weather forecast on a silent TV in the electrical shop window.

Excitingly, in the George Eliot Memorial Garden there is an assignation. It is not the kind, though, that happens in *Adam Bede* or *Scenes of Clerical Life*. A leather-jacketed boy is trying to put his hands inside his girlfriend's T-shirt. I assume it's his girlfriend anyway. Perhaps they have just met, which would explain her reluctance to let him continue his explorations. Anyway, she seems to be taking it in good part, judging by her high-pitched squealing and convulsive laughter and occasional outraged shout of 'Darren!!!!'

Through the garden winds the river Anker (a name that must provide some mirth for the Darrens of Nuneaton). It is slow and sluggish and the colour of an old snooker table. A few desultory ducks waddle about on the bank. Suddenly a man in – of course – a high-visibility tabard appears from nowhere waving his arms and scares them, flapping and squawking, back into the water. Can this be his job, I wonder?

Jubilee Bridge over the fast-flowing weir is 'part funded by the EU'. Across it you come into town by the back way, past the smartest loo ever and by the loading bay of Marks and Spencer. They have turned the jail into a bistro, which seems astonishingly enterprising. I see a keystone by the very handsome town hall proclaiming 'Prêt D'Accomplir'. My poor French initially reads this as 'We've already done it', which I think is the most brilliant motto ever, as casually boastfully dismissive as, 'Nuneaton: Yeah, Right, Whatever ...' Disappointingly, it actually means Ready To Achieve.

The Ropewalk shopping centre is as grisly and soulless as these things always are in every little town. Striplit and echoing with tinny muzak, filled with expressionless shoppers, it's like something from a George A. Romero movie. So you escape to the market square with relief, into its trees and little florist stalls and a branch of Thornton's where the staff were as sweet as the chocolates and lure the unsuspecting traveller with pralines and alpinis and noisettes.

I emerged from their clutches eventually and chanced upon a statue of what seemed to be a giant sprouting fungus or a bouquet made of hastily and roughly severed ears. I check the date. It is of course 2000, confirming that the millennium surely inspired more bad public art than any other event. But a hundred yards or so away was a much more edifying piece of statuary, George herself.

She's sitting on a kind of tree stump thing but it looks awkward. She seems slumped. Perhaps she's knackered from a hard day of penetrating psychological insights. Anyway it's very nice, sculpted by John Letts in 1986 on commission from the George Eliot Fellowship. And the square is filled with toddlers and mums, lounging students and pensioners chatting. All human life is here, still gossiping and hoping and regretting, just as they did when the lady cast in bronze amidst them noted their foibles and failings a century and a half ago.

A.S. Byatt said of *Middlemarch* that the name roots it in 'the central English provincial counties in which it takes place [but] It is a microcosm, local but also universal, containing bodies and minds, individuals, families and groups, birth and death, tragedy and comedy, Rome and Europe as well as middle England in Middle Earth.'

A.S. Byatt is a very clever woman, cleverer than me, which is perhaps why I don't quite understand that last allusion. But it suits me perfectly, since one of my undernourished but pet theories is that perhaps the most quintessentially Middle English writer is neither Jane nor Mrs G nor George, nor is it Jilly Cooper or J.K. Rowling or Anita Brookner. No, it's a pipe-smoking Brummie bloke who took the quiet virtues of stolid, beer-drinking Middle England, made them a little more furry and took them to hell and back.

The journey to Mordor began in Edgbaston. The Fellowship of the Ring was forged by a millpond off the A4040 in the Birmingham suburb of Hall Green. Middle England's most enduring and popular cultural export is almost entirely suburban Midlands in origin. John Ronald Reuel Tolkien was born in South Africa but raised by his widowed mother in the village of Sarehole on the fringes of Birmingham in the last few years of the nineteenth century. He loved it 'with an intensity of love that was a kind of nostalgia reversed ... I was brought up in considerable poverty but I was happy running about in that country. I took the idea of the hobbits from the village people and children. They rather despised me because my mother liked me to be pretty. I went about with long hair and a Little Lord Fauntleroy costume ... The hobbits are just what I should like to have been but never was – an entirely unmilitary people who always came up to scratch in a clinch.'

This seems to me to be an almost perfect summation of the virtues of Middle England in trouble. It's there in *Dad's Army* and in phrases like 'You can only push us so far'. They (We?) will never look for trouble but if it comes looking for us or bullying some of our weaker neighbours, then look out, chum, whether you're a nasty Austrian housepainter with ideas above his station or the wraithlike Sauron in his black tower of fire. Artistically, Sarehole was a touchstone for Tolkien, a reservoir of memory that he drew on for his later creations. In fact you could say it was hobbit-forming. Sorry.

Tolkien remembered it fondly in later life. 'It was a kind of lost paradise. There was an old mill that really did grind corn with two millers, a great big pond with swans on it, a sandpit, a wonderful dell with flowers, a few old-fashioned village houses and, further away, a stream with another mill. I always knew it would go – and it did.'

Well, sorry to gainsay the great man. But it didn't. I'm looking at it now and, if anything, it's in better nick than it was when trespassing Tolkien and his brother were chased away by the miller's white-haired son George Andrew, who they nicknamed the White Ogre as he was often covered in bone dust. Some think he may have found his way into the character of Saruman, or perhaps Gandalf. Just before his death in 1959, he told a neighbour 'the pair of them were perishing little nuisances'.

Birmingham once had fifty working water mills; Sarehole is one of only two that remain. It languished as a tip in Tolkien's old age. In 1968, Birmingham writer Keith Brace wrote that if you ignored the rusty buckets and mouldering tyres dumped in the river you could see 'a faded manuscript' of Tolkien's Shire. Soon after, though, and following years of neglect and vandalism, the city council restored it in the late 1960s. Tolkien gave it his blessing but was too infirm to attend any ceremonies. It is now fully restored as a beauty spot and museum and attracts thousands of visitors a year. Its website claims that it is 'famously mentioned in *The Lord of the Rings*', which is rubbish, of course, but let's not carp.

They've done a great job of restoring Sarehole, in the lovely little wooded valley of the river Cole. When I arrive, I see that they are to host a Tolkien Day in a month's time, and that hungry visitors can get a bacon butty at the Hobbit Café just across the roundabout. The nearby Moseley Bog, the model for the Old Forest, has been drained and improved but retains a penumbral, swampy, creepy air. The scent of wild garlic is heavy in the undergrowth. A sign reads: 'Danger! Invasive weeds in this area.'

I am shown around by a fantastically energetic and friendly young guide called Tim who apologises that he is 'no Tolkien expert' and then proceeds to be just that and in a casual and relaxed manner, as well as pretty hot on the history of water-milling. He gives me a good potted biography of the man, telling me that after Sarehole he moved to another suburb of Brum, Moseley, but 'didn't like it there. Too many students maybe', a wry reference to Birmingham's student bedsit, wi-fi café and import-record-shop capital. I ask him if this is his full-time job and with a smile he informs me that he is in the process of reapplying for his job, the official title of which is Seasonal Part-Time Temporary Visitor Assistant. Cancel your next fact-finding junket to Barcelona, councillor, and give this young man a proper wage. He earns it.

Head back into Birmingham city centre from Sarehole, and down the Hagley Road, and just after at the second stop after Five Ways traffic island and the Plough and Harrow, turn into Waterworks Road and there, towering above the newsagents, you will see Minas Morgul, the Dark Tower, lair of the Witch King Sauron. I wonder if he ever gives the people at number 62 any bother.

Perrott's Folly is Birmingham's oddest architectural feature. It rises a hundred feet above the residential streets of Ladywood, though they were fields and meadows when it was built in 1758 by John Perrott. Perrott's idea was to build a tower so that he could see the grave of his wife buried ten miles away. Unfortunately the intervening Clent Hills got in the way and his tower did not afford the expected view, thus earning it the epithet 'Folly'.

Perrott's Folly has just opened tentatively to the public. They are coming in their droves. You can gingerly ascend the cold, whitewashed stone, spiral staircase, peeking into the half dozen or so little rooms that lead off. You'll need these if someone's coming the other way. You can't go right to the top. Well, OK, you can if you're lucky enough to be making a TV documentary about it, as I was in 2007. It's a bracing, brilliant experience, like being atop the ramparts of a medieval castle in the middle of a residential neighbourhood in a major city. From here you can see those Clent Hills, and beyond those of Malvern and Clun, and, just down the road, you can see Orthanc, the second of the Two Towers.

The man from the Tolkien Society pointed it out to me. He was shouting up from below, though, as he said he had a bad leg. The reason, you see, that the visitors come is because after leaving the rural quiet of Sarehole, Tolkien's family came here to Sterling Road. Every day walking to school or looking from his bedroom window, Tolkien would have seen these two brooding, lowering Victorian edifices and the seed of the two towers of Middle Earth were sewn in his imagination. By the way, there are a lot of towers in *The Lord of the Rings* but Tolkien himself seems to have intended the 'two' to be Minas Morgul and Orthanc, not Minas Tirith. This may well mean nothing to you and I apologise but I am just attempting to pre-empt the inevitable deluge of mail. Tolkien does bring out the fanatic in people, as well as the daffily enthusiastic. One website features a group of people in full Elvish and Hobbit garb fannying about at Sarehole Mill without a whiff of embarrassment and its directions to Perrott's Folly read: 'I have always found the natives friendly here, but it pays to be cautious, young Hobbit, as this is now a run-down area attempting to regenerate itself, and as with many such areas, crime has been a problem. Walk with fellow travellers, if you can, and be cautious – you never know when an Orc might appear ...' Which is really silly but rather sweet.

It is fashionable to knock Tolkien. As with *Middlemarch*, I haven't looked inside for years but I'm bored by people who sneer at the Ring Trilogy. It is such a soft target. Also, Auden was a fan and if it was good enough for Auden, it's good enough for me. If it was good enough for Auden, it's good enough for anyone. Its essential high seriousness is why I liked it as a twelve-year-old. Bob Dylan said 'to live outside the law you have to be honest' and I think to be fantastical you have to be utterly serious. 'Whimsy' kills it, shows it up for the silliness it is. Which is why Terry Pratchett and *Red Dwarf* will never be for me, but I cried when Dr Who lost Rose into that other dimension that time.

This does mean, though, that there are no good jokes in Tolkien. In fact, there are no jokes at all. But I bet if you asked him he would have said that he had a great sense of humour. And in that he is as English as tea, biscuits, gardening, queuing and thrashing your broken car with a frond before head-butting your Spanish waiter.

CHAPTER 7
Beyond a Joke

A Middle Englishman will admit that he is useless in bed before he'll confess that he has no sense of humour. He would rather make the boys laugh than the women sing. He will confess to a tin ear, a glass back, a limp upper lip and even limper disappointments downstairs before he will admit to a non-functioning funny bone. You can tell Middle England – in fact, all of England – that it is smug, racist, dull, stupid, ugly, lazy or weak. But what you must not accuse it of is not being able to take a joke.

Even the phrase 'sense of humour' is very Middle English. There is no such thing as a 'sense of anger' or 'sense of sex'. You are simply angry or aroused. I always think the quaint phrase itself, 'a sense of humour', means something like 'I will tolerate laughter as a concept without having the faintest idea what laughter sounds like or how to induce it.' Having a sense of humour is both revenge of the downtrodden – the skiving, piss-taking employee – and the benison of the powerful, as in the boss or teacher who 'likes a joke as much as anyone else'. For the English, humour is weapon, crutch, aphrodisiac and social emollient.

A few years ago, I was browsing on one of the many floors of a Tokyo toyshop. Given the Japanese's charming but slightly suspect grasp of the English language, it was probably called 'Robot Death Trilby' or 'Land of Coughing!' Anyway, I found a series of souvenir mugs representing the nations of the world. Beneath the Stars and Stripes on the American mug was the legend: 'Our American cousins are brave and strong. We love their films and our new friendship!!' The French one mentioned cooking and clothes. The British one had a Union Jack and a phrase something like: 'To make us laugh and jolly all day is what our British friends do best.'

It was both cute and, if you think about it, ever so slightly depressing. The implication was that Britain, the country that had given the world bridges and atomic power and railways, was now a mere sideshow. We had become global jesters, a bit of fun when the serious business of inventing and economic powerhousing was over.

I exaggerate. A Brit invented the World Wide Web, a Brit designed the iPod – we are still pretty smart cookies when we put our mind to it. And if we are the funniest nation in the world, why didn't we do *The Simpsons*? But there is a point here and a nugget of truth. We may still invade and invent. But we are genuinely, even a little smugly, secure in our belief that we are the funniest race on earth.

This is fascinating; and it's infuriating. It's the latter when some pub bore chirps up about the Americans 'not getting irony'. Like, hello! If you don't think the Americans get irony, then presumably your telly didn't get the aforesaid *Simpsons*,

Friends, *Curb Your Enthusiasm*, *The Larry Sanders Show*, *Roseanne*, *Frasier* or *Seinfeld* and you've never heard of Woody Allen, Lenny Bruce, Richard Pryor or Sarah Silverman. American humour is rich in withering irony whilst, let's not forget, Britain's favourite comedy moment is David Jason falling over in a pub.

We love slapstick. Hot on the heels of David Jason's barroom pratfall in any list of 'classic' comedy clips beloved of Middle England would probably come the Michael Crawford/Frank Spencer famous rollerskating riff from *Some Mothers Do 'Ave 'Em* or John Cleese goosestepping his way through the foyer of Fawlty Towers. But *Fawlty Towers* also reveals another enduring trait of Middle English comedy, particularly TV comedy. The thwarted ambition, conceit and pettiness of the little man which has been making us laugh, perhaps a little uncomfortably, since Malvolio wore crossed yellow garters in the deluded belief they made him look hot.

The comic song of the disappointed little man rapidly became and remained a staple of our humour. *Punch* magazine's very first serial in 1845 was Mrs Caudle's Curtain Lectures, Douglas Jerrold's account of a hen-pecked husband looking for respite from his wife, and arguably a Dickensian *George and Mildred*. Half a century later *Punch* spawned George Grossmith's *Diary of a Nobody* and the legendary Charles Pooter, a self-satisfied, humourless middle-manager intent on keeping up appearances but always, to his own exasperation, failing to hit the right note. Echoes of Pooter can be found from Hancock to Basil Fawlty, from Captain

Mainwaring to Richard Briers' Martin in *Ever Decreasing Circles* and the various satirical portrayals of John Major.

As English novelist and critic Michael Bracewell has written, 'The British sitcom of yesteryear is shot through with the troubling conviction – a running theme in sitcom – that the best of life is somehow over, its opportunities botched by circumstances or fate.' Cleese's irascible Torquay hotelier is clearly a deeply disappointed man. This is not what he thought life would be. This is not what he thought his hotel would be. He imagined that it – and the guests – would be classier. He despises them both now because at heart he despises himself for how he's ended up. But he masks this in pomposity, just as Hancock does at 23 Railway Cuttings, just as Rigsby does in *Rising Damp*, just as young Steptoe does in the flyblown scrapyard and arguably just as David Brent does in *The Office*.

For better or worse, *The Office* has been the most influential British TV comedy of the last decade. It has set the tenor of much that has come after and I say for better or worse because, like Monty Python and *Viz*, other great English comedy institutions, it has inspired a raft of hugely inferior imitators. Just as Python encouraged the mistaken belief that saying 'nostril', 'ferret' or 'Outer Mongolia' was side splitting, particularly if delivered in a high-pitched squawk, and just as after *Viz* came a deluge of crude and unfunny comics, so Ricky Gervais and Stephen Merchant's talent has created a climate where embarrassment in and of itself has been seen as a substitute for jokes and where much less talented people than themselves have mildly prospered. It's a paradigm shift in what Middle England laughs at. Once upon a time witnessing someone's discomfiture, be it Les Dennis or someone with a built-up shoe, would have seemed a 'tough watch', even in drama. Nowadays it's a comedy staple. What seems to have been forgotten by the imitators is that in *The Office* the bleakness is leavened by the warmth of a love story, and that most of the people being mocked are essentially jerks and thus deserving of ridicule.

Which brings us to satire. We like to think that we love satire but what we really like is seeing people made fun of. *Have I Got News For You* gets more laughs for pointing out that, say, John Prescott is fat or Ann Widdecombe looks weird than for exposing parliamentary corruption or poverty.

In fact, the poor, as well as the fat and the old, are pretty much the stock Aunt Sallies of most of the radio comedy shows beloved of Middle England today, which, as comedian Rhona Cameron has pointed out, seem to exist to give employment to unfunny posh men. Geordies are fat, old people smell of wee, chavs don't recycle, George Bush is a bit stupid. It is actually the opposite of genuine satire, be that Swift or Chris Morris, in that it exists not to challenge but to reassure, to leave the listener feeling warmly superior and contented in their politics and worldview. Morris's *Brass Eye* specials were genuinely subversive and shocking, blisteringly funny and exposed real hypocrisy. For the nearest thing to their wit and intelligence these days, you must look to that irony-free and intellectually lightweight nation much lampooned by our 'satirists', the United States of America, and to *The Onion* and *The Daily Show*.

There's something a little troubling about this because, firstly, one of the cardinal virtues of Middle England, I think, is what J.B. Priestley called 'the natural kindness and courtesy of the English people'. Secondly, fed too much of this comfort food masquerading as satire, we're in danger of losing our nose for the blood scent of real humorous subversion. The funniest show to appear on Radio 4 for some years is a spoof phone-in called *Down the Line* which mocks both the inanity of the medium and the type of opinionated nitwit of every class, creed and race who phones in to such shows. Of course, these were exactly the sort of people who phoned in to the station to complain about the show in their hundreds. They hadn't realised it was a joke and, naturally, they hadn't realised that it was them being lampooned. Now the show has to be rather creakingly trailed and billed as 'a comedy by the creators of *The Fast Show*' for the benefit of the humourless, which is a little sad.

Another thread – often a pink one actually – in the rich tapestry of English humour is sex. It's there in Chaucer and Shakespeare and Fielding and it thrives still. Indeed for many years holidaying families in Skegness and Bognor would send home a cheery missive to Auntie Maud on the back of an illustration in which a shrivelled, sexually inadequate man recoiled in red-faced horror from the attentions of a rapacious nymphomaniac.

Punch said of Donald McGill that he was 'the most popular, hence most eminent English painter of the century'. Not for McGill, though, haywains or horses or even cows in formaldehyde. McGill's subjects were sexy shop girls, matrons with enormous bosoms, ruddy-faced Scotsmen in kilts, fat women in tight bathing suits and the aforementioned spluttering weeds with their trilby hats and their goggle eyes. At the height of their popularity in the middle of the last century, McGill's saucy, colourful, comic postcards sold two million a year in Blackpool alone. 'Saucy' is how we always refer to them; dirty seems wrong. They are not dirty, they are almost childlike. As George Orwell pointed out in his famous essay, 'The Art of Donald McGill': 'The four leading jokes are nakedness, illegitimate babies, old maids and newly married couples, none of which would seem funny in a really dissolute or even "sophisticated" society.'

For Orwell, the McGill cards are a sort of inoffensive safety valve for respectable society. 'They are a sort of saturnalia, a harmless rebellion against virtue. They express only one tendency in the human mind, but a tendency which is always there and will find its own outlet, like water. On the whole, human beings want to be good, but not too good, and not quite all the time ... There is one part of you that wishes to be a hero or a saint, but another part of you is a little fat man who sees very clearly the advantages of staying alive with a whole skin. He is your unofficial self, the voice of the belly protesting against the soul. His tastes lie towards safety, soft beds, no work, pots of beer and women with "voluptuous" figures. He it is who punctures your fine attitudes and urges you to look after Number One, to be unfaithful to your wife, to bilk your debts, and so on and so forth. Whether you allow yourself to be influenced by him is a different question. But it is simply a lie to say that he is not part of you …'

When the Tories returned to power in 1951, they set about cracking down on the moral turpitude they thought had set in during the Second World War. Committees were set up to judge taste and decency of artwork and literature; 167,000 books were censored. They even turned their attention to old Mr McGill, who they prosecuted under the century-old Obscene Publications Act. McGill, in his eighties, pleaded guilty to avoid imprisonment. He was found guilty and the punishment was a £50 fine and £25 costs. Quite apart from the financial burden to McGill, the result had a devastating consequence on the saucy-postcard industry. Postcards were destroyed and orders were cancelled. With the swinging sixties and a new liberalism abroad, McGill's postcards seemed a vulgar anachronism and declined in popularity. But their bawdy and essentially good-humoured comic worldview lived on in the TV shows of Benny Hill and the *Carry On* films, many of which are basically McGill postcards brought to grinning, leering life.

Interestingly, in an interview for the *New York Times*, that stalwart of the *Carry On* films, Jim Dale, pointed out how the saucy postcard is a touchstone of English humour. 'We are brought up on rude comedy … A four-year-old English boy would go to the seaside and send home to his 84-year-old grandmother what we would call a "dirty" postcard. He might pick out one with a picture of a very fat man standing in the ocean and making a mildly off-colour remark. He would send that to his grandmother, and she would get the joke and laugh at it.'

In the *Carry On* movies, Sid James is eternally priapic and lustful, a shabbily rampant version of the British male as also seen in the interminable *Confessions* movie series of the 1970s as well as *On the Buses* and *The Likely Lads*. Call me biased but *The Likely Lads* I find truthful and skilfully portrayed: their fondness for the girls is what still unites Terry and Bob beneath their different aspirations.

The other two, conversely, are absolute rubbish. In the *Confessions* films, Robin Askwith is seen as both sexually voracious and utterly irresistible, at least one of which is hard to countenance. The series represents a kind of anti-James Bond movie in that milkmen and taxi drivers are objects of female lust rather than test pilots or spies, and this is clearly a kind of morale booster for the working-class lads who comprised their audience. Even sociology, though, cannot explain the lasting popularity of *On the Buses*. It ran for just four years – 1969 to 1973 – though it felt like decades and was about as funny as an outbreak of smallpox. It was incredibly popular, though; one of the dismal movie spin-offs outgrossed *Diamonds are Forever*. Each week, the 'humour' revolved around the efforts of the late Reg Varney, a bus driver, and his mate the conductor, men in advanced middle age it seemed but still living at home, to get young women to snog them in their vehicles whilst parked in obscure locales. Even as I watched this as little more than a child I knew it was weird and wrong. Reg, you're fifty, I thought. Get a flat of your own and, who knows, maybe Ethel the clippie might even come back to your place for a glass of Blue Nun and some nibbles and, you know, sex.

Elsewhere in *On the Buses* lurked another staple of British sex comedy: the lugubrious, joyless husband unwilling or unable to entertain the carnal desires of a still sexual wife. In *On the Buses* it was Arthur and Olive. In *George and Mildred* it was, well, George and Mildred obviously, with the former forever disappointing the latter. Variations on this melancholic theme can be seen in Basil and Sybil, Rigsby and Miss Jones, Arkwright and Nurse Gladys Emmanuel and more. Here, you know, the bedroom is either terra incognito or an arctic tundra.

I don't really want to think about *Terry and June* in those terms, though. I don't really want to think about *Terry and June* at all. I'm sorry, it's a softer target than a baby seal pup, but *Terry and June* blighted many a teenage early evening with its curious, and generally humourless, version of life, which I simply didn't recognise. Viewed through the refracting prism of the 1970s sitcom, Middle English domestic life involved a dad who went to work with an umbrella and a folded hand-kerchief in his top pocket, who came home at seven to a Scotch and soda from the decanter and a wife who had spent all day making beef bourgignon in a casserole for when the boss came round for 'dinner' that night. As I sat eating my Findus crispy pancakes off my lap, this world of casseroles, rolled umbrellas and decanters may as well have been Papua New Guinea or Neptune. Did anyone live like this? Maybe they did in what the media analyst Andy Medhurst has called the Gnome Zone. In film director David Lynch's suburbia, as exemplified in the film *Blue Velvet*, darkness lay beyond the picket fence: kinky sex, oxygen masks, severed ears. In the Gnome Zone, what the respectability masked was mild panic and mishaps: burned souf-flés, borrowed golf clubs, putting your back out.

Tom and Barbara Good lived right in the heart of the Gnome Zone but they were somehow different from the Terry and Junes of the London commuter belt. For one, they looked like they actually quite liked each other. They kissed and hugged and stuff; possibly even more. They certainly didn't do decanters and casseroles unless the former contained peapod Burgundy and the latter lentil bourgignon. Mavericks they may have been, but their address was pure Sitcom Central.

To get to Surbiton from inner London you take the Basingstoke train from platform 2 at Waterloo. Even that sounds mildly funny. Two American girl tourists actually giggle when they hear Surbiton announced over the tannoy. Does it even ring comical to a teenager from Boise, Idaho? Perhaps they've been getting *The Good Life* on HBO.

The Good Life, one of the best-loved English TV sitcoms of the 1970s, is the most famous comic celebration of Surbiton. It's not the only one, though. Back in 1906, Keble Howard wrote *The Smiths of Surbiton: A Comedy Without a Plot*. Even then, it seems, the suburb had a reputation for amusing dull-ness. Much later, in the early 1980s, teenage Liverpudlian game programmer Matthew Smith set his hugely successful Manic Miner and Jet Set Willy ZX Spectrum computer games in 'the caves of Surbiton', clearly a Scouse joke at the distinctly unadventurous nature of the locale. Liverpool is actually said in the mid-1990s to have considered adopting the slogan: 'Liverpool – it's not Surbiton'. Around the same time, John

Sessions and Phil Cornwell's surreal comedy series *Stella Street* traded on the notion that celebrities like David Bowie, Marlon Brando, Keith Richards and Michael Caine lived on the same banal street in, got it in one, Surbiton.

But Surbiton has become this icon of blandly genteel suburbia thanks more than anything else to *The Good Life*, John Esmonde and Bob Larbey's proto-green 1970s sitcom starring Richard Briers and Felicity Kendal as the titular Goods, trying to throw off consumerist trappings and live 'sustainably' in suburbia, and Penelope Keith and Paul Eddington as their snobbish but decent neighbours. *The Good Life* seems a remarkably prescient comedy now, pre-empting our current worries about carbon footprints by decades. At the time, though, this was much less noteworthy than Felicity Kendal's delightful bottom, which became something of a national obsession.

To some, *The Good Life* was TV at its twee-est but this is unfair. The performances were first-rate and in its often issue-based subject matter – gentle eco-warriors in dyed-in-the-wool Tory commuter heartland – it showed far more imagination than the dreary glut of crass and unfunny stuff 'on the other side': the *Mind Your Languages*, *Bless This Houses* and *Love Thy Neighbours*. And it had Felicity Kendal's bottom. Did I mention that?

But *The Good Life* more than anything else cemented the borough's reputation as 'Suburbiton'. The name of course is a problem. It's a contraction of South Barton. Its slightly northerly neighbour Norbiton has no jokes about it. And then there's Alfred Bestall, who for years produced the Rupert stories for the *Daily Express*. Bestall was a confirmed and rather joyless bachelor, a pillar of the Surbiton Methodist church, who thought that his work for Lord Beaverbrook was an offering to God and, according to the *Guardian*, 'sought to purge from the stories that element of darkness he had fearfully detected in the work of his predecessor, Mary Tourtel. He was the essence, you might say, of narrow, fearful, suburban morality.' With its riverside location and air of bland prosperity, it seems to embody the self-satisfaction of Baron Macaulay's remark that 'an acre in Middlesex is worth a principality in Utopia'.

The American girls change for Thames Ditton and Hampton Court, like many of my fellow passengers. I stay on for Surbiton and 'detrain' at the really rather lovely station, rebuilt completely in 1937 in the art deco architectural vernacular of the day to a design by J. Robb Scott. It's a gem, rightly considered by many as one of the finest modern British stations, along with Ramsgate and Manchester Oxford Road. Many of the north's great railway stations bristle with civic machismo and pride. Surbiton's exudes a subtler, elegant 1930s Metroland smartness.

I have lots of time to consider this as I stand beneath its awning and watch stair-rods of rain and hail bounce off the pavements, sending Surbitonites scurrying for cover, their coats pulled over their heads. Sheltering with me are a very classily dressed wedding party looking anxiously at their watches ('We're OK for a while yet … after all, we don't want to arrive and the boat not be there') and a gaggle of well-behaved but drenched school children in dashing blue blazers. It is the second day of Wimbledon week, the height of the English summer.

Eventually, as will always happen in Middle England if you wait long enough, the clouds part and the sun comes out. Across the road from the station is a neat roundabout with pretty hanging baskets, faced on the other three sides with architecture and institutions that, according to my original notes, 'speak of stolidity, security and prudence: HSBC, Lloyds Bank, an estate agent's where a fairly ordinary semi is priced at half a million quid'. Little was I to know that within two months, the world's economies would unravel and the banking and housing sector would be in disarray. There is another sign on the roundabout, pointing the way to the local branch of the Samaritans. Then it seemed utterly incongruous. Now it may be getting more business than its three neighbours.

Down St James Road there is a Waitrose (obviously) and the squat and stout red-brick Surbiton Members' Club where a large sign proclaims, 'New members always welcome!!' So I go in. The man behind the bar is actually polishing the inside of a pint glass with a white tea towel, something I have only ever seen landlords in plays do. Splendid, I think, especially when he says loudly, 'Greetings!' Again, this is something I have only heard landlords in plays do. It reminds me of another cardinal virtue of the Middle English: heartiness.

I ask Geoff – he looked Geoff-ish – whether I have to live in Surbiton to join the club. He looks a little puzzled, as well he might. 'Well, that's a good one. Never thought about it.

You have to be proposed by a club member.' Oh well, never mind. 'You can apply online!' he adds cheerily as I leave. Later I take a look at the online application form but it doesn't clarify the residency qualification. What is does tell me, though, and I thought this a wonderfully Surbiton touch, is that the club requests that 'briefcases should be left in the outdoor area'. As I'm leaving, from the back room I overhear a woman's voice, in a tone of breathy excitement and confidentiality, saying, 'She said it was the best cheese on toast she'd ever had.'

By now of course it is actually too hot for comfort outside, something only the English climate can manage, and I'm mopping my brow as I stroll along the hinterland of residential Surbiton. Here 'The Mall' is not a hideous, echoing shopping arcade but a pretty suburban street. As editor of the *Architectural Review*, J.M. Richards wrote in 'The Castles On The Ground' that 'for all the alleged deficiencies of suburban taste … it holds for ninety out of a hundred Englishmen an appeal which cannot be explained away as some strange instance of mass aberration … the beauty of the despised, patronised suburb.'

St Andrew's Square is a neat and beautifully kept if faintly pointless garden. There is no dog poo, no empty plastic cider bottles and its year-old benches – they had plaques with the date on – are gleaming. On the gate is a poster advertising walking tours and a quote from Queen Victoria: 'Surbiton is, not and never will be a boring suburb', which it certainly isn't if a verse posted at Surbiton.com concerning the local YMCA is to be believed. It thanks the Village People for the tune.

Young man! there's no need to feel down. I said, young
man! Come to Surbiton town I said, young man!
There's a place you can go. There's no need to get a job
now!!
Young man, if you want to score weed. I said, young
man!
Crack cocaine, LSD. I said, young man!
Here I know you will find. Many ways to get out of
your mind
At Surbiton town's doss hole Y-M-C-A
The drugs and alcohol Y-M-C-A
They have nothing there that a young man won't enjoy!

I've never really understood who uses YMCAs. Well, it seems in Surbiton it's chiefly for the use of local young homeless men, which has stoked animosity among some locals. I know nothing about this matter so will refrain from joining in but the interchange is revealing about Middle England. Here's one correspondent struggling with the twin compulsions of reasonableness and outrage: 'Regrettably though, whilst we would all support the principles of the welfare state to give someone less fortunate than ourselves a hand up (as we may need it to do for us one day) there are those in society that abuse the system – and consequently plenty of "do-gooders" to jump on the bandwagon and to help them continue do so. In pandering to many of these so-called "homeless" people who have no sense of responsibility, shame, respect or morals (but plenty of money for drink, drugs, cigs and £150 Nike trainers), the YMCA, like many other do-gooders, social work-ers, judges etc and of course the Gov't, is helping to perpetu-ate the problem, not resolve it.'

The YMCA is in the bosom of town, and a rather nice bosom it is too. Heading inwards, the main street goes from the drabness of Jewsons and a clutter of dusty building work and car showrooms to, quite abruptly, the feel of a smart market town or an upscale village. The chalkboard outside the Lamb pub promises 'organic meat from the family farm in Dorset, Sunday papers, bookswap, home-made pork scratch-ings and organic soft drinks'. I think of Orwell and his famous fictitious pub, the Moon Under Water, which was too good to be true. Well, it sounds as if someone has built it on the High Street in Surbiton.

You can sense real local pride in the naming of the busi-nesses, all keen to show off their association with the town. There's Surbiton Glass, Surbiton Dry Cleaners, Surbiton Business Centre, Surbiton Café. There is an art shop where it's Buy One Get One Free on large canvases. It also sells 'silver paper shredders'.

Why would anyone want to shred silver paper, I think, as I sip my tall vanilla latte in the coffee shop. I blow at the froth and read about rainlashed Wimbledon. The coffee shop is packed, much busier than the pub next door, through the window of which I see a solitary business man tapping at his Blackberry. Maybe it's the same one I saw in Knutsford and he's following me. A very elegant lady of about fifty asks if she can join me. She's got a tall vanilla latte too. We are kindred spirits, she says. We swap papers and after a while, with a sigh straight out of Noël Coward, she says, 'This Andy Murray may well be marvellous at tennis but it's hard to warm to a man in a baseball cap.'

I'm still smiling at this on the train out of Surbiton and back to the grime and greasiness of London. Alongside me in the carriage sits a group of three people; a trendy middle-aged couple and a woman of about twenty-five languidly eating an apple. It turns out they are all teachers at the same college and the young woman is leaving Surbiton for a new job. The older woman has her iPod on and can't hear the other two's conversation.

'I may be doing the wrong thing but I have to. It's about taking my chances,' she says and then takes a thoughtful crunch.

There's a pause and then the man replies with a nod to his partner. 'She's distraught that you're leaving Surbiton.'

Another pause, another crunch. 'You've still got Sophie,' the young woman replies, a little tersely I think. 'Oh, I don't know … It's like that Clash song, Should I Stay Or Should I Go.'

At this point I really want to politely interrupt and say that she shouldn't be making big life decisions based on Clash songs, especially not that one as it doesn't make any sense. If he goes there will be trouble, if he stays it will be double. Well, he should go then. Do the math, Mick!

I don't say this, as it would be enormously inappropriate. A little human drama is being played out here. I get the feeling that it is the man and not his partner who'll be distraught to lose his apple-eating friend. I wonder whether Sophie will offer some consolation and whether the young woman will find her own Good Life somewhere beyond Surbiton.

I don't think she'd find it in Slough, though, and I hate myself for saying it. I hate lazy, prejudiced thinking and I hate soft targets. I grew up in Wigan and while I have no illogical allegiance to the town and am pretty candid about its short-comings, woe betide anyone who does comedy accents or jokes about whippets when they find out my provenance. I've lived on and off in the West Midlands for years and nothing irks me more than that class of mirthless wag who mocks Birmingham – a vibrant, 24-hour city in the middle of beau-tiful countryside and full of great people, bars, shops, restau-rants, music and culture – from their vantage point in stylish, debonair, futuristic Lewisham.

Thus it was with Slough. The place has a bad name and I was loath to make it any worse or add to the chorus of general sneering. Though Slough gets a kind of oblique mention in Shakespeare's *Merry Wives of Windsor* when Bardolph is mugged 'near Eton ... in a slough of mire', it's in the 1930s when the town's rampant industrial growth made it a comic target for several writers. In Aldous Huxley's *Brave New World*, the chimneys of Slough Crematorium are cited as a symbol of 'progress'. But it was in 1937 that the laureate of suburbia, John Betjeman, fixed Slough forever in the public imagination as a place of blight and despond. The poem 'Slough' is known to generations from schoolbook editions, so much so that I don't propose to repeat it here. Suffice to say that Betjeman hated the way that the rural quality of the area had been swamped by 850 factories and mass housing. He called for the 'friendly bombs' to come as it 'wasn't fit for humans now'.

By which he might have meant that it wasn't fit for wealthy ex-public school boys from Marlborough, of course. It was certainly fit and indeed welcoming to successive waves of immigrants seeking a better life. During the Great Depression of the 1930s, unemployed Welsh families walked here looking for work and found it, as did Irish families on the new trading estate. There were no homes for them so they lived in sheds on an estate called Timbertown. Now I like Betjeman a lot. But it's against this backdrop that we must read his scathing poem, which, as David Robson wrote in a *Daily Express* column, whilst 'purporting to be a lament for nature succumbing to modern ugliness and profit, it is also a privileged man's cruelty and contempt directed towards people who needed a job and home'.

He's right. 'A house for ninety-seven down/And once a week for half-a-crown' is easy to sneer at when you live in the Old Rectory, Farnborough, a Georgian country house recently voted 'Best Parsonage in Britain' by *Country Life*. Remember too that Betjeman's bomb reference was made at a time when everyone knew that Hitler was readying himself for war. It's a lot less cute as an opening line when you know that the Luftwaffe were starting their engines and loading the bomb-bays.

After the war, immigrants came from further afield, first the Caribbean and then Eastern Europe. Slough Council made history by electing the country's first black female mayor in

1984, and has the highest percentage of Sikh residents in the country. As I was to find out, diverse does not even begin to describe the town now. It is so kaleidoscopic as to be bewildering. None of which really explains why Slough should have been made fun of so famously by several generations. Slough attracts jokes and slurs like it attracts incomers: in droves, seemingly at random and to the exasperation of long-standing Sloughites. Comedian Jimmy Carr has a joke that goes, 'I grew up in Slough in the 1970s. If you want to know what Slough was like in the 1970s, go there now.' Sour ex-Goon Spike Milligan spoofed Slough as a holiday destination, a gag elaborated upon by prog rockers Marillion in the song 'Costa del Slough', with the town as a post-global warming coastal resort.

Ali G, the clueless wigger (white middle-class youth desperate for the cachet of being black) created by Sacha Baron Cohen, is supposed to come from nearby Staines and often 'disses' Slough as uncool. In a survey by the Campaign to Protect Rural England in 2006, Slough was voted the least tranquil place in England.

There are odd little things in the town's CV too. It is twinned with the Latvian city of Riga and was, in the 1960s, the HQ of sci-fi puppetmaster Gerry Anderson's Supermarionation film company. Slough is thus the home of *Thunderbirds*, *Stingray* and *Fireball XL5*. The latter would often venture to Mars, which gave its name to a chocolate bar. That bar was made in Slough. Perma-smiling ice-skaters Torvill and Dean trained at the ice rink here. The Slough Stench is the local term of abuse for the smell that emanates from the vast sewage treatment works just off the M4. Perhaps most damning of all, the Soviet KGB made detailed 1:10,000 maps of nearly all urban areas of the UK in preparation for invasion. They didn't bother with Slough.

Slough's most famous modern resident is certainly not enamoured of the former Poet Laureate's verses. He is proud of the town and took Betjeman to task on British TV in 2002.

'This is the poem "Slough" by Sir John Betjeman. Now – he's probably never been there in his life. Right. "Come, friendly bombs, and fall on Slough. It isn't fit for humans now." Right, I don't think you solve town-planning problems with dropping bombs all over the place, so he's embarrassed himself there ... "It's not their fault they often go to Maidenhead." There's nothing wrong with Maidenhead, no ... Maidstone's a shithole, but Maidenhead's a lovely town, so, nah ... Leamington – now I've been to a conference in Leamington, and it's a lovely spa town, especially compared to Coventry, down the road, which proves my point – you don't sort out a town by extensive bombing. So, y'know. And they made him a Knight of the Realm. Overrated.'

David Brent is, of course, the wince-inducingly deluded and self-important middle manager of the Slough-based paper company Wernham Hogg and, of course, he isn't real. He is a creation of the aforementioned Ricky Gervais and Stephen Merchant and the central character of the enormously success-ful sitcom *The Office*. Gervais and Merchant have been vague about their choice of location. 'Why Slough? Apart from it being onomatopoeic – Slooough – we wanted somewhere very ordinary and unglamorous. Not that I know, I've only been there once when I was a kid. It probably has changed … Apparently [Slough Tourist Board] wrote to the BBC after the first series went out. I can't remember exactly what they said, but the gist of it was that they wanted us to know that Slough's changed. I don't know what they expected, whether they wanted David Brent to look out of the window and say, "I love the new pedestrianisation of the city centre, it's great for shopping, isn't it? Anyway, Gareth …"'

In an interview with the *Guardian*, Reading-raised Gervais was more forthcoming.

'If you live in the Thames Valley, you've got Reading, Slough, Swindon and on to Bristol one way and London the other. It's your neighbourhood.' On the end-title sequence of *The Office*, he'd wanted to show the sign that says 'London, 25 miles'. 'Like they'd be saying, "look, that's all it is, 25 miles. All you have to do. You could walk it …" The message behind *The Office* is for God's sake don't come here. Be true to yourself.'

Ignoring Ricky's advice, I find myself on a grey wet Sunday in the most mocked town in Britain. No town looks its best, I guess, under these circumstances: sheets of filthy drizzle blown into your face by gusts of chilly wind. But Slough does seem to be looking particularly bleak. Part of the problem is the architecture. It's ghastly. Slough has ninety-six listed buildings but they must be well hidden since the first impression you get is of every gruesome architectural style of the last century vying for supremacy. Dreary subways, huge inhuman office blocks, grimly functional civic buildings like the college and library and the cavernous Brunel bus station known to millions as the depressing vista from the opening credits to *The Office*. Buckingham Gardens car park, too, is not as pleasant or verdant as it sounds. It is a squalid concrete patch, lowered over by monstrous tower blocks. Everywhere there seemed to be road-works, gouging the heart out of the town and making every-thing feel ad hoc, unfinished and provisional. This, coupled with the bewildering array of races and styles of dress displayed by the townsfolk, all miserably huddling from the rain or dash-ing who knows where, gives the town the feel of a post-apoc-alypse shanty town for the displaced refugees of the world.

Even the council acknowledge that Slough is not Florence. A promotional film they made a few years back contains a verse reply to Betjeman, in which they state that the town is: 'Not picture book pretty and not claiming to be/But a town that is working not dainty or twee'. This is admirable. But in the murk of a rain-sodden Sunday, unconvincing.

It didn't help that on my visit the people looked so down-cast and defeated. In 2005, the BBC aired a four-part series called *Making Slough Happy*, where a team of 'experts' attempted to bring happiness to the whole town. As would have been the case in Riga, Florence or Maidenhead, it was only partially successful but was well received outside Slough. Residents, though, understandably, felt that it was further contributing to the negative perceptions of the town – why did Slough in particular need cheering up? – and didn't reflect the town's mind-boggling ethnic diversity.

That diversity is both immediately apparent as you pick

your way through the puddle-lined main shopping thorough-fare and one of the more interesting and colourful things about the town. However exotic your shopping list, from plantain to blinis to Somalian otka jerky, you can pick it up here. There is Zimca, a Zimbabwean grocery also selling music and ornaments. There's an African wig shop. There are Lebanese food stores and Punjabi restaurants. There is a comprehensive array of 'pound shops' and Polski Sleps and outside each there seem to be a gaggle of shaven-headed young Polish men arguing and laughing. The town has had a Polish community since the war but that has been bolstered by the recent wave of EU immigration. Apparently the older Poles of the town, particularly the ladies with their crucifixes and neat scarves, are not too happy with the newcomers who swear, drink, miss mass and, they think, are giving the Poles a bad name.

Marwa, the big Asian superstore on the high street, is foodie heaven and I leave laden down with asafoetida and chapattis, rasmalai and roti and some kielbasa and sweet nalesniki from its several aisles of Polish groceries. I lug all of this down to Pro-Tuga, a Portuguese café on the high street. With its Portuguese newspapers, chain-smoking Portuguese clientele, flags and cakes, it's like a little piece of back-street Lisbon transplanted to Berkshire. The two men behind the counter are brusquely cheery as they hand me my egg custard tart and doughnut and strong black coffee (the Portuguese have a notoriously sweet tooth). I fall into a broken conversation with them – about football naturally – but what I really want to say is, before you leave England, visit the Lake District or the Cotswolds or Bath. Please don't go home thinking that Slough was England.

If you're from Slough, you may well be angry with me for that, and I apologise. I come from a town that's no oil painting either, which is why I feel I can be honest. Maybe it was the day or the mood or the rain, but Slough brought despond for me like it did for John Bunyan's Pilgrim. There are whitewashed windows and signs proclaiming 'Last few days!' everywhere. A jaunty accordionist on a street corner seemed horribly out of place, and the policemen on little chopper bikes wearing body armour are a disconcerting mix of the homely and the menacing. Outside the Queensmere shopping centre, two kids are throwing milk cartons at the poster of a pretty girl advertising a chain clothes store. Inside, in a dimly lit chain chicken joint, a young Asian couple are having what must be the grimmest Sunday lunch ever, unless you count the largely liquid repast being taken by the three men smoking and drinking premium lager behind a sheet of polythene. It is surely the antithesis of what café society should be. The pub they are outside is called Wernham Hogg's, the name of the paper company in *The Office*. Is this an act of defiance or defeat, I wonder? Either way, sausage, egg and chips is £3.99 and on Monday there's a Hawaiian party night.

The museum is supposed to be nice but it was closed. They say that it is very good on the town's various communities and the history of immigration, but my eye was drawn to an exhibit in the window, a grisly-looking bladed implement. It is labelled 'Pig Scud – a tool for scraping the meat off pig carcasses'. I'd have preferred a bonnet or a teapot, to be honest. I leave town vaguely cowering beneath the hulking monolith of the gigantic Fujitsu building and the Ice Arena where Jayne and Christopher brushed up their lutzes and triple salchows. It looks really horrid, like a giant colander inside a chrome lawnmower, surrounded by cheap quick-build offices everywhere. The overall feeling is that of a giant retail park that people have somehow colonised like rats. It isn't fit for humans now, said Betjeman. It was a sneer but it contained a sad wisp of truth.

It doesn't help that the drabness of Slough is surrounded by some of Berkshire and Middle England's prettiest spots. Windsor and Eton look snootily down on it, six minutes away by train. Gerrards Cross, Ascot, Beaconsfield are all nearby, as is Cobham, beloved of the painter Stanley Spencer. And not far away is the leafy setting for the most famous bit of crepuscular reverie in the English language.

The curfew is tolling the knell of parting day as I arrive in Stoke Poges churchyard, just as it was when Thomas Gray wrote those lines here three hundred and fifty years ago. Gray's 'Elegy Written In A Country Churchyard' is a beautiful, melancholy meditation on mortality and the transience of human affairs. Stoke Poges churchyard on a wet Sunday evening is a perfect spot for these kinds of thoughts: rain drips from the silent elms, a pony grazes in a twilit field, the gravestones stand in sweet, sombre ranks and there's an almost refreshing wistfulness about the place after the grime and grimness of Slough.

Gray's elegy contains a whole host of famous and quotable lines as well as the opening I've mentioned. 'The paths of glory lead but to the grave', 'Far from the madding crowd's ignoble strife' and, of course, 'The ploughman homeward plods his weary way/And leaves the world to darkness and to me.'

I was plodding homeward too. I had my travel sweets and my Ginsters Buffet Bar and my *AA Book of the Road* and my timetables. I was every inch the travelling Middle Englishman. Because the Middle Englishman takes his travel very seriously. And a journey of a thousand miles starts with a single mint humbug.

CHAPTER 8

Brief Encounters, Missed Connections

On the Manchester to Liverpool railway line just south of Golborne and halfway between the warring Rugby League towns of Wigan and St Helens, there's an old halt called Parkside. If, like me, you're from the area, you'll know Parkside's name because of the colliery, the last of the Lancashire coalfields to close in 1993 and where many of my family and friends' families worked. Some hundred yards east of the bridge that carries the busy A573 road over the railway, there's a marble tablet mounted on the base of an old water tower. It has to be here, but it's in an awkward, obscure spot. The best view of it is by train but only if you are crawling along; otherwise it's a blur flashing by your window. The only other way to see it is by trespassing on the line, sliding down the embankment through the condoms and coke cans and rough shrubbery and encroaching on the track. Clearly you're taking your life in your hands by doing this. And that's fitting, in a grisly way, as this monument marks the very spot where the railways claimed their first passenger victim, in blood and gore and horror, amidst the bunting and brass bands of

what should have been a day to remember for entirely different reasons.

As you'd imagine, the opening of the world's first passenger railway on 15 September 1830 was a grand affair and of
course a feverishly exciting one. Amidst a hubbub of anticipa-
tion, rumour and controversy and in the teeth of opposition
from vested interests, the great northern cities of Liverpool and
Manchester were to be linked via a new high-speed technology
that inspired fear, hatred and awe. About six hundred guests
took part in the event and there were thousands of spectators.
Among the distinguished guests was the Duke of Wellington,
George Stephenson, inventor of the *Rocket* locomotive, which
would enter service that day, and one William Huskisson, the
60-year-old reformist MP for Liverpool. In his terrific book *The
Last Journey of William Huskisson*, Simon Garfield recounts how
Huskisson may have been the most accident-prone MP ever. As
a child he was frequently laid low with chest complaints and
once broke his arm getting out of bed. He tried to jump a moat
one weekend at the Duke of Athol's residence in Scotland,
lacerating the tendons of his ankle so badly that he limped for
the rest of his life. In 1827 his trachea became inflamed, a condition that rendered his voice permanently rasping. Recovering
in Calais he tripped on a cable and nearly cut his foot off. He
was particularly unlucky with horses, regularly falling from them
and breaking limbs. He was nearly killed on honeymoon when
this time a horse fell on him – let's not ask, eh? – and had been
advised not to attend the opening of the railway because of
strangury, an inflammation of the kidneys and bladder, causing
him a 'constant but unfulfilled desire to pass water'.

But attend he did. He'd fallen out with Wellington over parliamentary reform and, ambitious and intelligent, saw this as an opportunity to make expedient amends. Huskisson was passionately pro-railway. Many were not. The canal owners knew that their inflated profits were at risk from a new mode of transport that could make in two hours the Manchester-Liverpool trip that took thirty-six by canal boat. The landowning and therefore ruling class (if this seems polemical rather than factual, consider that Manchester had no MP at all at the time) had spread the lie that people would asphyxiate on trains, pregnant women would miscarry and the milk of line-side cows would be soured. However, after six long years of backbreaking work and astonishing technical ingenuity, the passenger railway had arrived. Huskisson was in the leading coach of the eight trains that set off for Manchester witnessed by hundreds of thousands of excited onlookers on the banks and bridges.

When they reached Parkside just before noon, the engine *Northumbrian* stopped to take on water, drawing the Duke of Wellington's personal carriage up on a parallel line to observe the passing of the *Rocket* and its carriages. Many passengers, including Huskisson, got down to stretch their legs in the gap between the lines. Then a shout went up. 'An engine is approaching. Take care, gentlemen!' It was the *Rocket*, then potentially the fastest thing on earth but moving almost in slow motion at this point. But even so, unstoppable.

Most of the assembled dignitaries climbed to safety with ease, though Prince Esterhazy of Austria was yanked in by his lapels. But Huskisson panicked and dithered and ended up clinging to the side of the carriage as the *Rocket* approached.

He grabbed at the door, which swung out into the path of the *Rocket* and was hit. Huskisson fell beneath the wheels, which crushed and mangled his thigh.

It was, as one can imagine, a horrific scene. Huskisson lay on the track in gouts of blood, his split limb twitching. As society hostess Harriet Arbuthnot later observed, 'It is impossible to give an idea of the scene that followed, of the horror of everyone present or of the piercing shrieks of his unfortunate wife, who was in the car. He said scarcely more than, "It's all over with me. Bring me my wife and let me die."' Instead, the *Rocket*, driven by Stephenson himself at a then incredible speed of 36 miles an hour, rushed him to Eccles parsonage, where he was attended unsuccessfully by surgeons and where he died nine dreadful hours later.

I find the story of that fateful day awful, compelling and extraordinary. Obviously, it's a human tragedy. But it's more than that. If you scripted it, the reviewers would rightly call it far-fetched. At the unveiling and maiden voyage of an incredible new form of transport, a leading politician is killed at the very moment of his rapprochement with the Prime Minister and is rushed away from the scene in a doomed mercy dash by the pioneering inventor of the lethal technology. Imagine if, on the opening day of the new ultra-fast Virgin Monorail service between London and Edinburgh, Gordon Brown was knocked down by it as Tony Blair tried to pull him to safety and in the ensuing mayhem, Richard Branson took the wheel himself to rush the stricken man away. As some people are fond of saying, you couldn't make it up.

But what is even more incredible is that not only did we

not abandon there and then any ideas of this new-fangled, clearly lethal transport system, we embraced it. Embraced it so fondly and heartily in fact that it became a cherished part of our national psyche. In blood and chaos, England's love affair with the railways was born.

America's defining mode of transport is the road: an endless highway leading across vast and untamed spaces to a date with freedom, destiny and the unknown. But the railways are, or were, emblematic of England: complex, labyrinthine, a network of quiet intricacy and subtle branching, communal and yet deeply private, reflections in windows, glimpses of back gardens, missed connections, parallel lines. Railways are parting and meeting, loving and leaving, coming home and sallying forth. Railway stations are full of little human dramas – tearful lovers, a young girl setting off for university with Mum a gentle word away from crying, a granny arriving for Christmas in an anxious, happy fuss – that service stations can never be. When Auden wrote 'Night Mail' for the famous GPO promotional film of that name, his comments on the postal service are really comments about the railways that bring the letters:

> *Pulling up Beattock, a steady climb*
> *The gradient's against her, but she's on time*
> *Thro' sparse counties she rampages,*
> *Her driver's eye upon the gauges.*
> *Panting up past lonely farms*
> *Fed by the fireman's restless arms.*
> *Striding forward along the rails*
> *Thro' southern uplands with northern mails.*

The night-mail train was discontinued in January 2004. I said above that the railway network is or was emblematic of Middle England because our railway network was once far, far more lovely and mysterious. As I write these words, a short series of TV programmes on the BBC is 'celebrating' or rather commemorating the forty-fifth anniversary of an act of railway butchery unparalleled in these islands except perhaps for the unfortunate events of September 1830. In 1963, the Conservative government led by the patrician Harold Macmillan paused briefly in telling us that we'd never had it so good to make a decision that would make life signally and decidedly worse for every Briton. I presented one of the TV programmes just mentioned and in one section I stopped railway users at Manchester's Piccadilly station and asked them what they thought of one Dr Richard Beeching. Nearly everyone knew the name; the younger ones creased their brows and recalled some ancient bogeyman but the older ones became alive with contempt. I stopped a retired chemistry teacher, a genial, dapper man in beret, cream suit and neat knitted tie. Rarely have I seen such a sweet countenance darken and purple so quickly. 'Oh I know that name,' he spat, his eyes flickering with real hatred. 'That was the man, the traitor, who ruined the British railway system. A dreadful man, a butcher, a fool. And what really upsets me is that someone who called himself a chemist, who should have had an analytical, intelligent mind, should have been so stupid and short-sighted.'

By academic training, Dr Richard Beeching was actually a physicist but by the time his name became known – and subsequently loathed – by the public at large he was Technical Director of ICI Chemicals. A corpulent, bald, thinly smiling man, he could have come straight from the Ruthless Capitalist Bastard department of Central Casting. Macmillan's government had what they perceived as a problem with the railway network in the early 1960s. Thanks to increased car ownership, it was losing money and needed, of course, to be returned to profitability as soon as possible. They hired Dr Beeching to do just that and on a handsome stipend too; he would be given five years' leave of absence from ICI on his private sector wage of £24,000 per annum, or £367,000 pounds in today's money.

For this they got a report called *The Reshaping of British Railways*, 'reshaping' here being a great early example of the kind of sanitised weasel-word coinage that would later include 'downsizing' and 'friendly fire'. 'The Wholesale Slaughter of the British Railways' would have been a more accurate title but skilfully Beeching had acquired the services of an early spin doctor called John Nunneley. He employed twenty-five typists in the production of the report and destroyed every typewriter ribbon every night to prevent leaks. That sounds awfully costly and wasteful to me. Personally I'd rather have subsidised an uneconomic railway, but there you go. Tony Hancock was recruited to front what was essentially a wholly biased TV smear campaign against the railways. Seen now these ads are pretty repellent: full of snobbish dislike of fellow passengers and indeed of public transport as a concept as opposed to the status symbolism of car ownership. For this good work, Hancock asked for the same fee as Beeching: twenty-four grand, about a third of a million today. Nunneley offered him half. He took it.

The report was published and implemented at speed based on an equally hasty and skewed survey. Some people still find it dubious that the plans to prune the railways and therefore increase road traffic was green-lit by a transport minister, Ernest Marples, who was in the road-building business. Despite all this, Beeching's axe was wielded on the nod; a third of the British railway network was closed down in the face of massive and sustained public opposition. It wasn't just about people losing their jobs, though it threw seventy thousand people out of work; 'fine men now uncertain about their jobs', as Betjeman said. It wasn't just about social divisiveness, although it isolated many areas, particularly in the south-west, and condemned them to economic decline. No, it was more than that. Beeching tore some of the heart out of our country. A decent public transport system is, like libraries and schools and hospitals, the mark of a civilised society. It is how families stay in touch and how lovers find each other's arms, it is how we play and explore and get to work, it is how we city folk get to the lonely hills and how the folk from the lonely hills can enjoy the bright lights of the big cities. As Ian Hislop said in his 2008 TV documentary about Beeching, railways in England have a social and cultural dimension that motorways will never have and cannot be bean-counted. They mean more to us than that as a nation, something indefinable and nostalgic and romantic. As he says, though, 'For Beeching, the bottom line was, well, the bottom line.' Whole sections of the country had been given a death sentence.

Beeching became a bogeyman, caricatured, mocked, feared and even lampooned in rhyme. The *Guardian* published a lament for the lost stations that ran, 'We shall stop at you no more for Doctor Beeching stops at nothing.' A popular song went, 'Oh, Dr Beeching what have you done?/ There once were lots of trains to catch, but soon there will be none/I'll have to buy a bike, 'cos I can't afford a car/Oh, Dr Beeching what a naughty man you are ...' But by far and away the most poignant and lovely musical lament for the lost railways of England was written by the duo Flanders and Swann in 1963, the year that the mad axeman from ICI first began to terrorise the English countryside.

Flanders and Swann were a prim-ish, proper-ish duo, an owlish pianist and a hearty bearded man in a wheelchair, whose comedy feels a little quaint and easy to mock these days, and indeed they have been, albeit affectionately, by the modern comic duo Armstrong and Miller. Yes, 'The Slow Train' is a piece of sheer and unabashed sentiment and utter nostalgia. It is also quite wonderful and will have anyone with a heart dabbing at their eyes within a verse. To a languid melody and rhythm that evokes the gentle rattle of a mid-afternoon carriage down a quiet branch line, the duo sing that no more will they go...

> *to Blandford Forum and Mortehoe*
> *On the slow train from Midsomer Norton and Mumby*
>   *Road;*
> *No churns, no porter, no cat on a seat.*
> *At Chorlton-cum-Hardy or Chester-le-Street.*
> *We won't be meeting again, on the slow train.*

When they get to the bit about 'No one departs, no one arrives, from Selby to Goole, from St Erth to St Ives' and the guard's voice calls faintly, 'Cockermouth for Buttermere', even the most cold-hearted economic pragmatist must have been having second thoughts.

Wishful thinking. They didn't. The lines were closed, weeds came and choked the tracks and platforms, supermarkets were built across the lines rendering them useless for ever. The only good thing that came out of this nasty, myopic policy was that there are now any number of good walks and cycle paths along the disused lines. On a wet, claggy day when the high fells are out of bounds I can recommend the lovely stroll from Keswick to Threlkeld in the Northern Lakes along the old Penrith to Keswick line. I have to say that it would be even lovelier by slow train, winding above the gorges of the river Greta and curving along the contours of Blencathra and Skiddaw. But at least they haven't built a Tesco on it.

On the internet you can find lists of the old stations and learn of the various fates that befell them. Marple in Cheshire is now a cheery pub, Cotherstone in Teesdale is a lovely house. Bassenthwaite Lake station moulders forlornly at the far end of the silent stretch of Cumbrian water. At Barnard Castle and Under Whernside in the Yorkshire Dales, there are ghostly signal boxes that remind you, with a shudder, of the houses at the end of *The Blair Witch Project*.

The architectural critic Jonathan Glancey says that after the Beeching closures some of the poetry of the English landscape was lost for ever, and in one case he was nearly exactly right. One of the doctor's casualties has gone almost for ever.

But what remains is an old station sign almost hidden in a leafy bus shelter in a quiet Gloucestershire village and, on a plaque beneath, the text of a poem that speaks of a Middle England that was lost to us long before Beeching came with his ledger and abacus and axe.

Adlestrop is little more than a cluster of houses, a racing stables and a post office nestling under a little Cotswold hill off the quiet B road that links Chipping Norton and Stow-on-the-Wold. There's no pub so the drinkers amongst the eighty or so folks who live here must perforce seek out the notorious fleshpots of nearby Oddington. The local newsletter, *The Adlestrop Express*, tells that the stables have had a frustrating winter and lost a much-loved, rising young horse called Piano Player. Two grand old residents have died in their nineties, and it's noted in passing that all three of the much-missed Nell's daughters were married to the sound of the bells in Adlestrop church. On a note of renewal, though, the village welcomes the new couple at Leigh Cottage. Permission has been granted for a new village hall and 'it's been decided to arrange a day for the Spring Cleaning of the Church. Many other parishes do this on an annual basis. This has been set for 2.00–4.00pm on Saturday 24 March. It is hoped that it will be fun to get together with the opportunity also for convivial chatter! Please come along armed only with dusters and polish. We will provide everything else. Come for the two hours or just drop in for whatever time you can spare. We will finish up with a nice tea for those who last the course!'

I know people in the north and the south and the bustling Midlands who would sneer at all this niceness, as they sneer at the very notion of Middle England. I thought it sounded bliss-ful. You just know there is something fundamentally good about Adlestrop. It feels comfortable rather than showily rich, sleepy but not boring. In fact, according to the parish notice board, it's a social whirl. There's 'Yoga For Everyone!' at Shipton-under-Wychwood. There's an evening of jazz on Broadwell Hill and over the road at the village hall they're hosting a racing and general knowledge quiz with wine and cheese. I note with some chagrin that the mobile police station has been here on Main Street – there are only two streets – that very morning. I'd have liked to find out about patterns of local crime. I bet shoot-outs, armed robberies and crack deal-ing are at a premium. I'm sure there is the odd problem, though, and that local MP Jeffrey Clifton Brown ('Working for the Cotswolds') will be pleased to sort them out. With its charming thatched cottages, post office and sylvan setting and its leafy bus shelter with bench and timetables for Toy Lane, Little Compton, Kite Brook and Brock Hill Clump, it is exactly the sort of village where Americans and Japanese think we all live. We should be so lucky.

That's not why I first came there though. A clue to what brings me here lies in that fine old Adlestrop sign. It stood formerly on the platform of the old railway station and now has pride of place in the bus stop. Below it is a small brass plaque containing twenty-four lines of poetry. The first time I came to Adlestrop I was having a romantic weekend in a farmhand's caravan in a field in Evenlode, a village just down the road that makes Adlestrop itself seem like Chicago. The farmhand wasn't there, I should add. Tearing myself away from drinking champagne and such in front of the black and white telly that worked off a car battery, I noticed on the map that Adlestrop was just down the road. I had to make a pilgrimage. For Adlestrop is known all over the world to those who love getting their head in a book. Not for its Jane Austen connections – she visited the rectory often and is said to have based *Mansfield Park* here – but for a beautiful and much anthologised short poem that evokes both a specific time and a real sense of timelessness.

Edward Thomas was killed by a shell blast on the first morning of the First World War Arras offensive in 1917. All of his poems were written during the last three years of his life, leaving us to speculate on what he would have become. For myself, I think he would have become one of the giants of twentieth-century poetry, as what he left us is magnificent and mysterious, an almost whispered attempt to evoke the folk identity of an England that is both sweet and cherished and ancient and dark. 'Adlestrop' is his most famous poem and is, as the critic Adam Phillips has remarked, 'uncannily simple'. Over its four stanzas, in conversational tone, the poet remembers, a little vaguely, his train stopping unexpectedly one afternoon at the station in this tiny Gloucestershire village.

> *Yes, I remember Adlestrop –*
> *The name because one afternoon*
> *Of heat the express-train drew up there*
> *Unwontedly. It was late June.*

That's about it in terms of incident. It makes *Waiting for Godot* look like *Apocalypse Now*. But the poem casts a spell that captivates to this day. It survives rote learning in dusty class-rooms, it survives exams. It haunts one with its enigmatic brevity and luminous melancholy.

The steam hissed. Someone cleared his throat
No one left and no one came.

Note how Flanders and Swann in 'The Slow Train' echo that line about no one coming and no one leaving. Neat, I think. So the poet is left to his thoughts and to listen to 'all the birds of Oxfordshire and Gloucestershire' in the misty distance. Listening back to the voice notes I made on my handheld digital recorder that afternoon, I can hear those distant birds singing too. But that echo aside, it occurs to me, as it has to others, that the poem could not be written now. Thomas would find no ruminative silence on his train today, just a hubbub of mobile phone chatter ('Ask Simon if the estimate from Microsoft came through and tell him that I'm going to be late for the meeting ... God knows ... Adlestrop, wherever that is') and the occasional overloud under-informative announcement from the senior conductor.

Had Edward Thomas 'detrained' and strolled into the village he'd have seen very much the same things I note today: rows of pretty houses, the green, the church. But some things have changed. No trains will ever stop at Adlestrop again. Beeching saw to that in 1966. The station is abandoned and overgrown. It was a mile or so outside the village anyway, which confounds some pilgrims. So the poem now takes on another meaning and another aching dimension of loss. It is not just an elegy for the Edwardian innocence that was savaged and lost in the bloody mires of Ypres and the Somme. It's also, in a perhaps more trivial but sweetly sad way, an echo of the days when sleepy trains connected sleepy villages across a stranger, sleepier, slower England.

I went to the post office to pick up a souvenir. It used to be run by Dorothy Price, whose father worked at the station in 1914 and who therefore must have been there the day Thomas's train stopped 'unwontedly'. She's gone now but the new lady is brisk and chatty. She tells me that the pilgrims still come and some are disappointed to find the station gone. Actually, as she points out, it's not gone. 'It's a bit sad, though, all overgrown and fenced off. They still come, though, and take pictures. Nice people, generally ... well, I suppose they would be.' She chuckles in recognition of the fact that few devotees of old railways and poetry tend to be thuggish. I buy a strawberry cheesecake ice cream and four sepia postcards of the old station. In one, an awkward and moustachioed young man smiles sadly at the camera. It strikes me that it may have been Dorothy Price's dad.

As I leave the post office, I see clouds of steam belching from over the wooded and hedged barrier where I fancy the old line might be and I hear the unmistakeable sounds of movement and industry. For a magical, eerie moment I think that a ghost train is returning to sleeping Adlestrop or that I have stepped through some portal into the past. In fact, it was someone lopping branches with a chainsaw and chucking them onto a bonfire.

*

Beeching lopped branches with a chainsaw too, which is why you now go straight through Adlestrop on the London train without a second thought unless you're of a poetic cast of mind. I'm with Hislop and Glancey in that I think that railways are at the soul of England, Middle or Outer, Merrie or Darkest, and that they have permeated our national psyche; does any other nation produce trainspotters, I wonder? But the extent of this is debatable for some. For instance, the railway historian Jack Simmons states that: 'The success of the first steam railways evoked little interest from English imaginative writers.' And it has been claimed that, compared to France and Zola or Russia and Tolstoy, England has never produced a truly great railway novel.

Perhaps so. But England, Middle England specifically, has produced a great railway poem in 'Adlestrop', a great railway ghost story in Dickens' chilling 'The Signalman' and, of course, a great film. Perhaps the greatest British film ever made in fact: a beautiful and melancholy love story that might never have happened if Doctor Beeching had been around fifty years earlier.

It begins spellbindingly with a train whistle and a whoosh of steam. We are on a darkened railway station in midwinter, lit dramatically and romantically by the lights and fire and steam of an approaching train and by the glow of its carriage windows as it passes at speed. The ticket inspector, Stanley Holloway, crosses the track and enters the refreshment room where a couple are deep in thought and occasional, fragmentary conversation.

The beginning of *Brief Encounter* is also its end. The couple are meeting for the last time and she, Celia Johnson, is recounting in voiceover an imaginary conversation she is having with her husband. He isn't here and the man she is with is not her husband. And that's pretty much it. Two nice middle-class people, married but not to each other, have an unconsummated love affair after a chance meeting at a railway station. She gets cold feet and he goes off to South Africa.

What this bald plot summary cannot tell you is that *Brief Encounter*, written by Noël Coward, directed by David Lean and starring Celia Johnson and Trevor Howard, is a masterpiece. Now this will surprise some. If your idea of a truly great British movie is a Guy Ritchie gangster flick or possibly even *The Italian Job* (which actually stars the patrician writer of *Brief Encounter*) then you probably find *Brief Encounter* a bit twee. It has been parodied often, most affectionately and brilliantly by Victoria Wood, whose heroine begins her tale by stating, 'I'd gone into Wilverton to change my library book and order a coconut.' But she gets the mood and look just right and is clearly in love with the movie. Others, though, see it as the worst kind of repressed English melodrama and mock its cut-glass accents and dull milieu. Perhaps the worst insult of all is the ghastly 1974 TV remake featuring Richard Burton and Sophia Loren. It is mesmerisingly bad. Loren stumbles robotically through the most appalling dialogue and Burton exudes the desperate weariness of someone who was once the best Hamlet of his generation but is now looking forward only to the pubs opening.

Brief Encounter can take all of the above, and still emerge unscathed as a classic. It looks stunning, shot like a film noir by Robert Krasker, Lean's direction is masterly and the writing is easily the finest thing Coward ever did, a world away from his brittle and patronising worst, and Trevor Howard is great. But the film belongs to two things. First, there is Celia Johnson. She is simply superb, managing to evoke a world of desolation and interior pain with just a look. In one of her very first lines she says, 'This misery can't last.' But you know that it is going to last for the rest of her life. Her expression, luminous and wracked, as she pulls back from a suicidal leap beneath the train, is as astonishing as are her words: 'I meant to do it, Fred, I really meant to do it. I stood there trembling right on the edge, but I couldn't. I wasn't brave enough. I should like to be able to say that it was the thought of you and the children that prevented me but it wasn't. I had no thoughts at all, only an overwhelming desire not to feel anything ever again. Not to be unhappy any more ...' In a documentary about the film, the comic actor John Sessions puts it perfectly when he says, 'Only the most cold-hearted, Ray-Ban-wearing, *Face* reading, post-modern cynic could possibly not be moved by her.'

In the same documentary, the film's producer says that every time he watches it, he steels himself, gives himself a tough talking to and still cries. Me too. And I rage against it too. Because she does the wrong thing. She should have left Fred, the stolid and unremarkable hubby and to hell with propriety. In the end this is a film about a very un-Middle-English trait: cowardice, or as critic Jim Shepard has remarked, 'Decades of forbearance: slow-moving, mile-long freight trains of self-denial ... women [giving] up what they most wanted for somebody else's sake.'

In early previews, conservative commentators praised the film for its moral tone; exactly what exasperates me about it.

Look at the flirtatious station master and the tea-room matri-arch, the rude mechanicals of this piece. She has been married before, he lusts after her, and clearly their relationship, even if it does not last, will be joyous and warm and sexy. Now look at our heroes: these complacent, hidebound individuals don't go off with each other because they are gutless. Real love, real passion transcends and overcomes any boundary. Life is short, regret is long.

Compare it with Ian McEwan's *On Chesil Beach*, another Middle English masterpiece about a wrong turning and wasted, thwarted love. I am sure McEwan had *Brief Encounter* somewhere in mind but he's more forthright in his judgement. He does not conclude, oh well, you probably did the right thing. He says you did the wrong thing and, unlike *Brief Encounter*, his novel follows the action on, this time through the man's prosaic and second-rate life.

So I don't find the ending of *Brief Encounter* the happy reconciliation some do. For me, it's a study in defeat. She isn't crying with relief, she's in mourning. But that's just my opin-ion. And this is why *Brief Encounter* is great popular art. Because it entertains and it delights and it provokes and it makes you look into your own soul. I said that the film belongs to two things. The first is Celia Johnson, the second is Carnforth railway station.

I'm sitting at the very table where Celia Johnson and Trevor Howard said their botched, agonising goodbye. I feel I ought to be doing something more reverent than eating a toasted tea cake and jotting down notes about my surround-ings but, hey, I like toasted teacakes. My surroundings, I should point out before someone else does, are not those actually used in the film. That was built on a sound stage at Denham Studios. But that set was modelled on this very refreshment room at Carnforth, the station just north of Lancaster where all the movie's exteriors were shot. It is eerily identical.

Lean chose Carnforth for various reasons. The war was still on – just – and the station was remote from major cities and considered safe from attack. It was less hampered by blackout restrictions than a London or southern station would have been, and the long ramp from the subway was perfect for some of his set pieces. Even walking along them now brings a palpable tingle. Along the way are a sequence of framed poems by Lynne Alexander, who was the station's poet in residence in 2004. 'The Stations of the Clock' tells the story of Carnforth's famous clock, 'iconic' even, to use that abused phrase with justification here, from its manufacture in 1880 to its role in the film to its restoration along with the station.

After Beeching's cuts, the once proud station dwindled to the status of a branch line with the removal of the mainline platform, and then into dereliction in the 1970s. But in the 1990s a team of railway and film enthusiasts led by Carnforth businessman Peter Yates worked to restore the station with support from Railtrack and in 2003, Margaret Barton, the tearoom girl Beryl in *Brief Encounter*, cut the ribbon on the newly refurbished and handsome station. It's a great achievement but Peter Yates has said that they don't intend to rest on their laurels; their next objective is to get it back in use as a stop on London-Glasgow trains on the West Coast mainline.

If for years Carnforth station's place in British film history was overlooked, overgrown and under-acknowledged, it's certainly flaunting it now, and quite rightly too. The famous refreshment rooms now offer themselves for hire with a breezy 'Come And Have Your Brief Encounter At Carnforth Station'. They've done it all rather well: lots of period detail like urns, a bell for attention, adverts for long-lost stouts and such. Glenn Miller plays in the background and there are posters for a forthcoming – and entirely genuine – appearance by a swing band. It's Saturday afternoon and the place is packed. At a corner table sit a couple I take to be regulars: a loud, cheery man in early middle age with some kind of mild learning difficulty is eating scones – they are hugely popular with all the clientele – with a lady I assume to be his mother, silver-haired and chatty. The staff are attentive to them without being patronising, pleasant without being gushing. It's a touching scene. At the next table, two men in dark suits sit drinking orange juice, sharing a rock cake, whispering and poring over an old map. They seem to have strayed in here from another great British train film, namely Hitchcock's *The 39 Steps*, rather than *Brief Encounter*, and I am intrigued, especially when I notice that their whisperings are in German.

I would have followed them onto their train, disguised myself as the wine waiter, stolen what was clearly their top-secret map of English gun emplacements/radar installations and ended up being chased along the roof of the train whilst being shot at with a Luger. But I decided to look at the visitors' book instead. Nearly all have entered into the spirit of things, even if that is the rather exaggerated and inaccurate spirit. 'Spiffing!!' says a gentleman from Leeds. 'Quaint,' echoes a family from Kent. A darker note creeps in from Susan of Preston: 'Such a pity about the coffee!' 'Exquisite!' though, says a lady from Bath and, 'Oh, I have seem to have some grit in my eye!' writes a lady from the Wirral with a jolly nod to one of the film's most famous lines and the minor incident which brings the lovers together. That's a nice touch, I think, before I notice the next comment: 'As the film says, "We'll Be Back!"' Well, yes, except the film you're referring to isn't *Brief Encounter* but the much more modern, much more violent and vastly inferior *Terminator* starring the distinctly un-Celia-Johnson-ish Arnold Schwarzenegger. With a wince I note that the correspondent comes from my home town.

My pained reverie is interrupted as the Transpennine Express thunders through bound for Leeds. There were no Transpennines, Silverlinks, Arrivas and such in 1945 but, like today, there was a Great Western and similarly grandly named roll call of privatised train companies. Filming on *Brief Encounter* took place in the middle of the night, between 10 p.m. and 6 a.m., when the local rail services had ended. Every night, though, everything would stop for the midnight passage of the Royal Scot. As Lean recalled: 'I used to stand on the edge of the platform shaking with excitement, holding Celia's arm as the thing roared through within six feet of us. Just wonderful.' In between takes, Celia would huddle by the stationmaster's roaring fire and keep warm before heading back to the Low Wood Hotel in Ambleside at dawn for a snooze. She hadn't fancied the trip out of London and had told her husband that she'd got a job that entailed 'going up north for four weeks' location at some horrible railway station' but in the end, according to her letters, she really enjoyed the camaraderie of the production and the station. She played poker and did crossword puzzles and gave sweets and chocolates to the local kids, rare treats in those dark days.

Celia and Trevor's agonised goodbye is interrupted by the prattle of the well-meaning but irritating Dolly Messiter. I don't know if the kid in the replica Newcastle top is well-meaning but his table-top drumming is irritating. But it's too nice a day to be grouchy and I try to emulate the genial good manners of the staff, whose politeness and pleasantness is complimented on every page of the visitors' book.

Outside in the mild midsummer air and the sunlit platform, folks come and go. Some are actually going to places: assignations and appointments in Barrow, Lancaster and Sheffield. They check their watches, peer at timetables and chat on mobile phones. But they are outnumbered by my kindred spirits today, the amblers and the moochers and the tourists, just enjoying a sunny afternoon on the most famous railway platform in England, at least until J.K. Rowling came along.

Three people make haphazard and halting progress up the platform towards me. There is a tiny, birdlike elderly lady in mauve with cottonwool hair and a kindly, bewildered look, there is a small, haunted-looking man in an anorak and, completing the trio, a huge, luridly made-up woman in a preposterous fur coat who takes every opportunity to berate the other two at terrifying volume. My heart goes out to the cowering pair, who I take to be husband and mum-in-law, especially when the overbearing tyrant at their side demands that husband does up one of her slingbacks. And so he does, kneeling at her feet in the shadow of her enormous bulk, visibly quailing. It is like a Donald McGill postcard of a scene from Hieronymus Bosch. 'Oh, do hurry up, Arthur, what are you doing down there?' It is as if an old, bad, 1970s sitcom has come to dreadful life before my eyes. Don't be another Celia Johnson, Arthur, I want to shout. Don't stay in this hell out of duty. Leave her. Throw her under the train. Anything. I feel for Arthur especially when, with infinite gentleness, he rises and says to the elderly lady, 'Hey, Mum, do you want to go and see Noël Coward? He's through there.'

He isn't, of course. But his picture is. Next door to the Refreshment Room is a small visitors' centre which is, naturally, heavily themed around the film; it plays continuously in a small viewing area with comfy seats and I notice a young couple with backpacks and mousy hair holding hands as they watch Celia wander the rainy streets of Milford, distraught. You can buy the video here and I do, as well as a tea towel, a pamphlet about the station's history and several postcards, which I think will come in handy for quick jotted correspondence at moments of intense personal trauma and heartbreak. That kind of thing.

Carnforth's brush with cinematic immortality is not the only aspect of the station's life immortalised there. There are exhibits about the so-called Miracle of Hest Bank, an incident in 1965 in which a London-Glasgow express was derailed at high speed in the nearby village of the same name and, incredibly, none of the 119 passengers was killed. (Less fortunate were the twenty-three young Chinese cockle pickers who drowned on the treacherous sandbank nearby in 2004.) Under glass cases are kept prosaic but sweet little reminders of earlier and more luxurious days of steam – ashtrays and whisky glasses from the first-class cars of the Furness, Midland and LNWR Railways – as well as the kind of memorabilia and artefacts from the days of steam that will make some men sweaty palmed with excitement but simply baffle me. Exactly what is a fishplate spanner? It looked quite cute, though, in a small, oily kind of way.

Another treasurable feature of Middle Englishness is very much in evidence on this mild Saturday in Carnforth, that mainstay of many a rally, museum and open day: the volunteer enthusiast. We are a nation of both, and I like that. These days, when an arid, cultivated negativity is the default mode of the fashionable, people who are interested in things are viewed with disdain. Interested in certain things, anyway. It's OK to like football, it's almost obligatory in fact, but not, say, maps or Cluedo or swing bridges. A few years back you may remember that a holidaying party of aviation enthusiasts, or 'plane spotters' as the papers dismissively took to referring to them, were arrested in Greece on some ludicrous and trumped-up spying charges. The chatter across every dinner table in NW1 and on laddish phone-ins held that they deserved it anyway: they were sad, they should get a life.

I don't see the appeal in spotting trains or planes or vintage traction engines. But then again, I have no interest in cars or 'dark comedy' or Chelsea FC. I'm of the opinion that people who like *them* are in far direr and in more pressing need of a 'life' than someone willing to do chokey in an Athens jail for their love of planes. Each to their own, I say, and let's hear it for the British enthusiast, several of whom – grey-haired men in comfy sweaters all – made my day at Carnforth a lot more pleasant by, for instance, showing me around the large restored booking hall and telling me that people get married here these days and for pointing out that the curving platform was a pretty marvellous feat of geometry and civil engineering. I didn't ask them about the fishplate spanner, though, and so it remains an enigma, yet to reveal its dark and secret purpose.

I imagine that the Greek plane spotters probably got short, mirthful shrift from at least one of the presenters of a programme that is the TV flagship of the new Middle England – hugely ironic, given that it would probably hate to be thought of as such. For years, though, *Top Gear* would have been happy with that cosy designation. Launched in 1977 from Pebble Mill in the heart of Middle England's most car-friendly city, Birmingham, it was for many years helmed by William Woollard in driving gloves, talking about the Lombard RAC Rally and sumps. It reeked of Simoniz GT Wax and tinned travel sweets. Then some time early in this century, like many other previously straight-laced aspects of British life, it discovered irony. The new studio-based show is essentially a comedy programme with some sports cars in it, in which middle-aged men blow things up and mock each other's Lamborghinis or heap scorn on other, less testosterone-laden forms of transport, mainly any environmentally friendly new offering and caravans. *Top Gear*'s three-pronged attack of Jeremy Clarkson, James May and Richard Hammond has turned blokeishness, the hearty culture of the saloon bar, into an art form, and the viewers lap it up. It is astonishingly popular.

That it's popular with the 16- to 34-year-old male isn't surprising. That it regularly attracts 40 per cent of the available female viewers is. Amongst the explanations offered is that it appeals to the kind of woman who doesn't want the sappy schlocky dramas like *Heartbeat* on the other side. Or that Mum is just watching along with Dad and Darren. It's certainly easier to wax sociological on its male appeal. Like *FHM*, Jack Daniel's and Insignia body spray, it maybe serves as wish fulfilment for the kind of middle-ranking office furniture salesman who thinks that the fact he once visited a lap-dancing club called Elite in Sevenoaks makes him James Bond. He will never have a reckless, passionate affair with a beautiful woman or beat up a bully or silence a room with his brilliance. But he can gun his company Audi past a labouring caravan with a smirk and may give a half-decent best man's speech one day and he will take his jokey, blokey cue from what TV critic Andrew Anthony of the *Observer* called 'the kind of overemphatic irony and exaggerated indignation that, such is its popularity, threatens to become the blokeish lingua franca of Middle England'.

Having no interest whatsoever in cars, *Top Gear* is something of a closed book to me. Yes, I find its Tory populism slightly wearisome. But I may be confusing the show with the kind of person who likes it, such as the vein-in-temple-throbbing right-wing blogger of *Britain Today* who writes, and I quote, 'In Top Gear, white, middle class, public school educated men with a healthy appetite for the opposite sex get to haemorrhage huge quantities of licence payers' money on driving exorbitantly expensive cars in increasingly pointless and legally dubious ways [whilst] inarticulate and predominantly working class people gathering round much posher people in a studio and hanging on their every word ... fantastic entertainment ... When the BBC sticks to giving people what they actually want, which is things like Top Gear, and not things like Muslim women's fishing, the people are happy.'

Beyond finding this kind of guff tedious, I'm not really qualified to either praise or criticise the actual show. It is enormously successful and clearly very well made. It's just that as Morrissey once sang about old Radio One DJs (whom the *Top Gear* lads are endearingly reminiscent of), 'It says nothing to me about my life.'

So I do not know what the thing is about caravans. What can it be about these innocuous, beige boxes driven by middle-aged men that enrages other middle-aged men who drive dull, expensive German saloons? Perhaps it is precisely because they are innocuous and beige? Or perhaps it is because their reasonably sedate passage is preventing Simon in his BMW from a hot assignation with a Ginsters Scotch Egg Bar and the porn channel in a Travelodge near Reading. It is a curious thing, though: two bastions of Middle England maleness, each glaring at the other across the central reservation and thinking each other a bore.

Why am I not entirely qualified to dissect *Top Gear*'s worth as a motoring show, as opposed to a piece of light entertainment? Because I don't drive: a state of alienation from the common weal that some would say makes me about as un-Middle English as one can be. I wish I could claim some principled stand here, some brave and single-minded refusal to join in with the slow asphyxiation of the planet. The truth is less glorious: took driving test at nineteen, failed, not that arsed, lived in a town, plenty of buses, trains and taxis, liked a drink, then got job with the *New Musical Express* as a rock journalist who, if they are not, should all be prevented by law from having a driving licence.

For some years, I've presented regularly on Radio Two's *Drivetime* show. Like all *Drivetime* shows, it has nothing to do with cars, it's merely a designation regarding the time of day, borrowed from American radio. It has no more to do with fuel consumption or road tax than the breakfast show concerns itself with muesli or grapefruit or the best way to poach an egg. That, however, hasn't stopped at least one correspondent from sending me the email equivalent of a green-ink missive in which he rages against me having the gig. 'Excuse me, but how can a man who DOESN'T DRIVE PRESENT A DRIVETIME SHOW!!!!' Argument is futile. I've long since learned that where their cars are concerned, Englishmen become an illogical child race of angry air-conditioned hermits living on Dairylea Dunkers, service station lattes, Oasis and phone-ins.

Perhaps I'm biased but I don't accept that there is romance on the road as there is on the rails. In America, yes, as I've said. But in England, the railway is a kind of myth whilst the motorway is a means to an end. Journeying by train expands the experience of both the land and of the others moving in it. Car ownership is a matter of private pride – the Sunday afternoon car wash is a symbol for Middle England – and pure functionality.

For a certain kind of Middle Englander, the car is a kind of mobile house: private, domestic, full of kids' toys, books and food, a space jealousy guarded from intruders. This is what Maggie loved so much about the car: its narrow, personally owned domestic privacy as opposed to the unappealing public communality of the train. The car driver is an owner-occupier; the train makes council-estate dwellers of us all.

And this manifests itself not just in cute stickers and baby shades and Magic Tree air fresheners, but in road rage, that very English curse that turns bank clerks into thugs and thugs into murderers. Unlike Shylock, when you cut him up, it's you that could end up bleeding, and even the most undemonstrative of fellows is turned to a gesticulating pustule of impotent rage. You are, essentially, a burglar of the road to these men. The car is a castle and you have breached the drawbridge, entered the hermetic unreal bubble that drivers inhabit. As Betjeman puts it:

A man on his own in a car
Is revenging himself on his wife;
He opens the throttle and bubbles with dottle
And puffs at his pitiful life.

It's interesting that England's most loved car signifiers should all come from long, long ago, the honking, spluttering but ineffably romantic pioneering vehicles of the early twentieth century: the Darracqs and Spykers of the adored movie *Genevieve*, Mr Toad's sporty little number in *The Wind in the Willows*, *Chitty Chitty Bang Bang*.

But whatever the car, you could never have a *Brief Encounter*, however unsatisfying, at Charnock Richard, Newport Pagnell, Hilton Park or any of Britain's scores of service stations. Like airports and coach stations, no matter how beautifully designed they are, they have no mystery. Or rather, only one, and that is how they can charge six pounds fifty for beans on toast. Terrifyingly expensive, comfortingly faceless, almost Soviet in their statist regimentation, the motorway service station experience unites us all.

It used to be said that one reason the Catholic mass was held across the globe in Latin, dead language though it may have been, was so that whatever their race or nationality and wherever they were in the world, a Catholic traveller could enter a church and be comforted and uplifted by a familiar, shared experience. Perhaps then this is the logic underpinning our network of service stations. Know this, weary pilgrim motorist, wherever you are in England, however tired or lost or disorientated you may be, you are only a few miles from an overpriced baked potato, a Bumper Quiz Book the size of a suitcase, a dubious Bee Gees Greatest Hits CD that doesn't have anything from *Saturday Night Fever* on it and a notice that says, 'These toilets are cleaned and inspected regularly, but if you do find a problem please contact us.'

And yet, and yet, we clearly love them. Perhaps it is a deep residual longing for the turnpikes and the coaching inns but we seem loath to commit to a journey of more than a few miles and positively hostile to a motorway journey at all without the promise of a service station, the modern equivalent of some-where to get the horses stabled and a pipe and tankard. When the M40 was built, even the most committed environmentalist might have quietly, guiltily hailed it as a bit of a boon: 89 miles of brand-new motorway blasted through the Chilterns – I still give a 'wow' of admiration whenever I pass through that chalky steep-sided defile near High Wycombe – and providing a swift, neat alternative to the crowded corridor between the Midlands and London. It had been under piecemeal construction since the swinging sixties. It even appears in the second Thunderbird movie, *Thunderbird 6*, filmed in 1968; in one sequence, a Tiger Moth flies under one of its new bridges, much to the annoyance of the Ministry of Transport. It didn't open fully, though, until 1990. And when it did, hardly anyone used it. It was unnaturally quiet; so much so that the convenience seemed outweighed by the disquieting sense that some sci-fi disaster had befallen the rest of England and that you, in your Mondeo, Astra or Peugeot, were the last motorist on earth.

Nothing of the sort. The reason no one used it was that it had no services. The hell with the slashed journey times and limitless freedom, no one wanted to risk a journey from Brum to Hammersmith without the reassuring thought of a Julie's Pantry close at hand. It was regarded by most as as much of an oversight as if they had built it with no hard shoulder or slip roads. If you lived for danger or were truly masochistic, it was now possible to drive from Folkestone to Birmingham (M20, M26, M25, M40, M42) without the comfort of a comfort break. A chilling thought.

The comedian Harry Hill even worked it up into a comic riff. 'No services on the M40? What are we supposed to do?' Then, some minutes later, 'Take a packed lunch, that's it, take a packed lunch.' But, of course, a packed lunch is a poor substitute for a Whopper with cheese or a shrink-wrapped blueberry muffin. The nation breathed a sigh of relief when the first service station opened at Cherwell Valley in 1994, and two further service stations opened at Oxford and Warwick in 1998. Traffic is now much heavier. Phew!

The bulk of Britain's motorway services are run by one of three big hospitality and catering corporations, namely Moto, Welcome Break and RoadChef. The Welcome Break ones at Oxford are daringly futuristic, all sensual curves and sheer sides of glass and with a timber promenade deck where you can eat your bacon double cheese by a gushing fountain and pretend you're on the shore line at Lake Geneva for a while, if you ignore the bloodcurdling cries from the play area. It's rather pleasant really, certainly when compared to Forton on the M6, which seen from afar looks like an early 1970s Stasi Interrogation and Detention Centre somewhere in Rostock, but is actually much less welcoming inside. Or Sandbach, whose grim, dirty, urine-coloured footbridge is a much-loved landmark for those passing in haste bound for the Lake District.

Some motorway services have attained a semi-legendary status. Tebay off the M6 in Cumbria is talked of in hushed tones by middle-class drivers from Middle England making the trip north. Not only is the nearby scenery stunning – the famous heart-shaped wood on the side of one of the huge, gently elephantine Howgill Fells – but this is the Tuscany, the Waitrose, the Keira Knightley of service stations.

It looks different: sunken ponds, stony terraces, long, low, slate fort-style buildings all adorned with the distinctive antler logo. Forget Middle England. If they had service stations in Middle Earth, they would look like this; somewhere nice where Frodo could ask Gandalf to get him a carton of strawberry milk and a *Guardian* while he stopped off to use the loos en route to the evil realm of Mordor. You can actually get a table that overlooks the water. You probably have to book.

Tebay services – they're actually a pair spanning the motorway – are testament to the virtues of keeping it small, local and independent. It used to be an isolated farm until the construction of a major trunk road through the site in 1971. So the farmer and his wife decided to cut their losses and build a small rest area with just twenty-eight staff. Now they – or rather their daughter – employ over five hundred good people from hereabouts. There's a caravan park and a hotel, both of which routinely pick up awards, but what really sets it apart, what makes it totally irresistible, what drives us nice tasteful folk in our German cars on past Charnock Richard and Forton into the Cumbrian night against the demands of our bladders and screaming kids, is that, joy of joys, it's got a farm shop.

It's got two, in fact, one on each carriageway. Prince Charles opened them both in 2004. Of course he did. He may never be the Queen of our Hearts but he is, in many ways, the Prince of our Pork and Leek Sausages, the Baron of our All-butter Shortbreads. With its water features and organic produce, its locally sourced ingredients and community employer credentials, Tebay services is as PC and guilt-free as an institution devoted to facilitating the easy passage of the single most environmentally destructive invention ever can be.

For me, and for you as well, I imagine, motorway services are no place to linger. Whatever we in our different ways want from them – a wee, a fag, a nap, a dog walk, a John Grisham audio book, a massive bag of Hula Hoops – we want it quick and then to be away before the coachload of football fans arrives. Successive governments though have worried – unnecessarily I think – that left to our own devices we will forgo football and fireside and frolics of all kinds in order to spend all our time hanging around service stations. It is enshrined in policy that 'motorway services must be stop-off points, not destinations in their own rights'. For many years, the minimum distance between services was decreed as 25 miles (about a half hour's journey), now reduced to 15 but only for locations where there is a clear need for such a short distance between services on safety grounds. The implication is clear: without the firm hand of government the average Briton would be seduced away from work and family and spend all day hanging around Scratchwood or Hilton Park playing air hockey while the country ground to a halt. Frankly, I don't think they need to worry.

Tebay, though, is different. I could happily linger here. This is one service area where I can understand why people get out their *Daily Whatever* and Thermos and Tupperware and foldable canvas seat with net pouch in the arm for drinks and picnic in the shadow of an HGV. The view is great, the air is sweet-ish and, in case you've forgotten, there's a farm shop.

If only actual farms could be more like farm shops. No bulls, no body-warmers, no subsidised agro-barons, no black plastic bags, no NFU spokesmen, no barbed wire and illegally blocked off rights of way, no yapping dogs and ugly polytunnels. Just a selection of ripe cheeses and fancy ice creams and damson gin. The PR war would be over. We townies would support the Countryside Alliance wholeheartedly, stop caring about foxes and we wouldn't chuckle when John Prescott gets punchy or Bryan Ferry's son goes to jail.

The last time I was there was a dark Friday evening in midwinter. If the staff were eager to get to the sybaritic pleasures of Penrith or Sedbergh, they didn't show it. There was no rolling of eyes or pointedly looking at watches as I perused the shelves groaning with good stuff. A large, gentle, vaguely camp young man with an Emo/Goth fringe recommended a particularly smelly local cheese to me. 'On my wages I should really buy something cheaper but it's absolutely gorgeous. Melt it on toast when you come in drunk. Stinks the place out but it's heavenly.' His colleague, a girl of about twenty with a thicket of blonde hair piled up in a tartan bow, even offered me a taste of various biscuits to go with it. 'Some people rave about Bath Olivers but I always think they taste like beermats. You can't beat a digestive for me.'

Against this kind of gold standard, all other services will naturally be found wanting. But in the course of my researches I did diligently visit several others by means of arduous and extensive research. At Charnock Richard, there is an antiques fair every Sunday, a plucky little theme park called Camelot and, last time I was there if memory serves, a Bocca della Verità. These are surely the oddest amusements you will ever see: a fibreglass replica of the ancient marble image that hangs in the Santa Maria Church in Rome, as featured in the film *Roman Holiday*. A kind of Roman lie detector, the idea was that you put your hand in the image's mouth and, should you be a liar, it would bite said hand off. Not sure I would have bothered, to be honest. In the plastic version found at British service stations, you put your quid and your hand in, a few lights flash, a deep voice says something daft and a ticket emerges bearing a strangely cold and forthright assessment of your character. Mine said, 'You tend to be unfaithful … your capricious and inconstant nature will make it difficult for you to get on in life.' Thanks a bunch, Bocca.

On the aforementioned *Drivetime* show, certain names would ring through the travel bulletins like a Middle England mantra: the Air Balloon roundabout, the Hangar Lane gyratory, the Aston expressway, Clacket Lane services. This latter always made me chuckle, a name straight from an old *Hancock's Half Hour*, as British as boiled cabbage and drizzle.

It nearly wasn't called that. The story goes that the original planning application for the services had them down as 'Titsey Woods', but this was changed at the last minute because, so it's said, RoadChef feared no one would take the name 'Titsey services' seriously or would be able to pop in for a mochaccino and a muffin without giggling like small children. So they went for Clacket Lane; unmusically and bizarrely, as this is merely the unremarkable and undistinguished road where the emergency exits are.

I'm standing in front of a glass cabinet bearing the legend: 'The History of Titsey Woods'. I'm not giggling. It's all very educational. Well done, RoadChef. The chalk downs of this part of the Weald were once the haunt of wolves, pine martens and wild cats. Badgers would be hunted by the Celts who lived with their kin in the hilltop villages at Worms Heath, Walton Heath, Holmbury Hill, and Anstiebury on Leith Hill. In the glass case before me are several Roman artefacts dug up by workmen whilst the modern services were being built. These were left by Caesar's armies who drove the native Britons into the Surrey hills and settled in the North Downs with their own families.

Titsey Woods or Clacket Lane still gets its fair share of Roman invaders. And Spaniards and Hungarians and Poles. Clacket Lane is the first real services after the Channel Tunnel port of Dover and I notice the multilingual signs dotted about as I arrive on this rainy Sunday. The array of lorries and pantechnicons is dazzlingly multinational. Peaches from Portugal, cheese from Auvergne and whatever it is that funny man Norbert Dentressangle delivers.

Perhaps mindful of the nastiness of Forton and Sandbach, the finely tuned minds at RoadChef have tried to make Clacket Lane a more attractive prospect. The buildings are low, timbered and vaguely alpine, as if Grindelwald had been relocated to the M25. The children's play area is deserted but an Asian wedding party breaking their journey brings a welcome splash of colour and laughter, he in his crisp white three-quarter-length brocade jacket, she stunning in emerald green shantung, the Premier Inn forecourt horribly drab by comparison.

After this display of romantic optimism, it's pretty dispiriting to find an advert for a company offering 'Quickie divorces, 65 pounds' above the Durex machine in the gents' loos. But, emerging, I am heartened by the sight of one of Britain's last surviving Wimpys. These were Middle England's first greasy delicious taste of the burger revolution, and they are still vastly superior to any of their US rivals; full of what appears to be real beef and real lettuce and actual tomato and in a floury bap that leaves handprints on your jeans. Perfect.

In the car park I chance upon a strange assignation. Two men, one Asian and Pringle-sweatered, the other heftier, bald and Cockney, are haggling over a set of golf clubs at what is clearly a prearranged meeting. The stockier man takes out a driver and peers along its shaft one-eyed. He juggles it in his hand as if estimating its weight and then gives it a few swishes. 'Did we say a hundred quid?' His new friend seems pleased. Cash is counted, hands are shook. Why here, I wonder, on this damp slip road, as they drive away in their separate cars?

Another little Middle English mystery. And of course Middle England loves a mystery. For a place and a people so outwardly respectable, so proper, so decent, they are a bloodthirsty and savage and sinister lot. They rape and garrotte, they poison and gouge. They may nod and genu- flect and cross themselves, but they dance naked around fires and worship the horned one whose names are legion. They love ghosts and devils as much as golf and dinner parties. They may claim to keep the Sabbath holy but after mass, on dark Sunday evenings behind closed doors, they turn to their real god, Mayhem, who holds dominion in the secret killing fields of Buckinghamshire.

CHAPTER 9
In Darkest England

Sunday evening. All is quiet across the Shires of Middle England. The lawns have been mowed, the putts have been holed, the roasting tin is in the dishwasher. But this is the quiet before the blood-spattered storm. The Theremin, a weird sci-fi musical instrument invented by a Russian émigré and most famously used on 'Good Vibrations' and the *Star Trek* theme, is about as un-Middle English as you can get. But eight times a year (ish), its unearthly, keening tone calls Middle England to its lounges for two hours of worship, just as irresistibly as the muezzin calls the faithful of Teheran to prayer.

The extraordinary success of a Sunday evening ITV detective series called *Midsomer Murders* proves beyond doubt that Middle England, like Macbeth, is steeped in blood, 'unmannerly breech'd with gore', and bloated with 'slaughterous thoughts'. Ostensibly a cosy countryside entertainment for dozing Sunday-night stay-at-homes, it is actually a charnel house of glistening viscera, a bloodbath, a catalogue of frenzied stabbings, lust-crazed horror, perverted and ingenious slayings; indeed, an ongoing orgy of death.

Edgy comedies, lavish period pieces and controversial

documentaries may get the reviews and the column inches but *Midsomer Murders* gets the viewers. It is quite astonishingly popular. Sold to over two hundred countries, the series is one of British TV's greatest ever success stories. The thought of surbanites in Buenos Aires, factory workers in Ulan Bator, doctors in Accra and retirees in downtown Islamabad all watching Tom Barnaby investigating the rash of stabbings at his wife's watercolour class is both delightful and slightly bonkers.

Middle England has always had a dark side. As the horror writer Kim Newman says, we are 'one of the most blood-soaked islands in the world with a strange violent history'. We have been entertaining ourselves with ghouls, villains and horror since time immemorial. Beowulf, the tale of a terrorising monster, is set in Scandinavia but is thought to have been written in modern Warwickshire. From Staffordshire or Derby comes *Sir Gawain and the Green Knight*, in which an Arthurian round table is called upon to vanquish an elemental spirit. These were tales for the fireside, just as today, except the modern hearth is a plasma screen, but the purpose is just the same: wild and bracing entertainment with a valuable social function, a ring-fencing of darkness and disorder away from our normal lives, a safety valve, a catharsis.

Midsomer Murders is just the latest and most successful manifestation of the English love of murder, mystery and the macabre. We gave the world the notion of curling up with a good murder, the bizarre idea of manslaughter as comfort food. And before detectives came along to solve the crimes and put the world to rights, we were enjoying a drop of the hard stuff as our fireside entertainment with our old friends ghosts, witches and the undead. We are surely the only country in the world that, as part of its celebration of the birth of its saviour, the only begotten son of God, enjoys a date with the devil. The idea of the Christmas ghost story is typically English, a traditional part of our festive entertainment. But what a bizarre juxtaposition it is. I'm amazed that the new breed of crackpot fundamentalist Christians – the ones who think that Harry Potter and pizzas and Game Boys are conduits for Satan – haven't tried to ban the Christmas ghost story or at least banish it from our Yuletide screens. They would never succeed, though; ghoulishness and terror is as much a part of the classic English Christmas as Harvey's Bristol Cream, the *Radio Times* Xmas double issue and sage and onion stuffing. And when we settle down as a family to have our Christian values subverted and mocked by the notion of all-powerful, death-conquering evil, we do like it best if it's a nice M.R. James.

Montague Rhodes James was provost of King's College, Cambridge, and later of Eton, during the first decades of the twentieth century, and a noted medieval scholar and antiquary. But that is not what he will be remembered for. His fame, immortality even, rests upon the forty or so supernatural tales which are now considered perhaps the greatest ghost stories in the English language. Though almost a century old and set in a fusty antique England, James's stories are masterpieces of quiet terror. A classic Jamesian story will often concern some isolated, reticent don or clergyman, beginning with some mundane business, often academic or clerical in nature, and gradually descending into nightmare. They are lonely in mood and in setting: a deserted stretch of beach, the back room of a country inn, an empty church.

They are usually morality tales of a kind in that the main protagonist will be trying to meddle into something best left alone, to discover or dig up or get to the bottom of some relic's or painting's history. A nameless terror will be evoked, the sense of reality shifts, indistinct presences enter the world, partly hidden but getting ever nearer, until there is a revelation of some ghastly and disquieting kind. As James himself put it: 'An acrid consciousness of a restrained hostility very near us, like a dog on a leash that might be let go at any moment.'

Two of the very best such stories are 'A Warning to the Curious' and 'Oh, Whistle and I'll Come to You, My Lad'. In the first, an unemployed treasure-hunter awakens the malevolent spirits of long-dead Anglo-Saxon kings on the lonely Norfolk coast. In 'Oh, Whistle', a sceptical bachelor academic on a Suffolk seaside holiday accidentally conjures a baleful, unnamed demon. The moral of both stories is pretty clear. Next time you're at a loose end mooching about in some woods or down at the beach and you find an ancient crown, amulet, bone flute or such, leave it where it is. Whatever you do, don't blow down it. It's just not worth it.

Both of these stories were adapted for TV by the BBC in the 1970s as part of the fondly remembered *Ghost Stories for Christmas* season, which brought several of James's eeriest stories to the screen as well as Charles Dickens' superbly chilling 'The Signalman'. Most of these, definitely the best of them, are directed by Lawrence Gordon Clark, whose slow, almost somnolent direction suffuses the stories with a menacing stillness. 'Oh, Whistle', though, was directed by the young Jonathan Miller and casts Michael Hordern as Parkin, the meddling college professor. Disquieting, elegant, often funny, this and the Lawrence Gordon Clark adaptations have become DVD staples of Christmas *chez* Maconie. The climactic scene in which Parkin is confronted by the nightmarish wraith from the bedclothes, leaving him jabbering 'Oh no' like a child, has been known to reduce even the most gore-sated modern teen to silence.

The BBC has tried to resurrect the Christmas Jamesian adaptation of late with a terrific version of 'View from the Hill', and the repeats of the old classics roll around most Decembers. Nicely apt, as James had originally written the stories to be read for friends and pupils on Christmas Eves over a good port and before a crackling fire. James was something of an enigma; his biographer Michael Cox wrote, 'One need not be a professional psychoanalyst to see the ghost stories as some release from feelings held in check.' Many commentators have speculated that he was a repressed homosexual, even possibly with feelings towards his pupils. There is certainly a sense of revulsion or at least reticence towards physical expression. He abhors it in his chosen literature too. 'Sex is tiresome enough in the novels; in a ghost story, or as the backbone of a ghost story, I have no patience with it. At the same time don't let us be mild and drab. Malevolence and terror, the glare of evil faces, "the stony grin of unearthly malice", pursuing forms in darkness, and "long-drawn, distant screams", are all in place, and so is a modicum of blood, shed with deliberation and carefully husbanded.'

Taking a cue from James, the twentieth century was something of a golden age for the Middle English ghost story, or 'strange story', as some have preferred it. Walter de la Mare gave his stories that designation, and others have continued it. It's a good choice. This branch of very Middle English fiction has no clanking chains or severed heads but a disquieting sense of the lost and forgotten: branch lines, James's old churches, deserted farms, piers, windmills, weirs and remote woods. If you know de la Mare's haunting, melancholic poem 'The Listeners' from schoolroom anthologies, you will have some of the flavour of his tales.

So far, so sedate. But I love that one American internet aficionado of his work has put it more transatlantically: 'Trying to pick the ten best de la Mare tales is like trying to pick the ten best Beatle songs. You're screwed before you begin. It can't be done. Might as well give up now before you make a fool of yourself & piss everybody off in the bargain. Don't you want to have friends? What's wrong with you, anyway? Put down that pen. Better to keep silent & be thought an idiot than open your mouth & remove all doubt. Ahhhh, who am I kidding? Since when did I give a damn ...' And then proceeds to compile the list, comparing the two canons as they go, so that 'Seaton's Aunt' is 'Yesterday', 'Out of the Deep' is 'I Am the Walrus' and 'A.B.O.' is 'Blue Jay Way'. De la Mare's last words on his deathbed are so strange they might, as many have noted, have come from one of his own stories: 'All these on-lookers. There are so many of them. Where do they come from?'

Arthur Machen was an almost exact contemporary of de la Mare's and his writings grow more influential with every passing year, spreading beyond the literary world into realms like popular music. The contemporary English label Ghost Box attempts to recreate what we might call this Middle-English strangeness in sound, the sound of partially remembered school science programmes, Public Information Films, radio call signs, long-forgotten advertising jingles. One of their artists, The Belbury Poly, describe their music as: 'Soundtracks to televised versions of Arthur Machen tales, beautifully filmed in grainy day-for-night lighting, yet too disturbing and explicit ever to be broadcast.' There is a host of other writers in a similar vein, operating in Middle England through the late Victorian period and onwards: Oliver Onions, J.S. LeFanu, and H.R. Wakefield whose collection *They Return at Evening* is surely the best title for such a volume ever. The work of comedy troupe The League of Gentlemen and their stalwarts Jeremy Dyson and Mark Gatiss is indebted to them.

Dyson and Gatiss have dramatised on radio and film two of the best stories by one of the key figures of this very English literary scene, Robert Aickman, who, like de la Mare, called his pieces 'strange stories'. Aickman's Middle England is drab, lonely and unutterably weird. It's a place of cheap hotels, quiet estates, dowdy backstreets and tawdry fairs in Midlands towns. A fan and blogger Peter Coady has written: 'Robert Aickman would have enjoyed a visit to my home town, Leamington Spa, in the heart of the English midlands. With its air of foregone luxury and faded Georgian grandeur, it is the sort of place he would have approved of. There is a decent museum, and several art galleries to muse in, as well as two excellent second-hand bookshops. This time of year, mid-autumn, would have been an especially suitable time to come, when the few tourists have moved on and a melancholy calm pervades the damp streets. Autumn is a good time, too, to take account of the town's ghosts, timid and scattered as they may be.'

Aickman was a curious man, self-absorbed, moody, pessimistic. He wrote chiefly in his spare time, when not engaged in his day job at the Inland Waterways Association, which he helped found. He loved canals and boat people and viewed most of the trappings of the modern industrialised world with suspicion at best and usually downright hostility. Sex, viewed murkily as if in a weed bed, is never far from the surface of his fiction. In 'Ringing the Changes', a honeymooning young wife is seemingly lured away by undead beings in a nasty little seaside town and returns changed and strangely sexualised. In 'The Trains', two young women on a walking tour stray into a remote valley peopled by threatening yokels and see an isolated house by a railway line with desolate figures in the window. I won't spoil it for you beyond saying that they end up being the figures in the window, their pockets stuffed with railway tickets and the heady scent of lesbianism in the air. Appetite whetted? Aickman, like many of the above, can now be read in beautiful editions from private presses such as Tartarus and Ash Tree. The stock and reputation and level of interest in all these writers has never been higher.

So for me, Middle England's fascination, obsession even, with the dark and macabre runs like an icy underground river beneath the cosiness of the surrounding countryside and the respectable, proper veneer of the village and market town; all this in much the same way that David Lynch's movies expose the dark and disturbing interiors behind the white picket fences of Middle America. In every vicarage, country house and suburban semi, resentment, jealousy and revenge seethe, and murder waits its turn with revolver, rope and lead piping.

In February 1946, our old friend George Orwell contributed one of his most famous pieces to *Tribune* magazine. It began thus:

> *It is Sunday afternoon, preferably before the war. The wife is already asleep in the armchair, and the children have been sent out for a nice long walk. You put your feet up on the sofa, settle your spectacles on your nose, and open the News of the World. Roast beef and Yorkshire, or roast pork and apple sauce, followed up by suet pudding and driven home, as it were, by a cup of mahogany-brown tea, have put you in just the right mood. Your pipe is drawing sweetly, the sofa cushions are soft underneath you, the fire is well alight, the air is warm and stagnant. In these blissful circumstances, what is it that you want to read about?*
>
> *Naturally, about a murder ...*

Murder as comfort food, murder as toasted muffin if you like, is a very English concept. For Orwell, there was a very specific kind of slaying that went well with sleepy Sundays by the fire.

> *The murderer should be a little man of the professional class – a dentist or a solicitor, say – living an intensely respectable life somewhere in the suburbs, and preferably*

*in a semi-detached house, which will allow the neigh-
bours to hear suspicious sounds through the wall. He
should be either chairman of the local Conservative
Party branch, or a leading Nonconformist and strong
Temperance advocate. He should go astray through cher-
ishing a guilty passion for his secretary or the wife of a
rival professional man, and should only bring himself to
the point of murder after long and terrible wrestles with
his conscience. Having decided on murder, he should
plan it all with the utmost cunning, and only slip up
over some tiny unforeseeable detail. The means chosen
should, of course, be poison. In the last analysis he should
commit murder because this seems to him less disgrace-
ful, and less damaging to his career, than being detected
in adultery.*

To this I would add rivalry at the bridge club or scone envy at
the WI as possible motives. These teacup-rattling murders are
not just popular amidst the snoozing Shires of the Home
Counties. The Americans are a sucker for traditional Middle
English slaughter too. They may call it Clue not Cluedo and
Sherlockiana rather than Holmesiana, but the country-house-
murder board game and the deductions of the great detective
of Baker Street are both hugely popular across the Atlantic.
The long-running American TV series *Murder She Wrote* is,
essentially, Miss Marple relocated to New England and given
a job: writer of country-house-murder mysteries.

A *New York Times* piece in the late 1980s headlined
'Murder Most British; Homicidal Passion As National

Pastime' nicely articulates some of our felonious predilections. 'The British take particular delight in uncovering the secret scandals in such pockets of respectability. They excel at constructing tense, claustrophobic studies of homicidal passion, the burning-ember kind that smoulders behind a bourgeois facade of arch-propriety until flaring up in a desperate act of violence that shocks and thrills the neighbours and sends a shudder down society's moral spine.'

But in nearly every case, we want to see the damage done to the social order restored and repaired by detection, arrest and subsequent punishment. That is why we love reading reports of trials in our papers and why trial-scene set pieces feature so much in our crime dramas. They serve a nice double function. First they reveal all the juicy details, thus satisfying our prurience. Secondly, they show justice being done.

Who brings the miscreants to book? Well, you'd think it would be a pretty specialised job, wouldn't you? Requiring a bit of training or something? Not at all. In England, it appears, the investigation of serious crime and the apprehension of dangerous criminals is best left to little old ladies, chinless aristocrats, posh novelists, professors of literature or magician's assistants. The enduring popularity of Miss Marple, Lord Peter Wimsey, Paul Temple, Gervase Fen and Jonathan Creek are all manifestations of our love of the amateur sleuth. It is a love that writers and TV commissioning editors often stretch to breaking point, as they did with the ludicrous *Rosemary and Thyme* in which Pam Ferris and Felicity Kendal played crime-fighting horticulturists vanquishing the forces of evil across the begonias of Middle England.

Our love of the amateur sleuth says something fairly profound, I think, about our national character. We are nonconformists, and not just in the narrowly religious sense. Essentially, we are a nation of gentlemen adventurers and enthusiastic laymen rather than dull credentialled experts or state-sanctioned law enforcers. It speaks of our deep-seated mistrust of authority, of what the Americans would call 'big government'. Wimsey is only pretending to be a fool. He actually has a mind like a vice and, from time to time in the Dorothy L. Sayers stories, we see a flash of steel behind the silly arse demeanour. In this, of course, he echoes the greatest of all fictional detectives, Sherlock Holmes. Eccentric, unpredictable, dissolute even, but navigating by his own unerring and singular moral compass, he is clearly and deliciously the alpha male, the sine qua non, the intellectual heavyweight compared to Inspector Lestrade and the pompous second-raters at the Yard and the dead orthodoxy of the state's lawmen. This is very English. It is hard to imagine a Chinese Sherlock Holmes.

On the other hand, we will develop a fondness for policemen providing that they are mavericks, that they are flawed, that they, and this is axiomatic, 'do not do things by the book'. Sometimes, as I watch DCI Frost flying off the handle or Morse disobeying his superiors' orders, I fantasise about writing a detective drama about a cop who does things completely by the book, assiduously follows protocol and where whole episodes are taken up with him requisitioning new stationery or painstakingly writing up his notes with very minor witnesses before comparing his findings with a representative from the Crown Prosecutions Service and deciding, on balance, not to go any further with the case. Perhaps I could sell it to Burmese state TV.

In 1987, a writer called Caroline Graham introduced her policeman creation to the world in a book called *The Killing at Badger's Drift*, a title which immediately and cosily set the tone for her subsequent detective novels, all set in the fictional south-eastern county of Midsomer, and the colossally success-ful TV series to come. Tom Barnaby is, by the standards of Morse or Frost or Ian Rankin's John Rebus, not much of a maverick. Kindly, decent and happily married, the man who has brought Graham's creation to chubby and amiable life, John Nettles, says of him: 'Tom Barnaby is so normal, it almost hurts … He drives an Astra and likes to go to the garden centre. He dotes on his wife and daughter. He's moving house and because he's such a domestic soul, this represents a major event. But he also has a brilliant investigative mind and can solve crimes that would, in real life, take an entire police force years to penetrate. I find that juxtaposition rather fascinating.' He drives a Jag these days actually. But it hasn't gone to his head.

The TV series was originally called 'Barnaby' but its new name better reflects the sense of place. Barnaby's patch, the small town of Causton in Midsomer, is fictional but the series is filmed in the Vale of Aylesbury and around the M40 corri-dor. In the show the bloodstained villages of Midsomer are naturally given fictional names, nice ones too: Aspern Tallow, Martyr Warren, Goodman's Land, Midsomer Mallow, Morton Fendle. As well as them being aesthetically pleasing, one of the reasons for the invented names is to stop the actual locations becoming overrun by tourists and pilgrims from all over the globe. They still come, though, to the villages of Penn, Taplow, The Lee and Long Crendon (controversy here when filming in a local's house caused disruption in the small hours), and the towns of Aylesbury, Amersham and Beaconsfield.

The last of these three is where I'm headed now, on the neat blue Chiltern Line train from Marylebone, out beyond Neasden junction and through a tunnel beneath Lord's cricket ground, past the new Wembley, out beyond Denham golf club and Gerrards Cross to Beaconsfield, the 'clearing in the beeches'. There are Beaconsfields in Iowa and Nova Scotia, in Sydney and Melbourne, Perth and Queensland, and Beaconsfield Tasmania was once the richest gold town on that far-away island. But this is the very English Beaconsfield: prosperous, pleasant and frequently murderous, at least on telly.

The high street is replete with the staples of Middle England: a Waitrose, a Lloyd's chemist and a Help the Aged with an indigo DKNY blouse in the window. In amidst this standard fare are some oddities: one shop advertises 'Foreign Films converted' whilst its neighbour sells 'Specialist toys'. Evidence of Middle England's darkly passionate hidden nature? Probably not. Probably nothing more dubious than region-2 DVDs and wooden spinning tops. There's also a High Class Shoe Repairers, which implies that somewhere there's a Low Class Shoe Repairers; perhaps a beery man in a stained vest smoking a roll-up who says, 'I could put an elastic band round it for you.'

Beaconsfield is a model town and, appropriately, it has a model village: Bekonscot, perhaps the most famous in the world, and certainly the first. It was created in 1929 as a labour of love by one man, an accountant called Roland Callingham, who built the village in his back garden purely for his and his guests' amusement. Sweet, really, and again perfectly fitting as Middle England is the spiritual home of the hobbyist. All the proceeds from visitors, 13 million of them over the last seventy-five years, goes to charity. They've raised somewhere in the region of five million quid. Rather sadly, then, given all this good work, at the time of writing it has had its enormous sign pinched, a case for Tom Barnaby perhaps, if the killing spree in Midsomer Magna ever abates. This bit of petty thievery seemed a very un-Beaconsfield thing to happen. It's certainly very un-Bekonscot. The village is unashamedly and indeed gleefully stuck in a time warp, portraying an idyllic, idealised rural England as it was in the 1930s. There's no Starbucks, no KFC, no Bargain Booze. There's no CCTV or hoodies drinking cider in the bus shelter, although a policeman is chasing a bloke by the racetrack. Just six little villages set in a rolling, nostalgic land-scape of farm and pasture castles, churches, woods, lakes. Enid Blyton, who lived nearby, loved it here and visited often. A model of her house, Green Hedges, nestles in a leafy lane. There are trams and a zoo called Chessnade and piers and, in one corner, the tiny people are watching a game of cricket. There's no sledging, match-fixing or ball-tampering here, I'll bet.

The detail is touchingly, well, detailed. The station plat-forms are adorned with accurate period advertisements, you can almost smell the produce in the Chris P. Lettis (geddit?) grocery store and the seaside sojourners at 'Southpool' have ice creams whose flavours you can almost discern. Up until the 1990s the village was updated annually to keep up with the changing England outside, but after a couple of brushes with closure, it was decided to revert to the 1930s look of its halcyon days. A good move this, I think; Bekonscot is nicely and slightly eerily redolent of an idealised England that probably never actually existed. But in its quiet and impassive sense of tranquillity, a tiny world full of miniature people at peace and ease with themselves and their surroundings, it represents England as England wishes it was on a 1:12 scale. It's a fantasy, and a very attractive if slightly odd one. There are model villages in other countries like Madurodam in The Hague but no one has taken to them like us. Eccentric, gentle, funny, Bekonscot is quintessentially Middle English.

The day I'm there it's full of families, mums with toddlers and the odd mildly boisterous, jokey teenage boy or girl trying hard not to look as if they're enjoying it but clearly having a great time. There aren't that many forty-something blokes making notes, though, so it isn't long before I feel hugely self-conscious and decide to go in search of lunch.

Bekonscot sits halfway down the Warwick Road. On one side there's a Catholic church, St Teresa's (most famous congregation member one Gilbert Keith Chesterton). At the other end sits St Michael and All Angels, so this could be their Garvaghy Road, their flashpoint for sectarian conflict. But no. All is quiet. The green outside the church is delightful. Even the youths who congregate here are merely a handful of faintly lively teenage girls. St Michael's Court handsomely presides over all this. It must be mock-something (Tudor, Elizabethan, Baroque?), I reckon, and it simply must have been used in *Midsomer Murders*. It is crying out for a garrotting in the conservatory.

If this were to occur and Tom Barnaby had his hands full,

don't worry. Beaconsfield has its own police station. Actually it doesn't. It has what is essentially Trumpton's police station: hanging baskets effulgent with lobelias, a weather vane, a clock tower and a balcony where PC McGarry might appear and tell the assembled multitudes that there was nothing to worry about and to go about their business. It's actually offering 'surplus office space to rent', which seems to suggest that they're pretty much on top of crime hereabouts.

Lunchtime finds me in Smiles fish and chip shop. Instantly I'm aware that I'm not in a traditional northern chippy as haddock and chips is £7.50 and comes with a garlic and tartare dip, there's a wine list headed by pinot grigio and you can get mint tea. It's really very nice. Behind me I hear the young waiter say 'That's five pound forty short' to an elderly lady but before I can even begin to suspect some heartless scam, he then helps Eileen – clearly a regular – to the door and out onto the street where he makes sure she's got everything and waves her off.

Wandering through the streets I notice both an implausible amount of dry cleaners and the cheerily named Geezers Male Grooming. In the window, there's a poster run up on a PC showing a cheeky chappy with a mad, gravity-defying lopsided cockscomb dyed blond and a wonky grin. Below reads the legend, 'Welcome! New Stylist Neil formally [sic] of our Gerrards Cross branch'. Gerrards Cross features extensively in *Midsomer Murders*, as does the nearby town Aylesbury, which I decide to pop over to as there's a train in bound for it. It weaves through the Chiltern hills and through a succession of little villages used in the series, all of them adorable in the milky light of a spring afternoon. At Monks

Risborough there is a cross on the hillside and, as we sit at the station, a blonde woman with a huge bag of shopping seems to be doing a bit of negotiating with the driver. Then, a bit shiftily, she gets into the driver's cab. It all feels very rum, especially when, once we've moved off, the train makes erratic and jerky progress and after a minute or two the driver announces, a little shakily, that 'we are now approaching Little Kimble'. Are you now, I think. Is that what you call it round here?

Aylesbury is nicer than I thought it would be, which is an odd thing to say, I realise. Why didn't I think it would be nice? Evidently others have laboured under this misapprehension too, though, since a passionate posting on a local website from Steve P. gets really quite stirred up defending the town's honour. 'Aylesbury really is going from strength to strength, it is a lovely town – in my job I travel all over the country and anywhere north of Milton Keynes is unpleasant, HOW DARE those people last week send letter slagging off Aylesbury there is far far worse places how about Hull, Wigan, Manchester, Oldham, Birmingham .... shall I go on? Aylesbury is nice. Only 1hr-ish from London all major airports and most importantly NICE people!'

Steve is right to stick up gallantly for Aylesbury. It has much to recommend it. There are some pleasant winding terraces and funny, quirky little passages. There's a Roald Dahl museum, an adjunct to the Bucks County Museum which I have a wander into. The region's brick- and lace-making heritage is celebrated at what can be fairly enervating length if you're not really into bricks or lace. I rather like a painting called *The Jug* by John Morgan, which features various local dignitaries and yeomanry, the good men of Aylesbury, all stolidly Middle English. A little touchscreen tells you what they all did. In the Victorian room, you can measure yourself against 'the ruler', which is a cut-out silhouette of Queen Victoria who was, it seems, tiny. Then you can play match the kitchen utensil to the food. I can't see it taking over from the Nintendo DS.

The squares of Aylesbury were celebrated in 'Market Square Heroes', the debut single in 1981 by local prog-rock heroes Marillion. Singer Fish wrote the track in St Mary's grave-yard 'on the comedown from an acid trip and was completed as dawn came up and a ring of policemen moved in on my girlfriend and I who were acting "suspiciously"'. The song, inspired by the riots flaring across Britain at the time, posits a firebrand revolutionary emerging from the streets of Aylesbury and leading Middle England into a ferment of unrest and sedi-tion. It isn't going to happen this afternoon. There's not much to detain me beyond a water clock that is apparently never right. Also in the main square stand two statues of two very different local heroes, Disraeli the Tory PM, and John Hampden, an anti-Royalist during the English Civil War who refused to play the King's illegal naval tax. They probably wouldn't have got along so warmly and so it's kind of appropriate that they've been placed facing each other in a confrontational alignment that suggests that Disraeli is 'offering Hampden out'. Hampden brandishes a sword, Disraeli seems to have a sample swatch of carpet. So my money's on Hampden.

The underpass has a design award. Since, according to my friend Paula who lives here, it floods instantly and copiously after an inch of rain and becomes a kind of leisure-pool for the local rat population, we conclude that the award must have been given on the day it opened. Certainly before the first light shower. Apparently the town got very excited recently when land was acquired for a supermarket. Rumour had it that it would be a branch of Waitrose, that bastion of lovely bourgeois comestibles, and an expectant Aylesbury palpitated, dreaming of prime organic beef and fresh kiwi fruit and warm walnut bread. In fact, they got not one but two supermarkets; sadly for the gourmets of Aylesbury, they came courtesy of those two bleak, warring German discount chains: Aldi and Lidl.

As the dusk settles across the Chilterns, I head out of town for a snapshot of Midsomer. In a newsagent's in Cuddington I ask the shopkeeper, a briskly militaristic man standing to attention behind the *Telegraphs* and the Mini Cheddars, whether he watches *Midsomer Murders*. 'No. Too busy for that kind of thing. No, not for me, thank you,' he answers in a clipped, disapproving, even offended tone, as if I'd asked him did he go dogging or smoke crack. In another, though, in Turville I think, where that other iconic TV emblem of Middle England, *The Vicar of Dibley*, is filmed, a lady organising the pile of *Radio Times* told me that she loved it, thought John Nettles was 'lovely' and that 'it shows off this part of the world in a very good light', this last said sweetly and without a trace of irony. A hearty fellow in the Crown in Little Missenden told me that his mate had made a 'nice little packet' from hiring out his garden for 'the one where they find a body in the well, I think'.

These Chiltern villages are sublime, almost to the point of caricature: families of ducks on millponds, the shadows of ancient elms lengthening on tidy greens, higgledy-piggledy manor houses, weirs and a general sense of utter contentedness; apart from the constant slaughter, obviously. Buckinghamshire was, according to a recent survey, the most desirable place to live in Britain in terms of several indicators of quality of life. All new babies born here are expected to reach eighty. The percentage of Bucks residents owning their own homes is 80 per cent, well above average. GCSE results are better than normal too. The county enjoys more sunshine each week than the national average. The average salary in the county is £40,000 and some of the local residents do considerably better than that, thank you, for as well as wonderful wildlife like barn owls and red kites, celebrities haunt the Chiltern hills too; it is home to Cilla Black, Terry Wogan, John Mortimer and the Osbournes and successive lucky prime ministers since 1921 have Pimmsed and croqueted their weekends of R&R away at their country retreat, Chequers.

It is, then, where money made in London finds a sweeter, nicer, kinder home, tucked in the wooded hills far from the din and jangle and fumes of the West End, far from the shrieking sirens of Dalston and Stoke Newington. It isn't actually far from any of those; your Cornish pasty bought from the ever-welcoming stall at Marylebone will not even be cold before you enter the welcoming bosom of the Vale of Aylesbury. But it is a world away. In the window of an Aylesbury tobacconist I spotted a flyer advertising a production of *Summoned by Bells*: 'an evening of words and music celebrating John Betjeman'. Of course, I thought. This corner of Buckinghamshire – in the same way that nowhere was more typically English than the remote hill stations of Darjeeling – is the furthest-flung but perhaps most representative outpost of Metroland.

Betjeman's Metroland, as evoked in his classic BBC documentary of 1973, took its name from the Metropolitan Line's publicity slogan of the 1920s and 1930s, referring to the towns and villages to the north-west of London served by the new Metropolitan Line. It was clever marketing, promising a suburban idyll that was convenient for but entirely separate from grimy, bustling London. 'Metroland ... Beckoned us out to lanes in beechy Bucks,' as Betjeman put it. For him Metroland began at Baker Street and extended to the forgotten station of Quainton Road near Aylesbury, pictured in the last shot of the documentary. Metroland as a concept is a companion, then, to Middle England. They are real places and you can map them. But you cannot quite pin them down. They are regions of the mind and heart as well as the map.

North of Metroland lies Oxfordshire. The original and inventive rock band Radiohead are from Oxford and Colin Greenwood of that band once said of his home city: 'Oxford is in the centre of England, but it's not really a rock 'n' roll town.' To a degree, he is right. It's no LA. But on one level it rivals any US city, any ghetto or downtown or barrio, and that is in its crime rate. If at any rate we are to believe another Oxford Colin, Colin Dexter, and his most famous creation, another Middle English touchstone, Inspector Endeavour Morse of the Thames Valley Police.

Like Midsomer, the sheer wanton lawlessness of Oxford as presented in the Inspector Morse books and TV series has become something of a humorous cliché. The critic Phillip Wickham says that its murder rate must 'rival the Bronx' and many commentators have delighted in pointing out that, at such a rate of slaughter (one hundred and twenty-odd deaths in sixty-odd hours), the entire city would surely be depopulated before long. But crime and death stalked the streets long before Inspector Morse quit the army and signed up for the irascible, snobbish but essentially decent squad of Thames Valley police. There are two Sherlock Holmes cases set here. Dorothy L. Sayers had her Lord Peter Wimsey on the trail of a killer at a girls' college reunion in her wonderful *Gaudy Night*. Bruce Montgomery wrote the music for six *Carry On* films but, as Edmund Crispin, he also wrote six amusing, diverting, occasionally exasperating crime novels involving Oxford don turned detective Gervase Fen. And Sarah Caudwell's four detective novels, an acquired taste but a growing cult, feature amateur sleuth and Oxford law don Hilary Tamar, so enigmatic a personage that even his/her sex is uncertain (Caudwell apparently rejected the advances of TV because it would be necessary to reveal the detective as either male or female and this would ruin everything).

But Colin Dexter/Inspector Morse have done most to make Oxford Murder Capital UK. There is good reason to conflate creator and creation; both are diabetic, both enjoy real ale, opera, cryptic crossword puzzles and *The Archers*. I am sitting in the downstairs bar of the Randolph Hotel, beneath a selection of production stills from the series. A small plaque records that this is where in 1880 the Amateur Athletic Association was formed and is thus, in effect, the home of modern athletics. But it's dwarfed by a much bigger plaque recording Morse's comment that 'they serve a decent pint' at the Randolph. Predictably, perhaps, where I am sitting is now called the Morse Bar.

Crenulated and canopied and flying various flags, the Randolph has long been regarded as Oxford's traditional 'posh hotel'. It is sometimes claimed that Colin Dexter wrote some scenes whilst enjoying a pint in the bar, but whether this is true or not, the hotel's connections with Morse run deep. One short story revolved around Room 231, whilst in *The Jewel That was Lost*, an elderly lady snuffed it in Room 310. As I was planning my trip, Jasper Gerrard in the *Daily Telegraph* was a tad sniffy about the food in the old place, *viz.*: 'The Randolph, where parents have long toasted Firsts and commiserated with Thirds, is so bad that diners may feel they are being set up in a remake of *Candid Camera*.' But others love it, and I found the welcome warm from staff from a variety of nations under the skilful, suave, unfussy leadership of a brilliant bloke from the old North Riding of Yorkshire ('Cleveland, we say now') with salt and pepper hair and a winning smile. This conviviality was much appreciated since there'd been a bit of alarming business on the pavement outside when a very presentable and proper elderly lady, waiting her turn in the queue for the Playhouse theatre next door, had suddenly and very violently vomited all over her queuing companions and most of the pavement. A chair and water was fetched from the Randolph and she was made as comfortable as she could be, although clearly undergoing the kind of embarrassment that is bad enough in Middle England but in Japan, where a number of the vomited upon seemed to be from, would have necessitated immediate seppuku with a sharp-bladed Tando.

A little shaken but not unduly stirred, I get the key to my room, where I lie on the bed for a bit watching the football results – ever the adventurer – before heading off into town to eat at a Lebanese restaurant that, from my researches, has the most bewildering, contradictory and downright incomprehensible reviews I have ever come across. The only constant appears to be that it is 'a legendary Oxford venue' and 'unforgettable'.

I soon see why. The place is packed with diners. Except they aren't really, in that no one seems to be actually eating. There are a great many staff and all appear to be engaged in a whole host of noisy and complicated tasks involving phones, paper, tablecloths, but none that seem to involve the production of food or the delivery of said food to tables. No one else seems to care, though, so I instruct myself to stop being so Middle English and to 'chill out'.

Two young staff seem to be assigned to my table and I soon come to think of them as Heroin Girl and Afro Boy. In case this seems uncharitable, they were both extremely pleasant, but just striking in appearance and oddly disengaged. He sported, as you may have guessed, an enormous afro, certainly the most luxuriant if not the only one I have ever encountered on a person from the Middle East; she seemed so vague and blurry and distracted, if good-natured with it, that I begin to suspect something chemical – at the very least Benylin – must be involved. When she takes my order, she stands so close to me and seems so fragile that I think she's going to sit on my knee. This bothers me as I have no idea what the protocol is for this in the Lebanon. Then she goes away singing softly to herself and he brings me a large silver salver on which are arranged a veritable grocer's display of raw vegetables: a whole green pepper, a whole head of cabbage and a cos lettuce, several carrots and radishes. This is a customary Middle Eastern gesture but I have never encountered quite such an amount of veg of quite such elephantine proportions and of quite such, well, rawness. No one seems quite sure what to do with them and several are clearly wary of making a 'drinking the fingerbowl' style rookie ethnic error, so nearly every table is dominated by a large shopping basket of untouched vegetables, leaving little room for the mezze and baba ganoush and farkeh and such. I nibble a couple of radishes, 'Just so I could say I've had some,' as my mother would say.

The food and wine was heady and terrific from what I remember, though, which perhaps explains a) why Oxford seems to have fallen so headlong in love with Lebanese cuisine and has at least five such restaurants and b) how come I got so hopelessly lost on the short and straightforward journey back to the hotel. Still, if you're going to get lost, Jericho is as good a place as any to do so. On this balmy Saturday evening, young women who all look like Virginia Woolf's trendier, indie-kid sister spill out laughing from the Jericho Tavern. After a grisly spell as one of those themed horror pubs, this Oxford landmark, venue for the first gigs by Radiohead and Supergrass, is back to its former and happier self. Happy is how I feel too as I eventually find my way back to my room at the Randolph, full of radish and resolving not to get murdered.

The next day doesn't begin well. I try to get a reviving something or other on Gloucester Green and stray into an awful coffee shop. The only other customer is an Italian man with a terrible glossy wet-look perm and nasty, clearly expensive leather slip-ons, who is shouting loudly into his mobile phone. On the wall are pictures of Dylan and Sinatra and Green Day, and random quotes from each that are completely meaningless, bearing no relation to coffee or Oxford or indeed anything. It's just another example of that mind-numbing identikit tat that some blue-sky thinker in marketing thinks will say 'contemporary' and 'now' rather than 'cheap' and 'desperate'. Morse would have hated it. I hated it. And the staff were rude so in the end I leave my greasy latte undrunk and head for the more congenial and upscale ambience of the Ashmolean.

The Ashmolean museum was built in 1667 (opening in 1683) to house the treasures given by one Elias Ashmole to the University of Oxford. They used to have a stuffed dodo here and there's a persistent rumour that Christopher Wren did the original design, though it can't be proven. What is true beyond a doubt is that it contains one of the great Middle English treasures, the Alfred Jewel: a gorgeously decorated ornament carrying a portrait of Christ and discovered in 1693 near Athelney where Alfred the Great, the first man to style himself King of England, founded a monastery. It was certainly commissioned by Alfred. The inscription reads 'Alfred ordered me to be made', and it may even have been worn by him. It too finds its way into a Morse story, rechristened the Wilvercote Tongue and the source of many misadventures, not least for the dead lady in Room 310 of the Randolph across the road.

There's a lot else in here too, particularly if you're a fan of amulets and embalmed viscera in jars. But the sun is up and the day is hot and I decide to explore Oxford on foot. Strolling along, Morse tour printout to hand, negotiating Oxford's semi-permanent log jam of visitors from around the world, I find myself outside another Morse haunt, the Eagle and Child pub, also famous as the boozer where the Inklings met, that beery, blokey gang of middle-aged writer dons that included J.R.R. Tolkien and C.S. Lewis. I'm every bit as keen on beer and the like as they or Morse. But it's a beautiful day and the sun's barely over the yardarm so I pop into the café next door for an ice cream. There, the same charming, perplexing shambles that permeated last night's restaurant holds sway. For a start, they are playing 'Fitter Happier' by Radiohead, the one about 'a pig in a cage on antibiotics', delivered in a scary Stephen Hawking robot voice and the most gloomy and disturbing thing they have ever done. Nice bit of local pride but surely not even Thom Yorke wants this with his 99.

They don't do 99s though. They do seem to do Fairtrade ice cream but the genial, horribly pierced girl serving can't get the scoop into the cryogenically hardened ice cream. She shouts for 'muscles' and a scrawny blond kid comes out from the back room. He suggests soaking the scoop in lukewarm water. In the end I do it myself. Outside I realise that they, or rather I, have given me the wrong flavour. It's clearly catching.

By a nice coincidence it is actually 'Gaudy Night' tonight, this the title of maybe Dorothy L. Sayers' best Lord Peter Wimsey story. In it, his squeeze Harriet Vane goes back to her old college and gets mixed up in all kinds of proto-feminist skulduggery. Gaudy is short for 'gaudium' and is basically a reunion for students back at the old alma mater. It's Wadham's tonight and the old boys and girls, a little more lined and less lean than once perhaps but still bright-eyed and expectant, are bundling out of their Audis and Rovers with long velvet dresses and dinner suits on hangars. Perhaps there will be a murder, though of course no one would wish for that. The romantic in me does hope, though, that a little late-flowering passion might bloom again under the moonlight in the quad, some sweet unfinished business from 1973.

As I stroll through the quad of the Bodleian Library, where a brisk woman in a turban is waving her arms and declaiming at some delighted chaps from the Orient, I ponder on the uniform of the Middle English academic class. Not the cap and gown of the students or dons, but the crumpled cream jacket and Panama hat that, seemingly by law, every man over thirty in Oxford must wear during the summer months. Smarter perhaps than hoodies and tracksuits and baseball caps, but just as unthinkingly de rigueur.

I spot at least seven Panama hats atop seven greying handsome heads in the compact, crowded beer garden (beer forecourt may be closer to the truth) outside the Turf Tavern. No pub in Oxford is harder to find; common sense will tell you that you've gone wrong when you find yourself at the seeming dead end at the foot of Bath Place. But persevere. Have faith. And you'll be rewarded with the best pub in Oxford and one hard to beat across the whole of Middle England.

Don't blame me if you can't get a seat. 'They're like gold dust ... hurry,' said the nice woman in the shawl who beckoned me over to take her place as she finished her white wine and collected her shopping. Though unseen from any road and tricky to find, the Turf will be thronged day and night with happy people in the know. It's a gem that's been loved by successive generations of dreamers amongst these famous spires. Thomas Hardy in *Jude the Obscure* called it 'an obscure and low-beamed tavern up a court', which is completely accurate if a little prosaic. 'The Turf in Hell Passage knew us well,' hiccup Charles and Sebastian in that other hymn to Oxford student life, *Brideshead Revisited*.

Bill Clinton used to booze here in his Rhodes Scholarship days in Oxford. Some say it is the place where he smoked but did not inhale. Elizabeth Taylor and Richard Burton knocked back a few whiskies here when they were sojourning in the town. And it is Inspector Morse's favourite boozer, though he calls it the Lamb and Flag, possibly so that he and Lewis can put people off the scent and be certain of a seat. It is snug, cramped some would say, a warren of little rooms and stairways and the low ceilings threaten concussion if not decapitation. But it's worth it. It was much too warm for mulled wine on the day I was there but I can see why, muffled and scarved, you would hurry down that tiny passage on a December day to sit by the fire with a steaming glass and a copy of something poetic. Particularly at three pound thirty. When you learn that in the winter, huge charcoal braziers are lit to keep the beer garden warm and that kids are invited to toast marshmallows over them, you start to wonder whether, like George Orwell's Moon Under Water, the place might not be too good to be true.

Out again, reluctantly, and by a different way, into tiny St Helen's passage and onto Broad Street and here's another Oxfordian gem. Its real name is Hertford Bridge since it links together the old and new quadrangles of Hertford College, Evelyn Waugh's alma mater and the model for the college in Brideshead. Either for this wistful, nostalgic reason or more likely for its resemblance to the one in Venice, this small perfect arch with its leaded windows is known as the Bridge of Sighs. You will look up and sigh, and so will your neighbours from Seoul and Seville and St Petersburg because wherever you stand and however polite you are you will all end up in each other's pictures, the back of your heads obscuring this architectural delight.

I find myself lingering here, loath to move on, in a kind of wistful reverie. All things Brideshead, in fact all things redolent of 'the groves of academe', do this to me. They bring on a kind of romantic, aching sense of loss and attachment that some would say makes no sense for a boy who grew up on a council estate in a grimy Lancashire cotton town. Or does it make perfect sense? I am pining for a past I never had, a dream as sad and unfulfilled I guess as *Jude the Obscure*. When I was a bright kid doing A levels, I had all kinds of moral and political objections to 'Oxbridge', all of them I now see pretty half-arsed and self-serving. I'd have loved it here I think. Or at least I'd have hated it in some spectacular, glorious Malcolm McDowell in *If* way. Perhaps I'd have been 'put down' or 'rubbed down' or 'sent down' or whatever it is they do with miscreants and ne'er-do-wells. Watching the young men and women cycling down these lovely streets, arms linked, laughing gaily as they stroll, book-burdened, beneath the ivy and the deep green shadows of the tiny, serene quadrangle at Lincoln's, I feel a palpable twinge. It may all be guff. But it's still palpable.

But I am jerked from my reverie by the sight of a man carrying a really old plough in a Marks and Spencer plastic bag. Let's face it, it's hard not to be. He is sweating and swearing a little. The day is hot, the streets are crowded and the bag has been designed for baguettes and fruit, not antiquarian agricultural implements. I watch where he goes keenly. And I am amply rewarded.

Oh joy of joys! *The Antiques Roadshow!* Here is a programme that rivals both Morse and Midsomer as the ultimate TV emblem of Middle England from the cod Handel starchiness of its theme tune to its Sunday teatime slot with its echoes of apple pie and custard, tinned salmon and snoozing granddads. Since 1977 when Arthur Negus was its benign public face, this staple of the TV schedules has presented both the best of the English character – enthusiasm, hobbyism, a desire to preserve the best of the past – with hints of something darker, namely the avarice, greed and lust that flickers behind the eyes of even the cuddliest nan in Oxfordshire. Oh, they may pretend that all they want is a little information about how this trinket found its way into Aunt Dorothy's bottom drawer, but what they really, really want to be told by a teasing, smiling Eric or Geoffrey or Bunny is that they should insure it for two hundred and fifty thousand pounds.

And it's here today, in Waugh's old quad at Hertford. Not so much Brideshead Revisited as Bedstead Revisited, a stroke of absolute luck for the traveller from the far north come in search of Middle England. There are vans and cameras and coils of cabling and cheery chippies and sparks and who knows maybe even Fiona Bruce, feline temptress of the newsroom and surely a secret passion of every one of these Panama-hatted gentlemen of Oxford.

There are Panama hats galore in the little quad. And there is much much worse. Dotted here and there amidst the little umbrella-ed tables, the little sections marked 'Militaria', 'Paintings', 'Clocks and Watches' and the like, are many terrifying examples of how badly the posh Englishman will dress if you let him. One of the antique experts struts around in Ray-Bans, a mauve-striped blazer, revealingly tight cream slacks and a pair of tasselled loafers. Individually, these may not sound too bad. But it's the way they are worn, each item shouting at another like in a pub argument, the effect designed for maximum standoutishness.

Some people, the organisers I imagine, are sporting bright vermillion silk sashes and thus look like the Graham Norton wing of the Ulster Defence Association. There are also two policewomen in body armour lurking by the ceramics. What can they be expecting? A spray of gunfire from behind the porcelain stall? A score-settling shoot-out between two rival gangs of ruthless period-furniture salesmen from Banbury? Everywhere I look there is something so delightfully daft and English that it gladdens the heart. A clutch of white-haired septuagenarian ladies giggle as they watch a pony-tailed cameraman of about twenty take a long, astonishingly boring close-up of a candelabra.

I overhear a smart, exasperated women hissing into her mobile phone, 'Of course, he's brought his camera obscura and I'm sitting here like a lemon,' a line straight from the pen of Alan Bennett or Victoria Wood. I see the man with the plough again wandering by bemused like the lost and inexplicable recurring penguin in *Gregory's Girl*. I could have stayed there all day but Fiona was yet to be lured from her trailer and it was almost time for me to leave Oxford.

The Turl is a quaint street round the back of Brasenose, which served as the fictitious Lonsdale College in *Morse*. A little further up is Exeter College where Tolkien got his first in medieval history in 1915. A small group of men in gowns on a street corner are discussing 1970s British TV of the *Are You Being Served?* ilk before coming up to date. 'I love BBC1, I love *Traffic Cops*. Course, you being Swiss wouldn't know.' University Clothing on Turl must be where the poshos get their dreadful clothes: an unseemly eyewatering riot of turquoise ties and lime-green and salmon-pink striped shirts.

On route for the checkout at the Randolph, I pass through the famous covered market, which is quite staggeringly brilliant and therefore, obviously, endangered, from the evidence of the 'Save the Covered Market' posters. Here I found a butcher's that could furnish with me seven types of veggie sausage, such as sweet potato and chestnut, stilton and walnut, Glamorgan. The man in the cheese shop asks 'Would you like me to suggest something yummy?' of some delighted American tourists, and gives me and them a taste of mountain gorgonzola. It was so buttery and ripe it took my breath away. Under one roof you can get Manolo Blahnik shoes, a tan Italian briefcase, Hungarian gyulai sausage, fresh skate wings and North American pesto. The pasta shop sold me the best filled pasta I have ever tasted, though I wasn't to know this until a day or so later when I sat at home relishing it with my mountain gorgonzola and North American pesto and remembering how lovely Oxford was.

It almost made me forget about the place I'd gone to next: 22 Cromwell Street. Almost, but not quite. If you are going to delve into the dark side of Middle England, you cannot pretend it is all sleuthing spinsters and lovelorn bachelor policemen sipping real ale and solving crosswords to the sound of Wagner. There is a real darkness too, an almost unspeakable, near unnameable wickedness that doesn't just hide up on some rainy, blasted northern moor or in the glass-strewn stairwells of sink estates. Beowulf lives. And it can live quietly and horribly behind net curtains in nondescript Middle English residential streets in towns like Gloucester.

It was the second time I'd been here. I'd come a few years back making, of all things, a somewhat intellectual TV show about the portrayal of apes in Hollywood movies and the symbolism therein, filmed at a lovely old independent cinema in the city. The show was fun but I'd taken away a queer, unpleasant feeling about the place, which was probably unfair and really based on one incident. One lunchtime, the crew and I were having our tea and bacon sandwiches in the picture house's bar area along with the cinema staff. I'd taken a real dislike to one of them, a surly moustachioed maintenance bloke who cracked bad, crude jokes and made the girls ill at ease and clearly wanted it to be known that us fancy telly folk were pampered ponces who were no better than him. I happen to think he was wrong. But that's by the bye.

Over lunch, with a leer, he asked us, mouthful of sarnie,

'Who d'you think did some of the plastering and stuff in this place then?' Clearly, we didn't know. Or rather we guessed too late: Gloucester has only one famous builder. 'That's right,' he said with malevolent relish, 'Fred West.' Sharp breaths were drawn; an uncomfortable silence fell. He was enjoying it. 'Oh,' he huffed with exaggerated impatience at our soft liberal media sensibilities. 'He was all right, old Fred.'

'Yes, except he wasn't, was he?' I replied without hesitation. 'He wasn't all right at all.' Leaving behind an awkward silence, I quickly went out for some fresh air and thought about just how not all right old Fred was, what with the sadism and murder and child abuse and torture. Sorry, Gloucester, but that's the memory I took away with me.

And that's why I'm back, that and some much nicer reasons. But before I can come on to them I had to go to Cromwell Street, where Fred West, a slow-witted son of farming stock, had, along with his wife Rose, tortured, raped and eventually killed at least twelve young women in horrific circumstances over a period of years from 1973 onwards. And all the while the cars had passed and the kids had played and the milkmen had whistled.

I'd decided that I should go to Cromwell Street as it stands as probably the darkest corner of Middle England in living memory. But I didn't relish it. Driving through the anonymous, surrounding streets, I felt that even the sat-nav woman was admonishing me as she instructed me to take the second exit on the left and keep right up ahead. I knew that local people resented the ghoulish interest that West's old home continued to generate. In an interview in 2004 with the

BBC, the receptionist at the nearby surgery said, 'Somebody called in here once from abroad and asked me where it was and I thought, what in God's name do you want to be looking at that for?' But then added, 'West himself was actually very pleasant.' Well, yes, but – sorry to labour the point and everything – he wasn't, was he?

The Wellington Stores offers phone cards and Afro-Caribbean food. I think about going in and making casual enquiries. Then I think better of it. It is probably a trick of the mind, one brought on by associations and the oddly narrow, oppressive little street. But even on a day of bright sunlight, we seem to have fallen into shadow. And I am being watched, of that there's no doubt. I'm being watched by the haggard little woman on the corner. I'm being checked out by the shirtless toothless tattooed youth with a snooker cue. An old Jamaican man stops as he trims his privet hedge and stares at me. I turn away, awkward and ashamed, to the opposite side of the street where there's a curious gap in the middle of the row of houses.

After Fred West's arrest, trial and conviction, and after his subsequent suicide by hanging in Winson Green Prison, Birmingham, the council demolished 25 Cromwell Street. They even demolished the house next door just for good measure. In fact, once demolished, they powdered and incinerated every brick and piece of timber just to thwart any black-hearted potential souvenir hunter. There's a gap now, a passageway that we'd call a ginnel up north, blocked with bollards to deter cyclists and skateboarders and worse.

Many of Cromwell Street's residents were not here in the 1990s; many are asylum seekers who do not, or at least did not, know about their new street's grim history. Quite a few, though, were here while West was, and so you can sense and understand a weird, illogical but pervasive sense of guilt by association. Middle England, so it's said, likes to keep itself to itself. But here is one instance where a little more busy-bodied nosiness, a bit more prurient curtain-twitching would not have gone amiss.

That's about as much as I am willing to theorise about Cromwell Street. I just wanted to be away from there as quickly as I could. I knew that the cathedral was a stunner and I wanted to be somewhere vast and airy and noble as quickly as I could. The sat nav mocked me a little, took me down some shabby, quiet streets round the back of the Africa Café and Racial Equality Centre, where I spotted my sinister, scrawny, topless snooker-player friend again (I mean, that's why he had the cue, right?). But eventually I was away from this little maze of streets and with a real sense of relief.

I could have done without the John Hooper monument then. It stands in front of the cathedral and, before you can get inside and feel too lyrical, humbled and awe-inspired, reminds you of just what a nasty business religion is. Hooper was Bishop of Gloucester, a diehard Protestant, whose refusal to recant during the torrid religious climate of the Catholic or Counter Reformation led to his execution. It happened here, on the spot where I'm looking up at the fine vaulted statuary in his honour, and a terrible, gruesome botched job of a slaying it was.

Hooper was taken to the stake leaning on a staff, thanks to the painful sciatica brought on by prison life. Three times they tried to light the damp, green wood at his feet. It wouldn't take light properly though, only succeeding in subjecting him to intense, excruciating heat. He kissed two faggots, stuffed them under each arm and showed the executioners how to set the remaining ones around him so that he might burn quicker. Unfortunately, it was a breezy day and the burning faggots ended up in his hair, blistering and swelling the skin of his head. 'For God's love, let me have more fire,' he cried. More faggots were added, and then some gunpowder. This only succeeded in blowing the fire apart and some of Hooper with it.

Eventually, his tongue so swollen he could not even cry out any more, with the fat, water and blood dripping from his fingertips, he banged at his own chest with his arms till they dropped off. Forty-five minutes later, when his bowels fell out of the burning lower half of his body, he died 'as quietly as a child in his bed'.

There was a good turnout for all this splendid entertainment. Around seven thousand, they reckon. So next time some lazy, professionally scandalised demagogue of the press or TV is scaring you into believing that Middle England is going to hell in a handcart, remember how John Hooper died, his last pitiful agonies cheered and crowed over by a capacity crowd of decent, law-abiding, God-fearing folk in a busy Midlands market square.

Protestant, Catholic, Hindu, Muslim, Jew, Zoroastrian, Scientologist, Taoist, Shinto, Norse or Jedi: for me, every religion contains a kernel of life-denying madness and intolerance that will, left to its own devices, end up with blokes getting burned alive and young girls getting stoned to death. Sorry. But that's my faith and I ask you to respect it. I do, however, appreciate old hymn tunes, coffee mornings, bring and buy sales and a good cathedral. Gloucester is, if you'll pardon the expression, a bloody good cathedral.

It's almost hidden away, surrounded on three sides by unprepossessing semis and a prosaic estate. But there is nothing unprepossessing or prosaic about the cathedral itself. It is huge, and so filled with detail and interest and different rooms, chapels and structural splendours that you could lose yourself for a day in it. Church architecture on this scale is not a matter of practicality; it is about might and effect. It is designed to reduce you, or rather you as you might have been nine hundred years ago, to mute obeisance to God and all his works. These arches and aisles and vast, vaulted ceilings are as much about 'shock and awe' as the US bombing raids and aerial bombardments of Baghdad in the first Gulf War. Interestingly, then, one of the connections that brings American visitors to this glory of European architecture is that one John Stafford Smith is buried here, the man who wrote the tune to 'The Star-Spangled Banner'.

It has other draws and attractions for the modern secular tourist too. Gloucester Cathedral stars as Hogwarts School in several films of J.K. Rowling's Harry Potter books. The ranks of posh-boy wizards fannying about on broomsticks may be pure CGI but the cathedral itself is as you see it. It doesn't need much in the way of computer assistance. The Potter connection is thought to bring in hundreds of visitors a year now. Good for the rattle of coin in collection box but not without resentment and hostility from some.

The Dean of Canterbury Cathedral turned down a 'generous' offer from the movie company because he was concerned at the 'Pagan imagery' of the stories. The Very Reverend Nicholas Bury, Dean of Gloucester, was more amenable, saying, 'Gloucester is one of the most beautiful cathedrals, and its friendliness and human scale have often been remarked upon. It is an atmospheric place and good for a story about a boy making friends in his first year at school.' In the teeth of frothing opposition from fundamentalists, he went on to say of the Potter books: 'They emphasise that truth is better than lies, good overcomes evil, and the use of gifts should be responsible. They are extraordinarily wholesome books, and children should be encouraged to read them.'

I couldn't make any kind of headway with Harry Potter but he and J.K. seemed to be getting along without me just dandy. She strikes me as pleasant and principled and the words of the Very Reverend Nick seem to have the bracing and attractive whiff of common sense to me, as opposed to the overpowering aura of bull emanating from the Christian right and, indeed, religious fanatics of any hue. If the Potter money has helped the upkeep and preservation of this stunning building, then good. They certainly aren't milking it; a small, unofficial Harry Potter companion in the bookshop is the only hint of Harrymania.

Even an agnostic like me feels holy and humbled in the presence of the Gloucester cloisters where Daniel Radcliffe occasionally roams. They are amazing, disorientating almost, womblike, pulsing abstract cocoons of light and colour. Quiet intensity and emotional power are everywhere here: in the serene quad, the silent chapter house and the amazing chantry. The overall effect is mesmerising, as indeed must have been the sound made here in 1910 when one of the most powerful pieces of English music was premiered in the otherworldly acoustics of this extraordinary space.

The *Tallis Fantasia*, premiered in Gloucester Cathedral at the Three Choirs festival of 1910, was a product of Vaughan Williams' three months' study with Ravel in Paris where he acquired 'a little French polish'. Technically, it is an astonishing piece, composed for a strange and demanding orchestral arrangement: a large string orchestra, a chamber-sized string orchestra and a string quartet. And it was composed with the immense acoustics of this cavernous interior space in mind. It must have been an astonishing evening, that first experience of a piece that is almost a cathedral of sound in itself, overarching, massive, powerful and yet at the same time full of contemplative corners, whispered secrets, quiet reverie. I leave Gloucester Cathedral with it ringing in my ears, though the cathedral is silent.

Like his other emblematic work, *The Lark Ascending*, the *Tallis Fantasia* is English myth in sound. Middle England is as much myth as it is reality, as much about shared mystery as explicit fact. But myth is not just about historical ambiguity and enigma; it's not just about King Arthur and Robin Hood and some other blokes who may or may not have existed. In fact, the two defining Middle English mythic icons of our time are two women who most definitely did.

CHAPTER 10
Myth UK

In the sullen, workaday light of a damp East Midlands afternoon, it's a dismal spot. The ruthlessly efficient Bavarian sat nav couldn't find it at all, taking me aimlessly up the Barrowby Road, even past a pub called the Middle of Nowhere. On foot it became no clearer; the street badly signed and the trip entailing several deflating wrong turns and a plod around the back of a faceless, sprawling retail park. Whatever your feelings about 'her', whatever your take on 'that woman', whatever your politics, you would expect a more imposing or memorable site than this, a cramped, nondescript crossroads where that Barrowby Road meets the old A1 to Newark and Great Gonerby, a tarmac ribbon clogged with delivery vans and school-run mums and shiny-suited salesmen, all tetchy, all tired, all eager to be somewhere else.

Crossing is awkward and will earn you a grimace or two through the wipered fanlights of the misted windscreens, a jab of the horn or a sockful of filthy rainwater from a speeding tyre. When I do get across, I'm harassed and stressed, like the grainy, tired woman who passes me with her shopping in cheap, overfilled plastic bags and a fractious, grizzling toddler in a buggy. Harassed and, in truth, a bit disappointed.

The plaque is plain and vaguely home-made and fixed high on the drab brick wall, perhaps so it can't be accessed easily with chisel or spray paint or even bouquets. It sits glumly alongside what might have been her bedroom window and beneath a smaller, higher one, perhaps the room where she was born on 13 October 1925, daughter of Alf Roberts, the second most famous grocer ever of that name. The one played for decades by Bryan Mosley in *Coronation Street* may be better known but is rather less significant in the history of these islands.

Imagine again, as I asked you several hundred pages and miles earlier, that you are a very particular kind of Englishman or woman. Again, one burdened by strange and terrible fears. Maybe you're still terrified of the sea, still suspicious of the Scots and consumed by a loathing of France and all things French. Or maybe you've got an axe to grind about the Falklands War or the destruction of the British coalfields or the privatisation of the railways. Well, again, maybe this is where you would come. Number 2, North Parade, Grantham, Lincolnshire, just opposite the Catholic Church of Mary the Immaculate and the Abacus day-care centre ('government-funded', it says, ironically).

These days, number 2 is a chiropractic and holistic therapy retreat called the Living Well Centre. Its window is bedecked with rainbows, silver stars, mandalas and pastel exhortations to 'unwind', 'rebalance', 'pamper', and so on. I bet you can get your chakra realigned here and at a competitive price. If the practice had more of a sense of humour they'd have that quote from St Francis of Assisi somewhere: 'Where there is discord, may we bring harmony. Where there is error, may we bring truth. Where there is doubt, may we bring faith. And where there is despair, may we bring hope.'

It would be an appropriate enough slogan for a holistic therapist's and moreover a clever little nod to its former resident, the most controversial and divisive political figure of modern times. Depending on your point of view, either the true and truly unpalatable, mean, small-minded face of Middle England, or its most shining avatar and exemplar of hard work, backbone and decency. Such things are debatable. What is not is that, as the plaque says, this is 'birthplace of the Rt Hon Margaret Thatcher MP, first woman prime minister of Gt Britain and Northern Ireland'.

Maybe I came on the wrong day. Maybe on St George's Day or a decently warm August bank holiday it is thronged and buzzing and you can't move for coach parties, school trips, performance artists and megaphoned speakers from competing ideologies. But I found it a strangely muted little place and Grantham more than a little apologetic. The town's websites and literature mention the fact that Margaret Thatcher, longest-serving prime minister of the twentieth century, was born here, but could hardly be said to shout it from the rooftops. They make much more of another local lad, Isaac Newton, in that there's a big, ugly shopping centre bearing his name and a statue in the town square. Maybe this is understandable, as even the most passionate and confirmed Thatcherite would concede that the three laws of thermodynamics and the discovery of gravity is a bit more important than the setting up of Thames Water.

Although it's more northerly and easterly than anywhere else in this book, I knew from the start that I'd be coming to Grantham. It booked itself, you could say. Apparently Lord Salisbury first used the term 'Middle England' in 1882 but it did not really become a popular term in public discourse until Thatcher, and because of her. She herself branded it into our consciousness in the same way that Nixon had talked warmly of 'Middle America'. That's why I came to Grantham, because it is so central to the Thatcher myth, which in itself is a part of the modern notion of Middle England, a part that I find hugely problematic and contradictory.

However strong the association, and however much the marketing men and tourist boards and development agencies talk that association up, pretty much every one of our major cultural figures outgrows and transcends their origins. The brown signs on the M5 may call it Shakespeare's Stratford and understandably so. But has anyone ever thought of him as Stratford's Shakespeare? Has anyone ever watched Lear's impotent madness or Othello's terrible hurt and jealousy, Hamlet's existential doubt or Lady Macbeth's deranged remorse and said, knowingly, 'Ah, you see, you can take the boy out of Stratford but you can't take Stratford out of the boy. Only a chap from that small yet prosperous Warwickshire market town with its roots in the woollen trade can fully comprehend these myriad mysteries of the human condition.' I don't think so.

But Grantham's Thatcher? According to many, not least Margaret herself: yes. Grantham made her. This market town and its presumed values loom large in her created mythos. And it was a quite deliberate act of reinvention. When she emerged onto the political scene as MP for Finchley in 1959, she carefully cultivated an image as a posh Tory lady from the Shires, knowing that this was the only way to succeed within the entrenched snobbery and sexist milieu of Conservative politics at the time. But as time went on and her zeal and ambition as a conviction politician and ideologue grew until eventually she challenged for the leadership of the party in 1979, she effected a transformation. According to biographer John Campbell: 'In place of the Home Counties Tory lady in a stripy hat, married to a rich husband, whose children had attended the most expensive private schools, she forced the media to redefine her as a battling meritocrat who had raised herself by hard work from a humble provincial background.' Sincerely or cynically, she turned her provincial roots into a mother lode, and the grocer's daughter from Grantham was born. Again.

The truth of the exhaust-fumey, clamorous T-junction in this peripheral, overlooked part of town is unprepossessing. But, as Campbell astutely points out: 'The iconography of Grantham is almost as familiar as the manger in Bethlehem: Alfred Roberts' famous corner shop, with the Great North Road thundering past the window; the sides of bacon hanging in the back, the smell of baking bread, young Margaret weighing out the sugar; the saintly father, the homely mother, Victorian values – thrift, temperance, good housekeeping, patriotism and duty.'

The satirical puppet show *Spitting Image* turned this homespun Messianic mythology rather neatly into a song in the late 1980s, a piece of overheated schlock sung by their infamous Thatcher puppet.

The bottles of bleach cost thirty pence each
and Duraglit is forty-six pee
And family-size individual fruit pies
are a bargain at one twenty-three ...
I will sing the Grantham Anthem
that I learned at my father's knee
As I helped him in his corner shop
in Nazareth Galilee

For all this, as I said, and unlike Bath or Stratford or Liverpool and their attitude to their most celebrated offspring – unlike even the villages of Midsomer – there is no tour, no trail, no leaflet from the tourist office. It seems that this has been a long-standing reluctance, dating back from Margaret's pomp when the town was perhaps mindful of Maggie's powerful, polarising effect on people. A *New York Times* article from 1989 reports on how some locals were irked by this lack of civic pride: 'The Premier Restaurant, which occupies the old grocery store above which she was born, announced that it would serve a five-course meal featuring Chicken Margaret [but] The lack of enthusiasm being displayed for the home-town girl who made good was enough to make Joe Flatters take matters into his own hands ... "I just felt that we were underplaying things too much, which is a tendency that is part of Grantham's character ... So I did something about it myself. I think she's the greatest thing that's happened to this country since the war. She has given some pride to this little town, which was once accused by a radio station of being the most boring town in England."'

What Flatters did was to put up signs on the roads leading into Grantham reading, 'Congratulations, Margaret Thatcher. Ten Years as Prime Minister'. The council made him take them down. By then, many had already been ripped down or defaced. Undaunted, the splendidly Dickensian-sounding Mr Flatters planned to erect signs around town that said: 'Grantham, Birthplace of Margaret Thatcher.' He applied for permission this time. But didn't get it, it appears. Or gave up. Or got bored. Or had a Damascene conversion to Labour.

The Premier Restaurant, by the way, occupying Maggie's dad's old shop and now, as reported, a holistic therapist's, found that many of the town's residents boycotted the place. It was spattered with eggs so often that the owner ruefully considered hanging a sign that said, 'Omelettes Our Speciality'. By the way, in case you're curious about Chicken Margaret: 'We thought of sweet and sour sauce but decided against it … Then we thought of Chicken Margaret. It's soft on the outside and has hazelnuts on the inside to give it hardness. Apples give it a bit of sweetness and lemon sauce gives it zest.' Personally, the thought of biting into something as soft and succulent as fried chicken and coming up hard against a hazelnut sounds more distressing than appetising. Perhaps that why the Premier Restaurant isn't there any more.

So, in the absence of a Margaret Walk or a Thatcher Tour, I'm left to wander the drizzly streets of Grantham in a damp and desultory fashion. I really don't know if it's the most boring town in Britain as that impertinent radio show suggested; I'd have to spend a great deal more time in the town. And, frankly, I've no intention of doing that. It's no Bath, let's put it that way.

Without wanting to labour or contrive any political point, Grantham's ugly town centre is what happens when commercialism is let off the leash unchecked. Everywhere, the buildings of the old market town have been barnacled and carbuncled and muscled out by nasty new ones, mainly cheap and tawdry-looking retail outlets. One boasts, bizarrely, 'Hessian sandbags! In stock now!' I find myself wandering glumly in the George shopping centre; several of the shops are closed, there are dirty puddles on the floor reflecting the harsh fluorescent lighting and a bad, thin version of Joan Armatrading's 'Love and Affection' is piped around the echoing galleries. It's a dreary experience.

But what's most noticeable and most depressing is that Grantham today is more a slip road than a town. For every pedestrian I spot, a score of vans and cars come throbbing through the town at speed. The few of us on foot feel like an afterthought, an irrelevance, cowering and scuttling along the shopfronts while the lorries roar by.

In the half-empty bookshop I notice a volume called *Grantham in the News*, a collection of cuttings from the local paper. It ends abruptly in 1979, just before its most famous daughter becomes Britain's first and as yet only woman prime minister. I don't know about you but I, ever the hard-nosed newshound, might just have put that snippet in. Possibly even given it a whole page. No mention, though, although there is a nice piece on a local bullock that was too big to fit in his shed.

Eventually, down a back alley, opposite Griddle's snack bar and Korky's discount beers, I spot a dingy pub called Chequers, named after the PM's Chilterns hideaway. I don't go in. I don't imagine Reagan or Gorbachev ever did either, unless they were really keen on Blue WKD and Big Screen Sky Sports. It is, however, the only even vague allusion I have seen to Grantham's illustrious former resident: Alf's daughter from the grocer's shop. I wasn't tempted. Whatever the myth that Thatcher forged, whatever she and her image-makers may have wanted us to believe, Grantham didn't feel like Middle England to me, not in 2008 anyway. It felt like the edge and the fag-end of something.

Which cannot be said for the vast, sleek, futuristic new St Pancras station complex in London. Wandering around it felt like being inside one of those architect's scale models or artist's impressions: cool, spacious and clean, in which we little people moved around in awe almost, gently transported here and there by escalator and moving walkway. Newly opened, which so often in England means 'opened in a rushed, half-arsed way with no lifts or shops or running water and loads of bits cordoned off with yellow tape', this is actually a model of quiet efficiency. You can buy nice cheese from the deli and look at the sky through a canopy of glass and read the computerised display boards and feel that you are living in a near future that works.

I had come here to embark on a trip to a place that, though it meant little to a northerner, had come up in conversation a few times when I'd mentioned that I was going in search of Middle England. Grantham had been a myth, I felt, but this was the reality, according to people in the know. One of my colleagues at the BBC said it was 'so cosy and comfortable and nice that you'd feel like sneering at it, but you don't because you know secretly you'd love to live there. If you could afford a house that is.' My friend Mike who grew up in nearby St Albans told me that it was even more Middle England than his home town, 'and, believe me, that's saying something'. He also told me that he had nearly lost his virginity there. I felt I ought to go, if only to see if there was a plaque.

The moment I stepped from the train I knew what my friends had meant. Harpenden, Buckinghamshire embodies the entirely gruntled, utterly comfited, completely mayed spirit of Middle England, its quiet satisfaction, its ease and content. Now for all I know, underneath this calm and pleasant exterior is a hotbed of rage and discontent, a simmering, barely contained pressure cooker of suppressed anger. But I doubt it. It was on a very low light if it was.

Straight out of the station and past the elderly Muslim taxi drivers with their luxuriant beards, the first shop is a picture framer's (exhibition by Ivan Taylor at the moment) and I get an inkling that Harpenden may well be a cut above. But hot on the heels of this, or cheek by jowl if you prefer, are Harpenden Grill and Kebab and Jack's Famous Chippy. I have to say that this latter may be an idle boast. I had never heard of it, and I'm quite a connoisseur of chippies. I've heard of the Magpie in Whitby and George and Helen's in Harborne – a place of pilgrimage across the Midlands – and. Perhaps Jack's fame is more local, cultish, a sort of John Cassavetes or Van der Graaf Generator of chip shops. Mindful of the fact that I seem to be partaking of tasty but greasy, artery-clogging snacks in every town I visit, I walk briskly past, avoiding Jack's (if it is he) alluring grin. Perhaps this is what he is famous for. At the side of his shop, whence come aromas that test my resolve, is a large red billboard on a gable end that says, bluntly, 'Some People Are Gay. Get Over It!'

In the window of the (obligatory) Help the Aged shop, a man with Down's Syndrome in a huge, fluffy, white Fair Isle sweater is writing the prices on the CDs with infinite and infinitely touching patience and care. The street is crammed with darkly inviting Moroccan restaurants, quirky bookshops and bijou barbers. I could live here, I think, as I have found myself thinking with surprising regularity on my travels across Middle England. If I had the money, of course, since this is, according to the *Daily Telegraph*, the eighth richest town in Britain with an average house price of £500,000 as of spring 2008.

Turning right onto the grand parade, I am met with newsstands announcing that Kosovo has proclaimed its independence. Harpenden looks fairly independent too, independently wealthy anyway as I make my way down a wide, handsome, prosperous street crowded in the mid-afternoon with healthy, affluent, well-scrubbed people radiating a glow of satisfaction but not smugness. This part of town is known as the Village, which isn't as silly and affected as it sounds; with its unhurried, semi-rural feel, Harpenden does seem a lot further than 25 minutes from the jangle and roar of Central London. I can see why so many people with no connection with the area came to live here, from the Aussie yodeller Frank Ifield to enigmatic American film director Stanley Kubrick to Morecambe-born comic and national treasure Eric Morecambe, who was a famously passionate fan of nearby Luton Town football club. The lounge there is named after him, as indeed are Harpenden's public halls.

On the high street, there's a posh confectioner's and

women of all ages come and go, clutching beribboned boxes which must contain all manner of sinful pralines and forbidden fondants. They have the furtive, slightly embarrassed air of middle-aged men leaving a sex shop. Except much prettier and with more giggling. The Slug and Lettuce is full and the clientele spill out on to the pavement tables; most of the patrons are drinking big frothy lattes, though, rather than beer. The Methodist church seems to be having a coffee morning too. Outside is a poster of three smiling babies and the slogan: 'You are Unique. Copyright God.'

Pleasant though it is, walking the streets of Harpenden involves a certain amount of risk in that it is seemingly a town full of elderly ladies parking badly, reversing without looking, mounting pavements and crunching tyre walls against kerbs. There are estate agents galore and in this, the early months of the credit crunch, the prices are just this side of breathtaking for stolid, bland, detached houses. As I have found all across Middle England, every other shop on the high street is either a dry cleaner's or a charity shop.

The village feel is enhanced by a pretty church just off the high street whose grounds are dotted with spreading elms, a bit of the country right in the town. I take a turn around the churchyard, where Special Brew and shouting are noticeable by their absence. A teenage girl in a Franz Ferdinand T-shirt sits on a bench with her knees up reading Thomas Hardy's *Return of the Native*, whilst further away under the trees a silver-haired gentleman is trying to teach a bumptious spaniel to fetch. St Nicholas itself is closed but I content myself with a shufti in the foyer where there is a selection of parish notices and such. There's a flyer for an appearance by Eric Knowles, 'irreverent expert from Antiques Roadshow', dapper in trade-mark bow-tie, at the Harpenden Eric Morecambe public halls. 'Pre-show valuation at 6.30.' A hand-typed notice says, 'Handyman seeks work, I am honest and reliable.' It could be a detail straight out of the young girl's Hardy novel.

Returning at a leisurely pace to the high street, I stop at the parish noticeboard by the drop-in centre. Peter Lilley seems to be the local MP and is holding some kind of public meeting or surgery. I never liked him. At best, I used to think of him as Andrew Ridgeley to Michael Portillo's George Michael. The Marmalade for Marie Curie Cancer Evening sounds much more fun. Strolling on, I pass an attractive-looking specialist off licence. Or rather I don't. As I run my eye along the shelves full of lustrous wheat- and honey-coloured Aberlours and Caol Ilas, Laphroaigs and Taliskers, a quartet of smartly dressed young mums come in (yummy mummies as some might have it, even, ahem, MILFs), chatting and joking and obviously stocking up for a girls' night in. One small, dark-haired woman in a white fur-lined parka picks up a bottle of Lanson champagne and pretends to swig from it. She catches my eye, winks mischie-vously and says, 'Just getting ready for the school run.'

Sandra has lived in Harpenden for five years. She grew up not far away in Harlow New Town. 'Harpenden's much nicer but' – and here she grows a little wistful – 'Harlow was quite a fun place to be a teenager. Course I'm a sensible grown-up mum now,' she says with the distinct air of someone who isn't quite that yet. They're having a send-off drink tonight for Colleen who's going to live in Christchurch, New Zealand.

'Very pretty apparently and very respectable. Just like Harpenden in fact,' she says with a smile.

The young guy behind the counter chips in and asks me what I'm doing here. I tell him and he says, 'Oh, you've come to the right place. This is Middle England all right. The heart of the Shires,' and then tells me about the history of various local church towers, an interesting and unexpected specialism for a twenty-something with a dyed maroon asymmetric haircut. I treat myself to a nice 15-year-old Dalwhinnie, wish Colleen bon voyage and all the girls a good night in. 'Am I going to be in your book?' asks Sandra, putting an extra Slimline Tonic in her basket for good measure. Yes, you are, I say. And so she is.

The heart of the Shires. Yes, Harpenden did feel like that. But I had come to realise, indeed had probably known all along, that though phrases like Heart of the Shires, Gateway to the Cotswolds, Heart of England, Fulcrum of Median Albion (OK, I made that one up) abound on tourism websites and marketing brochures, they are place-specific but no one actually uses them. 'Middle England', on the other hand, is used thousand upon thousand of times a day, and, though every user may have a slightly different, nuanced concept in mind, it revolves around certain shared assumptions. It is not so much places as states of mind. And shared collective rituals. That sounds dauntingly sociological so I should point out that what I'm driving at is farmers' markets.

Farmers' markets are the ... well, I hate to say Nuremberg Rallies of Middle England because of the unpleasant connotations, but you know what I mean. They are Middle England made flesh and gathered in one place, actualising itself in a celebration of identity. But without the Horst Wessel song and the flaming torches. Though the notion may seem intensely English, farmers' markets have been a feature of street life in Latin America and Europe for centuries. And the first farmers' market as we know them now, or so they claim, occurred in 1934 and still occurs on the corner of Third and Fairfax in Los Angeles, of all places, the creation of a savvy advertising copywriter and a local businessman who invited eighteen farmers to sell their produce from the tailgates of their trucks. Thus was born the modern farmers' market, like the ploughman's lunch a romanticised, marketable nugget of wholesome, country living designed specifically for pressured, weary, eco-friendly city dwellers.

If that sounds disparaging, let me say that I love farmers' markets. In fact, they are about the only thing about farming I do love. I can spend hours and pounds there, under the stripy green canvas awnings and along the trestle tables, browsing the produce which, according to regulations, must be 'grown, reared, caught, brewed, pickled, baked, smoked or processed by the stallholder'. In theory, anyway; a *Times* article of April 2008 revealed that some farmers employed a bit of sleight of hand and passed off 'bought' produce as their own. One was quoted as saying, 'If you've got to buy it from the market, then just stick it in your own boxes before you go to the [farmers'] market. You've got to dress it up how you want it … Don't take it in the Spanish black box or take it in a box that says "Lincolnshire Produce". It's common sense. You can work it out. There are times of the year [the customer] knows you can't get it, so you have to be a bit shrewd.'

I still love them, though. At the farmers' market on the high street in Harborne, a leafy, affluent suburb of Birmingham, there's a stall run by the Handmade Scotch Eggs Company that sells thirty different varieties of the ovoid breadcrumby snack. One is called Baz. They do six vegetarian ones. When I was there last I spent twenty-six pounds, which I think may be the most amount of money ever spent on Scotch eggs, though it's hard to ratify this claim, of course. At a farmers' market in Kent I bought several jars of olives stuffed with all manner of ingredients: red pepper, lemon, garlic, probably kippers and liver and powdered Crunchie. I don't even like olives. I don't actually believe anyone does. Let's face it, they taste of TCP. But I still bought them. At the same market, I stood and drank a plastic cup of hot apple juice – again which I'm not wild about – just so I could pretend for a moment I was in Madrid or Cadiz. I bought more goat's cheese than anyone could have wanted, particularly since, yes, you've guessed it, I prefer Dairylea. I then spent a happy half hour in the company of Khalid Ishmael, proprietor of Ishmael's Mother, who made me eat a variety of ferociously delicious Asian curries and dals. The company motto is. 'Eat this, you'll like it', which I find winningly to the point. By his own admission, he's 'a good south London boy' with a nice line in cheeky patter with the mildly scandalised ladies. The dal 'sneaks up and takes you from behind' and the lamb mussaman 'will be the most interesting thing you've had in your mouth all year, madam'.

The spiritual cousin of the farmers' market is the craft centre. Also known as the 'craft centre cum antiques and shopping thingy'. There's a cracking example of the genre just outside Lichfield and called, yes!, the Heart of the Country Shopping Village. Well, I suppose it is a kind of village, if your definition of a village is 'no houses but with a boutique and a crêperie that's built next to an open prison'. Actually, this is unfair. It is genuinely an old farm dating back to the 1700s and in 1991 it received 'the Arthur Brown trophy, given in recognition of projects that have made a significant contribution to the preservation of Staffordshire's built heritage'.

The undoubted appeal of such places – and come here on a bank holiday Monday and you'll be engaging in hand-to-hand combat for a crêpe – is actually outlined in the village's own literature. 'In this age when high streets all over the country tend to look and feel exactly the same; be it shops, eating places or car parks with high fees; Heart of the Country Shopping Village provides a welcome alternative and in a way, a step back in time. Individual shops and distinctive restaurants, free parking, a safe, attractive and vehicle-free environment are the backdrop to a relaxed experience for our visitors. The Village strives to maintain the rural feel, and the buildings are unmistakably a former farmstead. The Village is particularly proud of the biodiversity in and around the buildings, quite apart from the adjoining woodland and hedgerows. There are 10 species of birds, including goldfinches and pied wagtails nesting in and on the buildings, and a colony of 40-50 bats breeding in one of the roofs.'

I didn't know any of this when I went. I just thought there might be some Scotch egg or stuffed olive opportunities. There weren't but there was pretty much everything else, including a microbrewery and a garden furniture shop that charged a grand for a frightening statue of a sinister cowled monk. He was a lot like the Spirit of Dark and Lonely Water in that 1970s Public Information Film, here making an unexpected second appearance in a book, surely some kind of record. I looked at some ace 'fire-pits', which are basically barbecues that wouldn't look out of place in a Shinto temple. I knew, though, that I wouldn't have anywhere to put it. And I was distracted that every bloke in the village was wearing autumnal cords and a scarf. Including me.

Given the village's location, there's a faintly French feel to it all. There are lads bustling around in aprons carrying baskets of baguettes. The furniture shop is called Ooh La La, which makes it sound like it sells knickers but in fact it sells little cane chairs and Beatrix Potter-ish beds and bottles of Crabtree and Evelyn shampoo and L'Occitane shaving oil. The girl behind the counter was from Coventry, though. She gave my friend Lydia, aged three, a chocolate egg, which I thought was very nice of her. In the Alessi shop I buy a stupidly expensive egg cup which sets off the fabulously camp young man (I hesitate to say that he was the only gay in the village) on dreamy reminisces of his childhood in the far-off days of, I guess, around 1989. 'OOOH, an egg cup! Do you know every Easter we'd have our Creme Eggs in an egg cup round at my gran's in Cannock. Do you think people still do that? Happy days!' I also buy yet another garlic chopper, something that will stone a mango – always a chore, don't you find? – and something ridged and silver whose use I had forgotten even before I got out of the store. As I leave I notice that the garden centre next door has just opened for business, and a passing gardener in green wellies clutching a hoe recognises me, saying, 'Hello, you could have been our guest of honour and cut the ribbon! Actually I don't know if we've got a pair of giant scissors.'

Not part of the village, in fact a separate entity (though surely ripe for annexation should a dictator ever arise from the Alessi shop), is Blackbrook's Antique Village. Again, it's not a village but it is a great place to while away an hour even if, like me, you have not the faintest interest in antiques. Not in the sense of old jugs anyway. The antiques at Blackbrook's are different, though, multifarious and a bit nuts. Here I thought about buying an early table-top football game made in Birmingham, some old typewriters, huge linen baskets cleared from the cotton mill in Wigan my mum used to work in, some Victorian tennis rackets, a ship in a bottle, a cage cum gazebo, the pews, crucifix and 'stations of the cross' from a disused church, and a massive fountain filled with goldfish for five thousand pounds, which makes the sinister cowled monk look like a bargain.

On a hillside on the North Weald I saw another instance of Middle England at play, one which was entirely new to me. It was sheer chance: what seemed to be an encampment, alive with fluttering pennants and noise, on the gently sloping rise ahead. It was late afternoon, the sun was on the wane but the coming evening was warm and sweet and the home-made sign taped to the folding table at the field gate said, 'Admission reduced to ten pounds a car'. I gave a tenner to the florid lady in the body warmer with the walkie-talkie and I was into my very first point-to-point.

A point-to-point meeting is essentially a rough and ready day at the races. The name is of the same derivation as 'steeple-chase', whose origins lie in a bet between Mr Blake and his neighbour Mr Callaghan in County Cork in 1752, who raced each other from the steeple – or point – of Buttevant church to Doneraile church some four and a half miles away. Though decidedly amateur, I guess point-to-point meetings are at the upper, posher end of what we might call Middle England. Certainly I have never seen so much brush-like ginger hair and pastel-pink polo shirts with the collars turned up. In the hubbub of voices I hear choice selections. A sizzled-looking chap in designer sunglasses and a floppy fringe is cradling his mobile phone between shoulder and ear. 'Yah, Simon, I'm over by the beer tent but I really fancy one of those ostrich burger thingies and some champers. I've had a skinful of Adnams and I need a sit down.' Two men who both look like Jeremy Irons's rugger-bugger brother have an exchange over glasses of red wine. 'We've got dinner with the Montgomerys tonight.' 'Oh, hard lines.' 'I know. Still, the food will be good even if the small talk is ghastly.' Over the tannoy comes a drawled, laconic announcement, 'We've got a small lost boy in the weighing enclosure. He's got an ice cream and an orange rugby shirt and we think he's called Jason. I don't know why.'

Throwing myself into the spirit of things, I decide to have a bet. There are proper bookies, most with little whiteboards and dry markers but some with digital displays which I am rather tragically impressed by. I peruse and deliberate for some time before placing my bet. As I receive my ticket, the gentleman gives some winnings to the little girl at the side of me. 'Thirty-eight pounds, well done, darling!' I take this to be a good omen.

I am wrong. For one thing, as I walk away clutching my

ticket I realise that what I thought were the odds were actually the horses' numbers, and so I have picked entirely the wrong horse. Not that my selection was to be trusted in the first place, of course. But now it is completely random. Jockeys and horses are paraded round to give potential punters a chance to size them up. My jockey is toothless, looks older than me and has the unconvincing confidence of a man who's been drinking aftershave all morning. I'm no judge of horse flesh but his steed will surely become Bostik and meat pies before the week is out. It doesn't bode well.

My horse came second, which would have been fine if I'd backed it each way. Or indeed backed the right horse. I screw my ticket up and throw it in the bin by the Countryside Alliance stand. Three men are talking over plastic glasses of beer and each is dressed in the full dress uniform of the Countryside Alliance: Barbour waterproof, white shirt with small yellow check, dull greeny-mustard tweed jacket, flat cap. They probably think of themselves as Middle Englanders but from my travels they are decidedly not. They are its lunatic fringe. As I leave the field in the setting sun, the man on the tannoy makes another weary announcement. 'So we now have one set of house keys, one dog, one iPod, one handbag and one little boy called, we think, Jason. Someone must remember losing these things.'

If point-to-pointing is an atypical Middle English pursuit, what could be more middling and suburban than gardening? Not that long ago, gardening threatened to become sexy, or so at least the Sunday papers and TV commissioning editors told us. They told us that benign horticulturalist Alan Titchmarsh was 'an unlikely sex symbol' (why do you never hear about 'likely sex symbols'?) and that Charlie Dimmock, voluptuous, bra-eschewing, Titian-haired temptress of the compost heap, was invigorating men of a certain age all across the Shires on *Gardeners' World* every Friday evening. They may even have said that gardening was, oh dear, 'the new rock and roll'. All that silliness is over now, gardening has returned to its proper place in the schedules – the middle – and the columnists have turned their attention to 'talent' and 'reality' shows, both of which richly deserve those ironic inverted commas, honest.

But we still garden. And even those of us who don't still crave or cherish the garden even if only as 'the extra room' it is glamorously sold as in all those makeover shows. Horticultural purists may grizzle at the ubiquity of decking and water features but for those of us with no appetite for dirt, worms and tetanus, the garden still remains an inviolate space of Middle England. A place for crafty fags and glasses of wine on fine evenings, a place for barbecues, bikes, swing ball and giant trampolines.

In the Botanical Gardens at Edgbaston, though, Middle England's religious love of gardening has found a shrine. Well, actually a Mount Rushmore. Gardening TV stalwarts Dimmock, Titchmarsh, Monty Don and Carol Klein have been immortalised here in a six-foot-high relief sculpture composed of 'peat-free compost-containing recycling materials'. It is charming but it is also completely ludicrous, especially since the bottom of Dimmock's jaw has sheared disastrously away like the Larsen B ice shelf, leaving her with a terrifying zombie rictus. On the subject of Alan, whilst calling him Middle

England's Gardening God, John Vidal writing in the *Guardian* hit that obligatory tone of metropolitan superiority when he opined, 'If he were a flower, he would be a busy lizzie – he thrives everywhere, comes up every year and offends no one. You could describe him as Terry Wogan without the wit. The less kind among us might prefer "Mr Bland". But that's the point of Titch, and the cult of Middle England now growing around him loves him for his ubiquity and inoffensiveness.' Successful, rich, good at his job and apparently lusted after, Titchmarsh is presumably immune to this kind of stuff. Let critics sneer if they like. They'll never get their own peat-free-compost Mount Rushmore, I thought, as I tucked into my mushroom soup and shepherd's pie in the cafeteria. It was full: full of ladies who lunch in cashmere wraps and young mums in Gap and Primark, retired couples and trios of teenagers and school parties with clipboards, all come to enjoy the Tudor knot garden and the national bonsai collection, the woodland walk and the tropical house that makes your glasses steam up. The new Middle England I'd say, coming together under leaded glass and creepers, just by a sign that says, 'These toilets are not in use. Please use the ones behind the parrot house.'

It didn't say why the toilets weren't in use but I imagine it was due to flooding. I say this because most of Middle England's woes for the past few years have fallen from the skies. Herefordshire, Worcestershire, Gloucestershire, Oxfordshire and Bedfordshire have been largely under water since about 2004, it seems. If this sounds jokey and flippant, the actuality has been biblical, apocalyptic even; thousands displaced from their homes, cars being washed away down the pretty streets of market towns, people taking to the roofs of their semis, rowing boats rescuing people from upstairs windows, people actually drowning. We have grown used to seeing such terrible images from Karachi, Sichuan or even New Orleans. But this is Tewkesbury.

Driving into Tewkesbury in the spring of 2008 I thought it was sweet, if a little sheep-like, to see that every, but every, semi-detached house in the residential suburbs on the outskirts of town had a caravan in the front garden. Did everyone really have to try so hard to emulate their neighbour and keep up with the Joneses? I felt ashamed a few minutes later when, of course, it dawned on me that these caravans were being lived in. The family homes behind were uninhabitable, a year after the waters had come to this pretty Gloucestershire town.

The Tewkesbury floods of 2007 were devastating, on a scale once unthinkable in England but now being repeated year after year. Whatever the climate change deniers may say – the ridiculous Nigel Lawson and those few mad scientists – the people of Tewkesbury know that all is not right up there beyond the clouds. Fifty thousand were driven from their homes. Three died. People who popped into Morrisons to get their Friday-night shop came out an hour later to find their cars submerged and useless. The main streets became rivers. The town looked like Venice. The magnificent abbey became an island, literally. Pictures of it from the air, surrounded by water, became the terrible icon of the floods. It soon filled with bedraggled, sodden refugees seeking shelter and sleeping on its stone floors. It was like something from Brueghel or Bosch, almost medieval.

I walk down Abbey Terrace a year later and every house is deserted. Through the curtainless windows, I can see that many still have industrial dehumidifiers with their huge trunk-like pipes dangling across the bare, concrete rooms where the furniture and carpets have gone. It is a melancholy sight. In the abbey itself, various pictures and displays tell of those terrible July days and how the abbey became a focal point for the town and an emblem of its quiet fortitude and generosity.

If you were to ask me what the best of Middle England is, I would say it is those qualities: fortitude and generosity with perhaps a side order of tolerance and stoicism and just a dash of spice and mischief. These are not the qualities, though, that some of the trumpeters of Middle England espouse, usually from newspaper offices in London. If you believed them, you'd think that Middle England was a nest of bitter and insular vipers, a frightened, mean-spirited people desperate to complain about something. When the Tewkesbury floods happened, most people in the town rolled their sleeves up, got a bucket and helped bail out. Some, though, preferred to stand around at a metaphorical distance, arms folded, and whinge. As comedian and columnist Mark Steel noted: 'One inevitable line of whining has been the one pursued by a columnist in the *Mail*, who complained: "If this biblical flooding was happening in some far-flung Third World country, pop stars would be falling over themselves to record a charity single." And someone in the *Sun* said: "If this was happening anywhere else in the world, the government would be sending wads of our cash." ... It is almost as if they're angry at how Middle England has suffered most, as if this were a politically correct flood that once again attacks the decent, silent majority, because these days a flood daren't devastate an inner-city area, in case someone accuses it of being racist!'

Steel is right. And such talk, trickling like the last of the flood water down Church Street from the newspapers to the readers who then parrot it, is bleating by any other name. It is not the authentic voice of Middle England. Ostensibly bullish but really querulous and whiney, it has only become the dominant key, the register, the default tone of Middle England relatively recently. Since 31 August 1997 in fact. I ended the last chapter by saying that the myth of Middle England owes much, not to Robin Hood and King Arthur, but to two women who very definitely did exist. Thatcher was one. It's time to consider the other.

The death of Diana, Princess of Wales following a high-speed crash in a Paris underpass in the summer of 1997 is, I'd argue, the most significant, indeed the defining moment, in English culture and society since the Second World War. It has been felt across every stratum of society but perhaps most in Middle England. Diana's death and the subsequent collective national derangement, that outpouring of grief and hysteria, has changed us utterly and for ever. Before Henri Paul, drunk and speeding, lost control of that Mercedes in the tunnel beneath the Place de l'Alma, Middle England had tended to be thought of as buttoned-up, repressed even, suspicious of gross displays of emotion, given to a little eye-rolling but not censorious, brisk, cheerful and above all sensible.

The ripples of madness left by the cataclysm of Diana's death are still with us. They are not the tides they once were but they are still an undertow that shapes our world. The stiff upper lip has been replaced by the trembling lower one. Stoicism has given way to sentimentality or 'the indulgence of feelings you don't really have' as I once heard it defined. Fortitude and generosity have been replaced by selfishness and judgementalism.

As you may have guessed, I don't think this change has been for the best. Don't get me wrong. This is nothing to do with Diana and is no comment on her. Her death was a human tragedy and only someone with a heart of stone could not have been moved, even if some of the excesses of those late summer days seem bizarre now. (When the Princess of Wales's coffin was driven up the M1, signs from a safety campaign saying 'Tiredness can kill, Take a break' were taken down to prevent anyone getting a photo showing the hearse juxtaposed with such a sign.) But the effect of that July night has been deleterious for us all. Nothing genuinely useful has changed (at one point it was felt that we trembled on the verge of republican). But we are that bit quicker to blub, quicker to take offence, quicker to shout the odds, quicker to complain, quicker to tell people exactly what we think of them. Every day, hours of the output of supposed news networks is given over to phone-ins in which the dim and the bigoted, the ill-informed bore who nonetheless is 'entitled to his opinion', the single-issue nutter and the monomaniac fundamentalist vie to see who can shout the loudest. And when the shouting day is done, we watch TV shows in which people's dreams are dashed by snickering juries. If you don't enjoy this shift, you are elitist, you are anti-democratic. Except this is not democracy. It's ochlocracy, as the Greeks called it. Rule by the *mobile vulgus*, the easily moveable crowd, or, in short, the mob.

I should say that I'm not pining for the days when we kept it all in, kept it under wraps and kept it in the family. I don't feel nostalgic for a golden age of backstreet abortions or the good old days when outwardly respectable bank managers were thrashing their wives – and worse – behind closed doors. But I wish we, and especially Middle England, wouldn't let it all hang out so readily. It's not genuine candour, it's just exhibitionism. If the next thing you say doesn't add to the sum total of human happiness, don't say it. As England used to say when we really were up against it, Be like Dad, keep Mum.

When I think of Middle England I think of tolerance and kindness. So it irks me that the phrase has become a byword for sour prejudice and insularity. The *Daily Mail*, generally regarded as the house journal for Middle England, has even tried to extinguish the phrase for what it deems the 'offensive' and 'outdated' stereotypes associated with its readership. Linda Grant, marketing services director at the *Mail*'s parent group Associated Newspapers, said of Middle England in 2008: 'People conjure up an image when they hear it but they can't really define it. The *Mail* and Middle England are synonymous but the idea of Middle England is outdated.' She argued: 'The results of the group's research, published today, claim that rather than being "old-fashioned, narrow-minded and conservative", Middle Englanders and *Mail* readers are people who are "influential, engaged and vocal" and the "ultimate consumers with the power to make or break almost any brand".'

The Labour Party, as I saw in Royal Leamington Spa, has long courted Middle England as its new power base, rather than its traditional constituency, the urban working class.

Labour strategist Philip Gould identifies it as a place populated by 'ordinary people with suburban dreams who worked hard to improve their homes and their lives; to get gradually better cars, washing machines and televisions; to go on holiday in Spain rather than Bournemouth'. If anything, though, research from bodies like MORI shows that Middle England is characterised not by entrenched loyalty to any party but by their floating, changeable allegiances. Ben Page, managing director of the MORI Social Research Institute, says that the label 'Middle England' is used as 'a convenient shorthand for the 25 per cent of the population who are not surgically wedded to one of the main parties – and who happen to live in marginal constituencies'. That's why parties of every hue want their vote.

Leftist commentator Martin Jacques has said that Middle England is a 'metaphor for respectability, the nuclear family, conservatism, whiteness, middle age and the status quo'. But this is metaphor, not mirror to reality. According to the National Centre for Social Research, Middle Englanders are becoming more tolerant and open-minded with regard to issues like homosexuality and women's rights, if not crime and immigration. And even here we should be careful not to assume that just because Middle England reads the *Mail* or the *Telegraph*, it agrees with every word. When censor-in-chief James Ferman passed Adrian Lyne's film version of *Lolita*, the *Daily Mail* attacked him for a 'gross betrayal of public interest', to which Ferman responded, 'Perhaps the problem is that those who claim to defend the values of Middle England may well be out of touch with Middle England.'

And anyway, from my sojourns in pub, hotel and tea shop,

they were just as likely to read the *Guardian*. For Ben Page, they're 'a bit Pooterish – a bit Margo from *The Good Life*; they are conservative but with a small "c". They may well be fiscally conservative, but they are mostly socially liberal.' It seems they hold lots of different opinions at the same time, and change their mind more often. More Muddle England than Middle England.

For instance, another contradiction. All those colonels risking thrombosis as they read the new crime figures in the *Daily Mail* are in fact criminal masterminds and Middle England itself is nothing like as law-abiding as it claims. A report, 'Law Abiding Majority? The everyday crimes of the middle classes', co-authored by criminologists Dr Stephen Farrall and Professor Susanne Karstedt, found that: 'Contempt for the law is as widespread in the centre of society as it is assumed to be rampant at the margins and among specific marginal groups. Antisocial behaviour by the few is mirrored by anticivil behaviour by the many ... Neither greed nor need can explain why respectable citizens cheat on insurance claims or in second-hand sales, and do not hesitate to discuss their exploits in pubs.'

According to their research, more than a third of the law-abiding majority beloved of politicians has paid cash to a cleaner, plumber or other tradesman to cheat the tax man. One in five has taken something from work, and a third if handed too much change in a shop would just keep it. One in ten doesn't pay their television licence. As the report concludes: 'These are the crimes and unfair practices committed at the kitchen table, on the settee and from home computers, from desks and call centres, at cashpoints, in supermarkets and restaurants, and in interactions with builders and other tradespeople.'

It seems that, having learned to love its foibles, I've been rather hard on Middle England for a paragraph of two. So while I warm up for my concluding eulogy, let me reflect, sadly, on another entry in the debit column: Middle England's capacity and appetite for censoriousness, a new zeal for judgement encouraged by the more rabid tub-thumpers of the press and TV. As I was coming to the end of my travels, the papers – some of them at least – seemed daily full of complaints. The redtop tabloids are still bracingly judgemental, which is exactly what they should be. *The Times*, 'The Thunderer', still thunders, I'm glad to say, albeit in a thoughtful, circumspect 21st century way. But somewhere in the middle lie writers and columnists and papers for whom 'The Whinger' would be a better nickname. Now a certain plaintive but stoic grumbling is part of our national make-up as our best comic writers have always known. It is there in Reggie Perrin's melancholy daily recital of the absurd reasons given for his delayed arrival by train at the office: 'Eleven minutes late, overheated axle at Berrylands.' 'Eleven minutes late, somebody had stolen the lines at Surbiton.' 'Twenty-two minutes late, badger ate a junction box at New Malden.' 'Twenty-two minutes late, escaped puma, Chessington North.' It is there in the quiet raging despair of Basil Fawlty's phone call: 'Ahh, yes, Mr O'Reilly, well, it's perfectly simple. When I asked you to build me a wall I was rather hoping that instead of just dumping the bricks in a pile you might have found time to cement them together ... you know, one on top of another, in the traditional fashion.'

But that small, clear, wry voice wasn't much heard at the end of 2009. It was drowned out by a clamour of outrage, sometimes justified maybe, but often babyish. Some bad jokes on a late evening radio show and the machinations of a celebrity ballroom dancing programme fought for coverage – and won – against the the horrific murder of a child called Baby P and the collapse of the world's economies. In a zeal to whinge, it seemed that some sections of Middle England's wailing media muezzin could not tell the difference between some puerile remarks on the radio and child abuse, could not distinguish the serious from the silly and the very same people who bleat about the nanny state seemed to need a nanny themselves to protect themselves from a few rude words or tasteless jokes.

I found this odd and slightly pathetic. This, after all, is the Middle England, the beating heart of the brave little country that once stood alone against the darkest, most malevolent evil the modern world has ever seen. When it gets its knickers in a twist over litter or Polish plumbers or lapses of taste, it lessens us all.

Late in the writing of this book I spoke at the Cheltenham Literary Festival. Towns do not come much more Middle England than this handsome Regency spa town, and as I lounged in my room at the Hotel Du Vin, strolled along the floodlit lawns before the town hall on the Saturday night, wandered in and out of the tents and bookstalls and venues of the festival or bought delicious fresh figs and paella at the continental market on the Sunday morning, I thought, again, I could live here.

This was interesting because the reason I was in town was to talk about a book of mine called *Pies and Prejudice*, a travelogue about the new north that is really a love letter. After the talk, I took questions from the audience and was surprised that many came from Leeds, Sheffield, Bury, Oldham, Bolton and the like. Had they come all this way just to hear me prattle? And of course they hadn't. These smart people were part of a diaspora. They were proud of their roots but they also loved living, for now maybe but quite happily, in Oxford or Chipping Norton, Moreton-in-Marsh or Cheltenham, surrounded by figs and paella and Jane Austen and loveliness.

Of course they were. They'd be mad not to be. These were not those folk, the worst of the north, who bang on about it being God's Country. It isn't. There is no God's Country. Unless it all is. Or unless it's Einstein's Country. Merely coming from the north per se is nothing to be proud of. You have to do something, go somewhere, be clever and beautiful and charming and, yes, maybe northern and share it with the world. Also, if you think God prefers Rotherham and Chorley to Bath and Ludlow, well, he's got a funny way of showing it, hasn't he?

Some northerners, maybe the ones who hoped this book would be a sustained sneer at Middle England, will be disappointed at this treacherous turn. Sorry, guilty as charged. But the England that made Vaughan Williams and Shakespeare is dearer to me than the England that made Bernard Manning and Liam Gallagher. And even if there are no jagged peaks here, the physical beauty of the place is still intoxicating, from the misty Chilterns to the luscious Cotswolds to the dreaming reverie of the university towns.

But the real lie about Middle England, the peddled myth that really should be exploded, is about its values. Middle

England's values, if you believe NW1, are a frenzied catechism of prejudice and rage underpinned by an ideology that's a sinister, alchemical blending of John Craven's *Countryfile* and *Mein Kampf*. In fact, I encountered much less casual racism and 'hang 'em and flog 'em' bloodlust than I hear in cabs and shops and pubs across the towns and cities of the north and south. It was nice, actually, not hearing 'paki' or 'twat' or 'bitch' quite as regularly as I'm used to, not seeing gaggles of fifty-year-old men drunk and swearing outside pubs at midday on Tuesday, or watching toddlers being struck and manhandled and hissed at in the street by their awful parents. I didn't see a lot of that in Middle England. Ah, they're only being polite, some will offer. Well, I have no problem with that. All any of us are doing is being polite. Love will fail, as Kurt Vonnegut said, but courtesy will prevail.

Almost by definition, Middle England is not extremist or lunatic. It doesn't smear fox blood on its children's faces or shoot little animals for fun. It doesn't go to Eton or Sandhurst. It goes to Waitrose and M&S. It doesn't shriek 'PC gone mad!' on message boards or write unhinged letters in green ink to local papers about abuse of parking discs or the loss of the word 'gay' to the English language. It hasn't got the time, to be honest, what with setting the pub quiz (all proceeds to charity) and clearing out the shed and watching the backlog of episodes of *Little Dorrit* and *The Blue Planet* it's got on Sky Plus. Maggie and Diana – blonde, remote and unknowable – are not their icons. It's Delia and Celia, dark, sweet and wistful.

I fell a little in love with Middle England. I could quite enjoy being her 'bit of rough' if she'd have me. Everyone thinks they know her. But they don't know the first thing about her. She didn't stay with old Fred, for instance, though she's still in touch obviously because of the kids. Trevor Howard was fun for a while but in the end she chucked him too. She's going out tonight with the girls and, as she texts them, big gin and tonic in one hand, Nokia in the other, Radiohead and *The Lark Ascending* on the iPod, she looks out over those broad sunlit uplands Mr Churchill talked about and thinks maybe her finest hour is still to come.

Could I borrow your hankie? I think I must have something in my eye.

Stuart Maconie is a broadcaster, journalist and writer familiar to millions from his work on radio and TV. He is a stalwart of Britain's most popular network, Radio 2, where he co-presents the *Radcliffe and Maconie* show during the week and his own regular Saturday show. His BBC 6 music show *The Freak Zone* is a global cult and he has written and presented dozens of other shows across BBC radio and TV. His work as a journalist has appeared everywhere from *NME* and *Q Magazine* to the *Daily Telegraph* and the *Oldie*. His previous books include the official biographies of Blur and James as well as the bestsellers, *Cider with Roadies* and *Pies and Prejudice*. He lives in exile in the West Midlands and is happiest fell-walking with Muffin the dog.

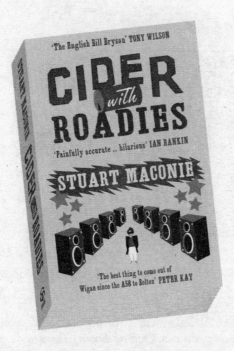

'The English Bill Bryson' TONY WILSON

CIDER with ROADIES

'Painfully accurate ... hilarious' IAN RANKIN

STUART MACONIE

'The best thing to come out of
Wigan since the A58 to Bolton' PETER KAY

'The perfect pop fan's life ... effortlessly articulate' *The Times*

'The rarest of rock memoirs – hilarious, erudite and
endearingly humble ... Maconie's reminiscences are rich
with both anecdote and insight' *Q Magazine*

'If you only read one personal music odyssey,
make it this one' *GQ*

'Maconie makes a jovial, self-deprecating narrator.
Sharp and funny' *Guardian*

'Stuart Maconie is the best thing to come out of
Wigan since the A58 to Bolton' Peter Kay

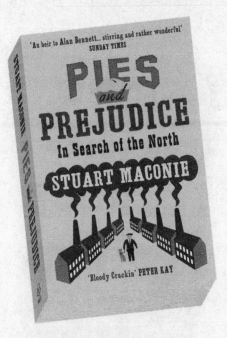

'An heir to Alan Bennett ... stirring and rather wonderful'
Antony Quinn, *Sunday Times*

'Funnier than Bill Bryson. There's lots to love about
Maconie's North – even for Southern Jessies' *Metro*

'Affectionate, informed, conversationally honest, polemical'
Daily Telegraph

'One of the delights of Pies and Prejudice is Maconie's prose
... behind Maconie's crafted wordplay is a serious thesis: that
the North is more than its image' *The Times*

'The book succeeds ... because of his care and wit in
revealing something of these wonderful cities' *Observer*

'[Stuart Maconie's] search for his northern soul has just the
right balance of pies and prejudice to be right good'
Independent

'A witty and illuminating travelogue' *Sunday Times*